the Antichrist

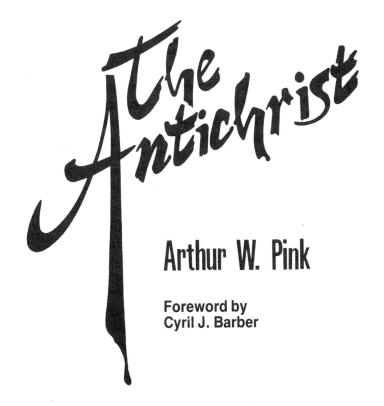

The Antichrist

Arthur W. Pink

**Foreword by
Cyril J. Barber**

krēgel
PUBLICATIONS

Grand Rapids, MI 49501

The Antichrist by Arthur W. Pink

Published in 1988 by Kregel Publications, a division of Kregel, Inc., P.O. Box 2607, Grand Rapids, MI 49501. Kregel Publications provides trusted, biblical publications for Christian growth and service. Your comments and suggestions are valued.

Cover design: Alan G. Hartman

Library of Congress Cataloging-in-Publication Data
Pink, Arthur Walkington, 1886–1952
   The antichrist / Arthur W. Pink.
     p. cm.
   Originally published: Swengel, Pa.: Bible Truth Depot, 1923.
   1. Antichrist. I. Title.

| BT985.P5 | 1988 | 236 | 87-29898 |
| | | | CIP |

ISBN 0-8254-3539-0

Printed in the United States of America

5 6 7 8 9 / 01 00 99 98 97

CONTENTS

FOREWORD

The writings of Arthur Walkington Pink have become popular since his death in 1952. Born in England, Pink held pastorates in Australia and in the United States, and in his later years enjoyed a widespread ministry throughout the English-speaking world.

The chapters which comprise *The Antichrist* were first published in *Studies in the Scriptures*—a monthly magazine edited by Mr. Pink and devoted to the exposition of the Word. In 1923 these essays were gathered together and published in book form.

The prominence of the Antichrist in Scripture has not always been apparent. Believers in Christ are exhorted to fix their gaze on the Lord Jesus and appropriate the work of the Holy Spirit in their lives. For this reason many have neglected the teaching of the Word on Satan and his emissaries, and considerable false teaching (and not a little ridicule) abounds on the subject of the Antichrist. Furthermore, a systematic study of the prophetic Scriptures is seldom attempted because it is all too easy for the would-be student to become confused over the terms used to describe the devil and his Antichrist. This dilemma need no longer face us. Arthur Pink has provided Bible students with a clear and thorough summary of the teaching of God's Word on the subject of the Antichrist, his character, the time of his appearance, his work, and his end. In doing so he corrects the popular error which seeks to identify Antichrist with the papacy.

Prominent in Pink's presentation is the relationship of the Antichrist to Israel. He believes that this person will be a Jew, and he advances seven reasons, some logical and some Scriptural, in support of his view. He does not raise the issue of whether the 'son of perdition' will come from the tribe of Dan, but wisely leaves the matter unresolved.

Of value in Pink's treatment is his handling of different passages of Scripture such as Ezekiel 21 and 28, Daniel 7–11, Isaiah 14, and Revelation 11 and 13. He takes literally the position that the Antichrist will be the physical son of Satan—a position different from his later writings in which he tended toward excessive typology.

Throughout the book Pink exhibits his mastery of the subject matter. For example, his description of the dragon who stands up on the sand of the sea (Rev. 13) is at once complete and draws together the teaching of various portions of Scripture on the subject. Pink advocates the view that the Antichrist's authority includes both religious and political realms and that, in keeping with Christ's prediction in John 5:43, he will exercise a prophetic office even to the extent of working miracles (Rev. 13:13–14).

The Antichrist is a thorough exposition of the whole teaching of the Scripture. While all readers cannot be expected to concur with the author's point of view, the fact remains that Arthur Pink has succeeded in providing a fine exposition of the biblical text.

And now, as the time of the Antichrist's appearance draws closer, we take delight in commending this work to you as one which is worthy of serious study.

Cyril J. Barber

INTRODUCTION

ACROSS the varied scenes depicted by prophecy there falls the shadow of a figure at once commanding and ominous. Under many different names, like the aliases of a criminal, his character and movements are set before us. It is our intention to write a series of papers concerning this one who will be the full embodiment of human wickedness and the final manifestation of satanic blasphemy. Many others have made reference to this mysterious personage in their general expositions of prophecy, but so far as our examination of the literature on this subject has carried us (and we have endeavored to make it as thorough as possible) there seem to have been very few attempts made to furnish a *complete* delineation of this Prince of Darkness. We do not know of any exhaustive treatment of the subject, and for this reason, and also because there is no little confusion in the minds of many concerning the character and career of the coming Man of Sin, these papers are now submitted to the attention of Bible students.

For upwards of twelve years we have studied diligently and prayerfully what the Scriptures teach about the Pseudo-Christ. The deeper we have carried these studies, the more surprised we are at the prominent place which is given in the Bible to this Son of Perdition. There is an amazing wealth of detail which, when carefully collected and arranged, supplies a vivid biography of the one who is shortly to appear and take the government of the world upon his shoulders. The very fact that the Holy Spirit has caused so much to be written upon the subject at once denotes its great importance. The *prominence* of the Antichrist in the prophetic Scriptures will at once appear by a glance at the references that follow.

The very first prophecy of the Bible takes note of him, for in Gen. 3:15 direct reference is made to the Serpent's "Seed". In Exodus a striking type of him is furnished in Pharaoh: the defier of God; the one who cruelly treated His people; the one who by ordering the destruction of all the male children, sought to cut off Israel from being a nation; the one who made fair promises only to break them: the one who met with such a drastic end at the hands of the Lord. In the prophecy of Balaam, the Antichrist is referred to under the name of "Asshur" (Num. 24:22),—in future chapters evidence will be given to prove that "Asshur" and the Antichrist are one and the same person. There are many other remarkable types of the Man of Sin to be found in the historical books of the Old Testament, but these we pass by now, as we shall devote a separate chapter to their consideration.

In the book of Job he is referred to as "the Crooked Serpent" (Job 26:13): with this should be compared Isa. 27:1 where, as "the Crooked Serpent", he is connected with the Dragon, though distinguished from him. In the Psalms we find quite a number of references to him; as "the Bloody and Deceitful Man" (5:6); "the Wicked (One)" (9:17); "the Man of the Earth" (10:18); the "Mighty Man" (52:1); "the Adversary" (74:10); "the Head over many countries" (110:6); "the Evil Man" and "the Violent Man" (140:1), etc., etc. Let the student give special attention to Psalms 10, 52 and 55.

When we turn to the Prophets there the references to this Monster of Iniquity are so numerous that were we to cite all of them, even without comment, it would take us quite beyond the proper bounds of this introductory chapter. Only a few of the more prominent ones can, therefore, be noticed.

Isaiah mentions him: first as the "Assyrian", "the Rod" of God's anger (10:5); then as "the Wicked" (11:4); then as "the King of Babylon" (14:11-20 and cf 30:31-33); and also as the "Spoiler"—Destroyer (16:4). Jeremiah calls him "the Destroyer of the Gentiles" (4:7); the "Enemy", the "Cruel One" and "the Wicked" (30:14 and 23). Ezekiel refers to him as the "Profane Wicked Prince of Israel" (21:25), and again under the figure of the "Prince of Tyre" (28:2-10), and also as "the chief Prince of Meshech and Tubal" (38:2). Daniel gives a full delineation of his character and furnishes a complete outline of his career. Hosea speaks of him as "the King of Princes" (8:10), and as the "Merchant" in whose hand are "the balances of deceit" and who "loveth to oppress" (12:7). Joel describes him as the Head of the Northern Army, who shall be overthrown because he "magnified himself to do great things" (2:20). Amos terms him the "Adversary" who shall break Israel's strength and spoil her palaces (3:11). Micah makes mention of him in the fifth chapter of his prophecy (see v. 6). Nahum refers to him under the name of "Belial" (Heb.) and tells of his destruction (1:15). Habakkuk speaks of him as "the Proud Man" who "enlargeth his desires as hell, and is as death, and cannot be satisfied, but gathereth unto him all nations, and heapeth unto him all peoples" (2:5). Zechariah describes him as "the Idol Shepherd" upon whom is pronounced God's "woe", and upon whom descends His judgment (11:17).

Nor is it only in the Old Testament that we meet with this fearful character. Our Lord Himself spoke of him as the one who should "come in his own name", and who would be "received" by Israel (John 5:43). The apostle Paul gives us a full length picture of him in 2 Thess. 2, where he is denominated "that Man of Sin, the Son of Perdition", whose coming shall be "after the working of Satan with all power and signs and lying wonders". The apostle John mentions him by name, and declares that he will deny both the Father and the Son (1 John 2:22). While in the Apocalypse, the last book in the Bible, all these lines of prophecy are found to converge in "the Beast" who shall ultimately be cast, together with the False Prophet, into the lake of fire, there to be joined a thousand years later by the Devil himself, to suffer for ever and ever in that fire specially "prepared" by God.

The appearing of the Antichrist is a most appalling and momentous subject, and in the past, many well-meaning writers have deprived this impending event of much of its terror and meaning, by confusing some of the antichrists that have already appeared at various intervals on the stage of human history, with that mysterious being who will tower high above all the sons of Belial, being no less than Satan's counterfeit and opposer of the Christ of God, who is infinitely exalted above all the sons of God. It promotes the interests of Satan to keep the world in ignorance of the coming Super-man, and there can be no doubt that he is the one who is responsible for the general neglect in the study of this subject, and the author, too, of the conflicting testimony which is being given out by those who speak and write concerning it.

There have been three principal schools among the interpreters of the prophecies pertaining to the Antichrist. The first have applied these prophecies to persons of *the past,* to men who have been in their graves for many centuries. The second have given these prophecies a *present* application, finding their fulfillment in the Papacy which still exists. While the third give them a *future* application, and look for their fulfillment in a terrible being who is yet to be manifested. Now, widely divergent as are these several views, the writer is assured there is an element of truth in each of them. Many, if not the great majority of the prophecies—not only those pertaining to the Antichrist, but to other prominent objects of prediction—have at least a twofold, and frequently a threefold fulfillment. They have a local and immediate fulfillment: they have a continual and gradual fulfillment: and they have a final and exhaustive fulfillment.

In the second chapter of his first epistle the apostle John declares, "Little children, it is the last time: and as ye have heard that Antichrist shall come, *even now* are there many antichrists; whereby we know that it is the last time" (v. 18). In strict harmony with this, the apostle Paul affirmed that the "mystery of iniquity" was *"already"* at work in his day (2 Thess. 2:7). This need not surprise us, for many centuries before the apostles, the wise man declared, "The thing that *hath been,* is that *which shall be;* and that which *is* done is that which *shall be* done: and there is no new thing under the sun" (Ecc. 1:9). History works in cycles, but as each cycle is completed we are carried nearer the goal and consummation of history. There have been, then, and there exist today, many antichrists, but these are only so many forecasts and foreshadowings of the one who is yet to appear. But it is of first importance that we should distinguish clearly between *an* antichrist and *the* Antichrist. As we have said, there have already been many antichrists, but the appearing of the Antichrist is yet future.

The first school of interpreters referred to above, have lighted upon Antiochus Epiphanes as the one who fulfills the prophecies respecting the Antichrist. As far back as the days of Josephus (see his *"Antiquities"*) this view found ardent advocates. Appeal was made to the title he assumed *(Epiphanes signifying "Illustrious") ;* to his opposition against the worship of Jehovah; to his remarkable military achievements; to his diplomatic intrigues; to his defiling of the Temple; to his sacrificing of a pig in the holy of holies; to his setting up of an image; and to his cruel treatment of the Jews. But there are many conclusive reasons to prove that Antiochus Epiphanes could not possibly be the Antichrist, though undoubtedly he was, in several respects, a striking type of him, inasmuch as he foreshadowed many of the very things which this coming Monster will do. It is sufficient to point out that Antiochus Epiphanes had been in his grave for more than a hundred years when the apostle wrote 2 Thess. 2.

Another striking character who has been singled out by those who believe that the Antichrist has already appeared and finished his course, is Nero. And here again there are, admittedly, many striking resemblances between the type and the antitype. In his office of emperor of the Romans; in his awful impiety; in his consuming egotism; in his bloodthirsty nature; and in his ferocious and fiendish persecution of the people of God, we discover some of the very lineaments which will be characteristic of the Wicked One. But again it will be found that this man of infamous memory, Nero, did nothing more than foreshadow that one who shall far exceed him in satanic malignity. Positive proof that Nero was not the Antichrist is to be found in the fact that he was in his grave before John wrote the thirteenth chapter of the Revelation.

The second school of interpreters, to whom reference has been made above, apply the prophecies concerning the Antichrist to the papal system, and see in the succession of the popes the fac-simile of the Man of Sin. Attention is called to Rome's hatred of the Gospel of God's grace; to her mongrel combination of political and ecclesiastical rule; to her arrogant claims and tyrannical anathemas upon all who dare to oppose them; to her subtlety, her intrigues, her broken pledges; and last, but not least, to her unspeakable martyrdom of those who have withstood her. The pope, we are reminded, has usurped the place and prerogatives of the Son of God, and his arrogance, his impiety, his claims to infallibility, his demand for personal worship, all tally exactly with what is postulated of the Son of Perdition. Antichristian, Roman Catholicism unquestionably is, yet, even this monstrous system of evil falls short of that which shall yet be headed by the Beast. We shall devote a separate chapter to a careful comparison of the papacy with the prophecies which describe the character and career of *the* Antichrist.

The third school of interpreters believe that the prophecies relating to the Lawless One have not yet received their fulfillment, and cannot do so until this present Day of Salvation has run its course. The Holy Spirit of God, whose presence here now prevents the final outworking of the Mystery of Iniquity, must be removed from these scenes before Satan can bring forth his Masterpiece of deception and opposition to God. Many are the scriptures which teach plainly that the manifestation of the Antichrist is yet future, and these will come before us in our future studies. For the moment we must continue urging upon our readers the importance of this subject and the timeliness of our present inquiry.

The study of Antichrist is not merely one of interest to those who love the sensational, but it is of vital importance to a right understanding of dispensational truth. A true conception of the predictions which regard the Man of Sin is imperatively necessary for an adequate examination of that vast territory of unfulfilled prophecy. A single passage of scripture will establish this. If the reader will turn to the beginning of 2 Thess. 2 he will find that the saints in Thessalonica had been waiting for the coming of God's Son from heaven, because they had been taught to expect their gathering together unto Him before God launches His judgments upon the world, which will distinguish the "Day of the Lord". But their faith had been shaken and their hope disturbed. Certain ones had erroneously informed them that "that day" *had* arrived, and therefore, their expectation of being caught up to meet the Lord in the air had been disappointed. It was to relieve the distress of these believers, and to repudiate the errors of those who had disturbed them, that, moved by the Holy Spirit, the apostle wrote his second epistle to the Thessalonian church.

"Now we beseech you, brethren, by the coming of our Lord Jesus Christ, and by our gathering together unto Him, That ye be not soon shaken in mind, or be troubled, neither by spirit, nor by word, nor by letter as from us, as that the day of Christ is at hand. Let no man deceive you by any means: for that day shall not come, except there come a falling away first, and that Man of Sin be revealed, the Son of Perdition; Who opposeth and exalteth himself above all that is called God, or that is worshipped; so that he as God sitteth in the temple of God, showing himself that he is God. Remember ye not, that, when I was yet with you I told you these things? And now ye know what withholdeth that he might be revealed in his time. For the mystery of iniquity doth already work: only He who now letteth (hindereth) will let, until He be taken out of the way. And then shall that Wicked One be revealed, whom the Lord shall consume with the spirit of His mouth, and shall destroy with the brightness of his coming: Even him whose coming is after the working of Satan with all power and signs and lying wonders, And with all deceivableness of unrighteousness in them that perish; because they received not the love of the truth, that they might be saved. And for this cause God shall send them strong delusion, that they might believe a lie: That they all might be damned who believed not the truth, but had pleasure in unrighteousness" (2 Thess. 2:1-12).

We have quoted this passage at length to show that the Day of the Lord cannot come until after the Rapture (v. 1), after the Apostasy (v. 3), and after the appearing of the Man of Sin (v. 3), whose character and career are here briefly but graphically sketched. The Antichrist is to run his career of unparalleled wickedness *after* all Christians have been removed from these scenes, for it is under him, as their leader, that all the hosts of ungodliness shall muster to meet their doom by the summary judgment of God. Has, then, the Wicked One been revealed? or must we still say, as the apostle said in his day, that while the "mystery of iniquity" is even now working, there is something "withholding" (restraining), that he should be revealed "in his time"? The vital importance of the answer which is given to these questions will further appear when we connect with this description of the Antichrist given in 2 Thess. 2 the other prophecies which reveal the exact length of time within which his course must be accomplished. Our reason for saying this is because the majority of the prophecies yet unfulfilled *are to be fulfilled* during the time that the Antichrist is the central figure upon earth. Moreover, the destruction of the Antichrist and his forces will be the grand finale in the age-long conflict between the Serpent and the woman's Seed, as He returns to set up His kingdom.

The dominant view which has been held by Protestants since the time of the Reformation is that the many predictions relating to the Antichrist describe, instead, the rise, progress, and doom of the papacy. This mistake has led to others, and given rise to the scheme of prophetic interpretation which has prevailed throughout Christendom. When the predictions concerning the Man of Sin were allegorized, consistency required that all associated and collateral predictions should also be allegorized, and especially those which relate to his doom, and the kingdom which is to be established on the overthrow of his power. When the period of his predicted course was made to measure the whole duration of the papal system, it naturally followed that the predictions of the *associated events* should be applied to the history of Europe from the time that the Bishop of Rome became recognized as the head of the Western Churches.

It was, really, this mistake of Luther and his contemporaries in applying to Rome the prophecies concerning the Antichrist which is responsible, we believe, for the whole modern system of post-millennialism. The Reformers were satisfied that the Papacy had received its death blow, and though it lingered on, the Protestants of the sixteenth century were confident it could never recover. Believing that the doom of the Roman hierarchy was sealed, that the kingdom of Satan was rocking on its foundations, and that a brief interval would witness a complete overthrow, they at once seized upon the prophecies which announced the setting up of the kingdom of Christ as immediately following the destruction of the Antichrist, and applied them to Protestantism. It is true that some of them did not seem to fit very well, but human ingenuity soon found a way to overcome these difficulties. The obstacle presented by those prophecies that announced the *immediate* setting up of Christ's kingdom, following the overthrow and destruction of Satan's, was surmounted by an appeal to the analogy furnished in the overthrow of Satan's kingdom—if this was a tedious process, a gradual thing which required time to complete, why not so with the other? If the rapidly waning power of the papacy was sufficient to guarantee its ultimate extermination, why should not the progress of the Reformation presage the ultimate conquering of the world for Christ!

If, as it seemed clear to the Reformers, the papacy was the Man of Sin, and St. Peter's was the "temple" in which he usurped the place and prerogatives of Christ, then, this premise established, all the other conclusions connected with their scheme of prophetic interpretation must logically follow. To establish the premise was the first thing to be done, and once the theory became a settled conviction it was no difficult thing to find scriptures which appeared to confirm their view. The principal difficulty in the way was to dispose of the predictions which limited the final stage of Antichrist's career to forty-two months, or twelve hundred and sixty days. This was accomplished by what is known as the 'year-day' theory, which regards each of the 1260 days as 'prophetic days', that is, as 1260 years, and thus sufficient room was afforded to allow for the protracted history of Roman Catholicism.

Without entering into further details, it is evident at

once that, if this allegorical interpretation of the prophecies regarding Antichrist can be proven erroneous*, then the whole post-millennial and 'historical' schemes of interpretation fall to the ground, and thousands of the voluminous expositions of prophecy which have been issued during the past three hundred and fifty years are set aside as ingenious but baseless speculations. This, of itself, is sufficient to demonstrate the importance of our present inquiry.

Not only is the *importance* of our subject denoted by the prominent place given to it in the Word of God, and not only is its *value* established by the fact that a correct understanding of the person of Antichrist is one of the chief keys to the right interpretation of the many prophecies which yet await their fulfillment, but the *timeliness* of this inquiry is discovered by noting that the Holy Spirit has connected the appearing of the Antichrist with the Apostasy: "Let no man deceive you by any means: for that day shall not come, except there come *a falling away* (the 'Apostasy') first, *and* that Man of Sin be revealed, the Son of Perdition" (2 Thess. 2:3). These two things are here joined together, and if it can be shown that the Apostasy is already far advanced, then we may be certain that the manifestation of the Man of Sin cannot be far distant.

There is little need for us to make a lengthy digression here and give a selection from the abundance of evidence to hand, which shows that the Apostasy *is* already far advanced. The great majority of those whom we are addressing have already had their eyes opened by God to discern the Christ-dishonoring conditions which exist on almost every side. It will be enough to barely mention the gathering of the "tares" into bundles, which is taking

* Erroneous in the sense that it is but a shadowy and secondary fulfillment, rather than the ultimate and primary.

place before our eyes; the rapid spread of Spiritism, with its "seducing spirits and doctrines of demons", and the significant and solemn fact that thousands of those who are ensnared by it are those who have *departed* from the formal profession of the faith (1 Tim. 4:1) ; the "form of godliness" which still exists, but which alas! in the vast majority of instances "denies its power"; the alarming development and growth of Roman Catholicism in this land, and the lethargic indifference to this by most of those who bear the name of Christ; the denial of every cardinal doctrine of the faith once delivered to the saints, which is now heard in countless pulpits of every denomination; the "scoffing" which is invariably met with by those who teach the imminent return of the Lord Jesus; and the Laodicean spirit which is now the very atmosphere of Christendom, and from which few, if any, of the Lord's own people are entirely free—these, and a dozen others which might be mentioned, are the proofs which convince us that the time must be very near at hand when the Divine Hinderer shall be removed, and when Satan shall bring forth his Son to head the final revolt against God, ere the Lord Jesus returns to this earth and sets up His kingdom. This, then, shows the need of a prayerful examination of what God has revealed of those things "which must *shortly* come to pass". The very fact that the time when Satan's Masterpiece shall appear is rapidly drawing nearer, supplies further evidence of the importance and timeliness of our present inquiry.

The *practical value* of these preliminary considerations should at once be apparent. What we have written in connection with this incarnation of Satan who is shortly to appear, is not the product of a disordered imagination but the subject of Divine revelation. The warning given that the appearing of the Antichrist cannot be far distant springs not from the fears of an alarmist, but is required by the Signs of the Times which, in the light of Scripture, are fraught with significant meaning to all whose senses are exercised to discern both good and evil. The many proofs that the manifestation of the Man of Sin is an event of the near future are so many *calls to God's own children* to be ready for the Return of the Saviour, for before the Son of Perdition can be revealed the Lord Himself must first descend into the air and catch away from these scenes, unto Himself, His own blood-bought people. Therefore, it behooves each one of us to make "our calling and election *sure"*, and to heed that urgent admonition of the Saviour "Let your loins be girded about, and your lights burning; and ye yourselves like unto men that wait for their Lord" (Luke 12:35, 36).

1

THE PAPACY IS NOT THE ANTICHRIST

I AM come in My Father's name, and ye receive Me not: if another shall come in his own name, him ye will receive" (John 5:43). These words were spoken by the Lord Jesus Christ, and the occasion on which they were uttered and the connection in which they are found, invest them with peculiar solemnity. The chapter opens by depicting the Saviour healing the impotent man who lay by the pool of Bethesda. This occurred on the Sabbath day, and the enemies of Christ made it the occasion for a vicious attack upon Him: "Therefore did the Jews persecute Jesus, and sought to slay Him, because He had done these things on the Sabbath day" (v. 16). In vindicating His performance of this miracle on the Sabbath, the Lord Jesus began by saying, "My Father worketh hitherto, and I work" (v. 17). But this only served to intensify their enmity against Him, for we read, "Therefore the Jews sought the more to kill Him, because He not only had broken the Sabbath, but said also that God was His Father, making Himself equal with God" (v. 18). In response, Christ then made a detailed declaration of His Divine glories. In conclusion He appealed to the varied witnesses which bore testimony to His Deity:—the Father Himself (v. 32); John the Baptist (v. 33); His own works (v. 36); and the Scriptures (v. 39). Then He turned to those who were opposing Him and said, "And ye will not come to Me, that ye might have life. But I know you, that ye have not the love of God in you. I am come in My Father's name, and ye receive Me not: if another shall come in his own name, him ye will receive" (vv. 40,

42, 43). And this was immediately followed by this searching question—"How can ye believe which receive honor (glory) one of another, and seek not the honor (glory) that cometh from God only?" (v. 44).

Here is the key to the solemn statement which begins this article. These Jews received glory from one another; they did not seek it from God, for they had not the love of God in them. Therefore it was that the One who had come to them in the Father's name, and who "received *not* glory from men" (v. 41) was rejected by them. And just as Eve's rejection of the word of God's truth laid her open to accept the serpent's lie, so Israel's *rejection* of the true Messiah has prepared them, morally, to *receive* the false Messiah, for he will come in his own name, doing his own pleasure, and *will* "receive glory from men". Thus will he thoroughly appeal to the corrupt heart of the natural man.

The future appearing of this one who shall "come in his own name" was announced, then, by the Lord Himself. The Antichrist will be "received", not only by the Jews, but also by the whole world; received as their acknowledged Head and Ruler; and all the modern pleas for and movements to bring about a federation of the churches and a union of Christendom, together with the present-day efforts to establish a League of Nations—a great United States of the World—are but preparing the way for just such a character as is portrayed both in the Old and New Testaments.

There will be many remarkable correspondences between the true and the false Christ, but more numerous and more striking will be the *contrasts* between the Son of God and the Son of Perdition. The Lord Jesus came down from Heaven, whereas the Antichrist shall ascend from the bottomless Pit (Rev. 11:7). The Lord Jesus came in His Father's name, emptied Himself of His glory, lived in absolute dependence upon God, and refused to receive honor from men; but the Man of Sin will come in his own name, embodying all the pride of the Devil, opposing and exalting himself not only against the true God, but against everything that bears His name, and his deepest craving will be to receive honor and homage from men.

Now since this parallel, with its pointed contrasts, was drawn by our Lord Himself in John 5:43, how conclusive is the proof which it affords that the Antichrist will be a single individual being as surely as Christ was! In further proof of this 1 John 2:18 may be cited: "Little children, it is the last hour: and as ye heard that Antichrist cometh, even now hath there arisen many antichrists; whereby we know that it is the last hour" (R. V.). Here *the* Antichrist is plainly distinguished from the many who prepare his way. The verb "cometh" here is a remarkable one, for it is the very same that is used of the Lord Jesus Christ in reference to *His* first and second Advents. The Antichrist, therefore, is also "the coming one", or "he that cometh". This defines his relation *to the world,* —which has long been expecting some Conquering Hero —as "the Coming One" defines the relation of the Christ of God *to His Churches,* whose Divinely-inspired hope is the return of the Lord from Heaven.

Nor does this by any means exhaust the proof that the coming Antichrist will be a single individual being. The expressions used by the apostle Paul in 2 Thess. 2—"that Man of Sin", "The Son of Perdition", "he that opposeth and exalteth himself", "the Wicked One whom the Lord shall consume with the spirit of His mouth", "he whose coming is after the working of Satan"—all these point as distinctly to a single individual as did the Messianic predictions of the Old Testament point to the person of our Lord Jesus Christ.

Now, in accordance with these texts, and many others which might be quoted, we find that all the Christian writers of the first six centuries (that is all who make reference to the subject) regarded the Antichrist as a real person, a specific individual. We might fill many pages by giving extracts from their works, but three must suffice. The first is taken from a very ancient document, entitled "The Teaching of the Apostles", which probably dates back to the beginning of the second century:—

"For in the last days the false prophets and the destroyers shall be multiplied, and the sheep shall be turned into wolves, and love shall be turned into hate. For when lawlessness increases, they shall hate and persecute and deliver up one another; and then shall appear the world-deceiver as Son of God, who shall do signs and wonders, and the earth shall be delivered into his hands, and he shall do lawless deeds such as have never yet been done since the beginning of the world. Then shall the race of men come into the fire of trial, and many shall be offended and shall perish, but they who have endured in their faith shall be saved under the very curse itself".

Our second quotation is taken from the writings of Cyril, who was Bishop of Jerusalem in the fourth century:

"This aforementioned Antichrist comes when the times of the sovereignty of the Romans shall be fulfilled, and the concluding events of the world draw nigh. Ten kings of the Romans arise at the same time in different places, perhaps; but reigning at the same period. But after these, the Antichrist is the eleventh, having, by his magic and evil skill, violently possessed himself of the Roman power.

Three of those who have reigned before him, he will subdue; the other seven he will hold in subjection to himself.
At first he assumes a character of gentleness (as if a wise
and understanding person), pretending both to modera-
tion and philanthropy; deceiving, both by lying miracles
and prodigies which come from his magical deceptions,
the Jews, as if he were the expected Messiah. Afterwards
he will addict himself to every kind of evil, cruelty, and
excess, so as to surpass all who have been unjust and impious before him; having a bloody and relentless and piti-
less mind, and full of wily devices against all, and especially against believers. But having dared such things
three years and six months, he will be destroyed by the
second glorious coming from heaven of the truly begotten
Son of God, who is our Lord and Saviour, Jesus the true
Messiah; who, having destroyed Antichrist by the Spirit
of His mouth, will deliver him to the fire Gehenna".

Our last quotation is made from the writings of Greg-
ory of Tours, who wrote at the end of the sixth century A.
D.:—

"Concerning the end of the world, I believe what I have
learnt from those who have gone before me. Antichrist
will assume circumcision, asserting himself to be the
Christ. He will then place a statue to be worshipped in the
Temple at Jerusalem, as we read that the Lord has said,
'Ye shall see the abomination of desolation standing in
the holy place' ".

Our purpose in making these quotations is not because
we regard the voice of antiquity as being in any degree au-
thoritative: far from it; the *only* authority for us is "What
saith the Scriptures?". Nor have we presented these views
as curious relics of antiquity—though it is interesting to
discover the thoughts which occupied some of the leading

minds of past ages. No; our purpose has been simply to show that the early Christian writers uniformly held that the Antichrist would be a real person, a Jew, one who should both simulate and oppose the true Christ. Such continued to be the generally received doctrine until what is known as the Dark Ages were far advanced.

It is not until we reach the fourteenth century (so far as the writer is aware) that we find the first marked deviation from the uniform belief of the early Christians. It was the Waldenses,—so remarkably sound in the faith on almost all points of doctrine—who, thoroughly worn out by centuries of the most relentless and merciless persecutions, published about the year 1350 a treatise designed to prove that the system of Popery was the Antichrist. It should however be said in honor of this people, whose memory is blessed, that in one of their earliest books entitled "The Noble Lesson", published about 1100 A. D., they taught that the Antichrist was an individual rather than a system.

Following the new view espoused by the Waldenses it was not long before the Hussites, the Wycliffites and the Lollards—other companies of Christians who were fiercely persecuted by Rome—eagerly caught up the idea, and proclaimed that the Pope was the Man of Sin and the papacy the Beast. From them it was handed on to the leaders of the Reformation who soon made an earnest attempt to systematize this new scheme of eschatology. But rarely has there been a more forcible example of the tendency of men's beliefs to be moulded by the events and signs of their own lifetime. In order to adapt the prophecies of the Antichrist to the Papal hierarchy, or the line of the Popes, they had to be so wrested that scarcely anything was left of their original meaning.

"The coming Man of Sin had to be changed into a long succession of men. The time of his continuance, which God had stated with precision and clearness as forty-two months (Rev. 13:5), or three years and a half, being far too short for the line of Popes, had to be lengthened by an ingenious, but most unwarrantable, process of first resolving it into days, and then turning these days into years.

"The fact that, in the 13th chapter of the Apocalypse, the first Beast or secular power, is supreme while the second Beast or ecclesiastical power is subordinate, had to be ignored; since such an arrangement is opposed to all the traditions of the Roman system. Also the circumstances that the second Beast is a prophet and not a priest, had to be kept in the background; for the Roman church exalts the priest, and has little care for the prophet. Then, again, the awful words pronouncing sentence of death upon every one who worshipped the Beast and his image, and receives his mark in his forehead or in his hand (Rev. 13), seemed—and no wonder—too terrible to be applied to every Roman Catholic, and, therefore, had to be explained away or suppressed" *(G. H. Pember)*.

Nevertheless, by common consent the Reformers applied the prophecies which treat of the character, career, and doom of the Antichrist, to Popery, and regarded those of his titles which referred to him as "that Man of Sin, the Son of Perdition", the "King of Babylon" and "the Beast", as only so many names for the head of the Roman hierarchy. But this view, which was upheld by most of the Puritans too, must be brought to the test of the one infallible standard of Truth which our gracious God has placed in our hands. We must search the Scriptures to see whether these things be so or not.

Now we shall hold no brief for the pope, nor have we

anything good to say of that pernicious system of which he is the head. On the contrary, we have no hesitation in denouncing as rank blasphemy the blatant assumption of the pope as being the infallible vicar of Christ. Nor do we hesitate to declare that the Papacy has been marked, all through its long history, by impious arrogance, awful idolatry, and unspeakable cruelty. But, nevertheless, there are many scriptures which prevent us from believing that the Papacy and the Antichrist are identical. The Son of Perdition will eclipse any monstrosities that have sprung from the waves of the Tiber. The Bible plainly teaches us to look for a more terrible personage than any Hildebrand or Leo.

Undoubtedly there are many points of analogy between Antichrist and the popes, and without doubt the Papal system has foreshadowed to a remarkable degree the character and career of the coming Man of Sin. Some of the parallelisms between them were pointed out by us in the previous chapter, and to these many more might be added. Not only is it evident that Roman Catholicism is a most striking type and harbinger of that one yet to come, but the cause of truth requires us to affirm that the Papacy is *an antichrist,* doubtless, the most devilish of them all. Yet, we say again, that Romanism is not *the* Antichrist. As it is likely that many of our readers have been educated in the belief that the pope and the Antichrist are identical, we shall proceed to produce some of the numerous proofs which go to show that such is not the case. That the Papacy cannot possibly be *the* Antichrist appears from the following considerations:—

1. The term "Antichrist" whether employed in the singular or the plural, denotes a person or persons, and *never a system.* We may speak correctly of an anti-Christ-

ian system, just as we may refer to a Christian organization; but it is just as inadmissible and erroneous to refer to any system or organization as "the Antichrist" or "an antichrist", as it would be to denominate any Christian system or organization "the Christ", or "a Christ". Just as truly as *the Christ* is the title of a single person, the Son of God, so *the Antichrist* will be a single person, the son of Satan.

2. The Antichrist will be a lineal descendant of Abraham, *a Jew.* We shall not stop to submit the proof for this, as that will be given in our next chapter; suffice it now to say that none but a full-blooded Jew could ever expect to palm himself off on the Jewish people as their long-expected Messiah. Here is an argument that has never been met by those who believe that the pope is the Man of Sin. So far as we are aware no Israelite has ever occupied the Papal See—certainly none has done so since the seventh century.

3. In line with the last argument, we read in Zech. 11: 16, 17, "For, lo, I will raise up a Shepherd *in the land,* which shall not visit those that be cut off, neither shall seek the young ones, nor heal that that is broken, nor feed that that standeth still: but he shall eat the flesh of the fat, and tear their claws in pieces. Woe to the Idol Shepherd that leaveth the flock! The sword (of Divine judgment) shall be upon his arm (his power), and upon his right eye (intelligence): his arm shall be clean dried up, and his right eye shall be utterly darkened". *"The* land" here is, of course, Palestine, as is ever the case in Scripture with this expression. This could not possibly apply to the line of the Popes.

4. In 2 Thess. 2:4 we learn that the Man of Sin shall sit "in the Temple of God", and St. Peter's at Rome cannot

possibly be called *that*. The "Temple" in which the Antichrist shall sit will be the rebuilt temple of the Jews, and that will be located not in Italy but in Jerusalem. In later chapters it will be shown that the Mosque of Omar shall yet be replaced by a Jewish Temple before our Lord returns to the earth.

5. The Antichrist will be *received by the Jews*. This is clear from the passage which heads the first paragraph of this chapter: "I am come in My Father's name, and ye receive Me not: if another shall come in his own name, him *ye* will receive"; but the *Jews* have never yet owned allegiance to any pope.

6. The Antichrist will make a Covenant with the Jews. In Dan. 9:27 we read, "And he shall confirm the covenant with many for one week". The one referred to here as making this seven-year Covenant is "the Prince that shall come" of the previous verse, namely, the Antichrist, who will be the Head of the ten-kingdomed Empire. The nation with whom the Prince will make this covenant is the people of Daniel, as is clear from the context—see v. 24. But we know of no record upon the scroll of history of any pope having ever made a seven-year Covenant with the Jews!

7. In Dan. 11:45 we read, "And he shall plant the tabernacles of his palace between the seas, in the glorious holy mountain; yet he shall come to his end, and none shall help him". The person referred to here is, again, the Antichrist, as will be seen by going back to v. 36 where this section of the chapter begins. There we are told, "The king shall do according to his will; and he shall exalt himself, and magnify himself above every god, and shall speak marvelous things against the God of gods, and shall prosper till the indignation be accomplished; for that that

is determined shall be done". This is more than sufficient to identify with certainty the one spoken of in the last verse of Dan. 11. The Antichrist, then, will plant the tabernacles of his palace "between the seas", that is, between the Mediterranean and the Red Sea. By no species of ingenuity can this be made to apply to the pope, for his palace, the Vatican, is located in the capital city of Italy.

8. The Antichrist cannot be revealed until the mystic Body of Christ and the Holy Spirit have been removed from the earth. This is made clear by what we read in 2 Thess. 2. In verse three of that chapter the apostle refers to the revelation of the Man of Sin. In verse four he describes his awful impiety. In verse five he reminds the Thessalonians how that he had taught them these things by word of mouth when he was with them. And then, in verse six he declares "And now ye know what withholdeth that he might be revealed in his time". And again he said, "For the mystery of iniquity doth already work: only He who now letteth (hindereth) will let until He be taken out of the way". There are two agencies, then, which are hindering, or preventing the manifestation of the Antichrist, until "his time" shall have come. The former agency is covered by the pronoun "what", the latter by the word "He". The former, we are satisfied, is the mystical Body of Christ; the latter being the Holy Spirit of God. At the Rapture both shall be "taken out of the way", and then shall the Man of Sin be revealed. If, then, the Antichrist cannot appear before the Rapture of the saints and the taking away of the Holy Spirit, then, here is proof positive that the Antichrist *has not yet appeared*.

9. Closely akin to the last argument is the fact that quite a **number** of definite scriptures place the appearing

of the Antichrist at that season known as the End-Time. Dan. 7 and 8 make it plain that the Antichrist will run his career at the very end of this age (we do not say this 'dispensation' for *that* will end at the Rapture), that is, during the great Tribulation, the time of "Jacob's trouble". Dan. 7:21-23 declares, "I beheld, and the same horn made war with the saints, and prevailed against them; Until the Ancient of days came, and judgment was given to the saints of the Most High; and the time came that the saints possessed the kingdom". Dan. 8:19 places his course (see 8:23-25) at "the last end of the indignation", i. e. of God's wrath against Israel and the Gentiles. Dan. 9 shows that he will make his seven-years' Covenant with the Jews at the beginning of the last of the seventy "weeks" which is to bring in "the end" of Israel's sins and "finish the transgression" (9:24). If the time of the Antichrist's manifestation is yet future then it necessarily follows that Rome cannot be the Antichrist.

10. The Antichrist will deny both the Father and the Son: "He is Antichrist, that denieth the Father and the Son" (1 John 2:22). This scripture does not speak of virtual, but of actual and formal denial. But Rome has always maintained in her councils and creeds, her symbols of faith and worship, that there are three persons in the Godhead. Numerous and grievous have been her departures from the teaching of Holy Scripture, yet since the time of the Council of Trent *(1563 A. D.)* every Roman Catholic has had to confess "I believe in God the Father . . . . and in the Lord Jesus Christ . . . . and in the Holy Ghost, the Lord and Giver of life, which proceedeth from the Father and the Son".

As a system Romanism is a go-between. The 'priest' stands between the sinner and God; the 'confessional' between him and the throne of grace; 'penance' between him and godly sorrow; the 'mass' between him and Christ; and 'purgatory' between him and Heaven. The pope acknowledges both the Father and the Son: he confesses himself to be both the servant of God and His worshipper; he blesses the people not in his own name, but in that of the Holy Trinity.

11. The Antichrist is described as the one "who opposeth and exalteth himself above all that is called God, or that is worshipped; so that he as God sitteth in the Temple of God, showing himself that he is God" (2 Thess. 2: 4). This is what the popes have never done. Not even Leo ventured to deify himself or supersede God. The popes have made many false and impious claims for themselves; nevertheless, their decrees have been sent forth as from the 'vice-gerent' of God, the 'vicar' of Christ—thus acknowledging a Divine power *above* himself.

12. In Rev. 13:2, 4 we read, "And the beast which I saw was like unto a leopard, and his feet were as the feet of a bear, and his mouth as the mouth of a lion: and *the dragon gave him* his power, and his seat, and great authority . . . . and they *worshipped the dragon* which gave power unto the beast". By comparing these verses with Rev. 12:9 we learn that the Dragon is none other than Satan himself. Now by almost common consent this first beast of Rev. 13 is the Antichrist. If, then, Romanism be the Antichrist, where, we may ask, shall we turn to find anything answering to what we read of here in Rev. 13:4 —"And they *worshipped the dragon* which gave power unto the beast"!

13. This same 13th chapter of Revelation informs us that the Antichrist (the first Beast) shall be *aided* by a second Beast who is denominated "the False Prophet"

(Rev. 19:20). The False Prophet, we are told "exerciseth all the power of the First Beast before him, and causeth the earth and them which dwell therein to worship the *First* Beast" (Rev. 13:12). If the First Beast be the Papacy, then who is the False Prophet who "causeth the earth and them which dwell therein to worship" her?

14. Again; we are told that this False Prophet shall say to them that dwell on the earth "that they should make an image to the Beast, which had the wound by a sword and did live" (Rev. 13:14). Further, we are told, "And he had power to give life unto the image of the Beast, that the image of the Beast should both speak, and cause that as many as would not worship the image of the Beast should be killed" (Rev. 13:15). Where do we find anything in Popery which in anywise resembles this?

15. In Dan. 9:27 we are told that the Antichrist "shall cause the *sacrifice* and the *oblation* to *cease*". And again in 8:11 we read, "Yea, he magnified himself even against the Prince of the host, and by him the daily sacrifice was *taken away*". If Romanism is the Antichrist how can these scriptures be made to square with the oft repeated *"Sacrifice* of the Mass"?

16. The *dominion* of the Antichrist shall be *world-wide*. The coming Man of Sin will assert a supremacy which shall be unchallenged and universal. "And all the world wondered after the Beast" (Rev. 13:3). "And power was given him over *all* kindreds, and tongues, and nations" (13:7). It hardly needs to be pointed out that half of Christendom, to say nothing of Heathendom, is *outside* the pale of Rome, and is antagonistic to the claims of the Papacy. Again; in 13:17 we read "No man might buy or sell, save he that had the mark, or the name of the Beast, or the number of his name": and when, we ask, has any

pope exercised such commercial supremacy that *none* could buy or sell without his permission?

17. The *duration* of Antichrist's career, after he comes out in his true character, will be *limited* to forty-two months. There are no less than six scriptures which, with a variety of expression, affirm this time restriction. In Dan. 7:25 we learn that this one who shall "speak great words against the Most High", and who shall "think to change times and laws", will have these "given into his hand until a time, and times, and the dividing of time": that is, for three years and a half—cf. Rev. 12:14 with 12:6. And again in Rev. 13:5 we are told, "And there was given unto him a mouth speaking great things and blasphemies; and power was given unto him to continue *forty and two months*" (Rev. 13:5). Now it is utterly impossible to make this harmonize with the protracted history of Romanism by any honest method of computation,

18. In Rev. 13:7, 8 we read, "And it was given unto him to make war with the saints, and to overcome them: and power was given him over all kindreds, and tongues, and nations. And *all* that dwell upon the face of the earth shall worship him, *whose names are not written* in the book of life of the Lamb slain from the foundation of the world". Here we are expressly told that the only ones who will not "worship the Beast", i. e. the Antichrist, are they whose names are written in the Lamb's book of life. If then the pope is the Antichrist, all who do not worship him must have their names written in the Lamb's book of life—an absurdity on the face of it, for this would be tantamount to saying that all the infidels, atheists, and unbelievers of the last thousand years who were outside of the pale of Roman Catholicism are saved.

19. In 2 Thess. 2:11, 12 we are told, "For this cause

God shall send them strong delusion, that they should believe a lie: that *they all* might be damned who believed not the truth, but had pleasure in unrighteousness". The context here shows that "believing a lie" means accepting the claims of the Antichrist. Those who believe his claims will "receive" him (John 5:43), and not only so, they will "worship" him (Rev. 13:8); and 2 Thess. 2:12 declares that *"all"* who do this will be "damned". If, then, the pope is the Antichrist, then it necessarily follows that *all* who have "believed" his lying claims, that *all* who have "received" him as the vicar of Christ, that, *all* who have "worshipped" him, will be eternally lost. But the writer would not for a moment make any such sweeping assertion. He, together with thousands of others, believes firmly that during the centuries there have been many Roman Catholics who, despite much ignorance and superstition, have been among that number that have exercised faith in the blood of Christ, and that lived and died resting on the finished work of Christ as the alone ground of their acceptance before God, and who because of this shall be forever with the Lord.

20. That the Antichrist and the Papacy are totally distinct is unequivocally established by the teaching of Rev. 17. Here we learn that there shall be ten kings who will reign "with the Beast" (v. 12), and act in concert with him (vv. 13, 16). Then we are told "these shall hate the Whore (the papacy), and shall make her desolate and naked, and shall eat her flesh, and burn her with fire" (v. 16). Instead of the Antichrist and the Papacy being identical, the former shall destroy the latter; whereas, the Antichrist shall be destroyed by Christ Himself, see 2 Thess. 2:8.

Perhaps a word of explanation is called for as to why

we have entered into such lengthy details in presenting
some of the many proofs that the Papacy is not the Antichrist. Our chief reason for doing so was because we expect that many who will read this paper are among the
number who have been brought up in the belief which
was commonly taught by the Reformers and which has
prevailed generally since their day.   For those readers
who had already been established on this point, we would
ask them to please bear with us for having sought to help
those less fortunate. Our next chapter will be one of more
general interest, for in it we shall discuss the *person* of the
Antichrist—*who* he will be, from *whence* he will spring,
and what marks will serve to *identify* him.

2

THE PERSON OF THE ANTICHRIST

IN our last chapter we pointed out how that the Antichrist is not a system of evil, nor an anti-Christian organization, but instead, a single individual being, a person yet to appear. In support of this we appealed to the declaration of our Lord recorded in John 5:43; "I am come in My Father's name, and ye receive Me not: if another shall come in his own name, him ye will receive". Here the Saviour both compares and contrasts the Man of Sin with Himself. The point of comparison is that, like the Saviour, he shall offer himself to Israel; the contrast is, that unlike Christ who was rejected by the Jews, the false messiah shall be "received" by them. If, then, the Antichrist many be compared and contrasted with the Christ of God, he, too, must be a person, an individual being.

Again; we called attention to the expression used by the apostle Paul in 2 Thess. 2:—"That Man of Sin", "the Son of Perdition", "he that opposeth and exalteth himself", "the Wicked One whom the Lord shall consume with the spirit of His mouth", "he whose coming is after the working of Satan"—all these point as distinctly to a single individual as did the Messianic predictions of the Old Testament point to the person of our Lord Jesus Christ. Assured, then, that "the Antichrist" signifies a specific individual, our next concern is to turn to the Scriptures and learn what God has been pleased to reveal concerning this Personification of Evil.

I. THE ANTICHRIST WILL BE A JEW

The Antichrist will be a *Jew,* though his connections, his governmental position, his sphere of dominion, will by no means confine him to the Israelitish people. It should, however, be pointed out that there is no express declaration of Scripture which says *in so many words* that this daring Rebel *will be* "a Jew"; nevertheless, the hints given are so plain, the conclusions which must be drawn from certain statements of Holy Writ are so obvious, and the requirements of the case are so inevitable, that we are forced to believe he *must* be a Jew. To these 'hints', 'conclusions' and 'requirements' we now turn.

1. In Ezek. 21:25-27 we read: "And thou, profane wicked prince of Israel, whose day is come, when iniquity shall have an end, Thus saith the Lord God; Remove the diadem, and take off the crown: this shall not be the same: exalt him that is low, and abase him that is high. I will overturn, overturn, overturn it: and it shall be no more until he come whose right it is, and I will give it him". The dispensational place and scope of this passage is not hard to determine. The time-mark is given in v. 25: it is "when iniquity shall have an end". It is the End-Time which is in view, then, the End of the Age, when "the transgressors are come to the full" (Dan. 8:23 and cf. 11: 36—"Till the indignation be accomplished"). At that time Israel shall have a "Prince", a Prince who is "crowned" (v. 26), and a Prince whose "day" is said to be "come" when "iniquity shall have an end". Now, as to *who* this "Prince" is, there is surely no room for doubt. The only "Prince" whom Israel will have in that day, is the Son of Perdition, here termed their "Prince" because he will be masquerading as "Messiah *the Prince*" (see Dan. 9:25)! Another unmistakeable mark of identification is here given, in that he is expressly denominated "thou, *profane wicked* Prince"—assuredly, it is the Man of Sin who is here in view, that impious one who shall "op-

pose and exalt himself above all that is called God". But what should be noted particularly, is, that this profane and wicked character is here named "Prince *of Israel*". He must, therefore, be of the Abrahamic stock, a *Jew!*

2. In Ezek. 28:2-10 a remarkable description is given us of the Antichrist under the figure of "the Prince of Tyrus", just as in vv. 12-19 we have another most striking delineation of Satan under the figure of "the king of Tyrus". In a later chapter we hope to show that, beyond a doubt, it is the Antichrist who is in view in the first section of this chapter. There is only one thing that we would now point out from this passage: in v. 10 it is said of him "Thou shalt die the deaths of the *uncircumcised*", which is a very strong hint that he *ought not* to die the deaths of the "uncircumcised" because *he* belonged to the Circumcision! Should it be said that this verse cannot apply to the Antichrist because he will be destroyed by Christ Himself at His coming, the objection is very easily disposed of by a reference to Rev. 13:14, which tells of the Antichrist being wounded to death by a sword and rising from the dead—which is prior to his ultimate destruction at the hands of the Saviour.

3. In Dan. 11:36, 37 we are told, "And the king shall do according to his will; and he shall exalt himself, and magnify himself above every god, and shall speak marvelous things against the God of gods, and shall prosper till the indignation be accomplished: for that that is determined shall be done. Neither shall he regard the God of his fathers". This passage, it is evident, refers to and describes none other than the coming Antichrist. But what we wish to call special attention to is the last sentence quoted—"The God of his fathers". What are we to understand by this expression? Why, surely, that he is *a Jew,*

an Israelite, and that his fathers after the flesh were Abraham, Isaac and Jacob—for such is the invariable meaning of "the fathers" throughout the Old Testament Scriptures.

4. In Matt. 12:43-45 we have another remarkable scripture which will be considered briefly, in a later section of this chapter, when we shall endeavor to show that "The Unclean Spirit" here is none other than the Son of Perdition, and that the "house" from which he goes out and into which he returns, is the Nation of Israel. If this can be established, then we have another proof that he will be *a Jew,* for this "house", which is Israel, is here termed by Antichrist *"my* house". Just as Solomon was of "the House of David", so Antichrist shall be of the House of Israel.

5. In John 5:43 we have a further word which helps us to fix the nationality of this coming One. In speaking of the false messiah, the Lord Jesus referred to him as follows, *"Another* shall come in his own name". In the Greek there are four different words all translated "Another" in our English versions. One of them is employed but once, and a second but five times, so these need not detain us now. The remaining two are used frequently, and with a clear distinction between them. The first "allos" signifies "another" *of the same kind or genus*—see Matt. 10:23; 13:24; 26:71, etc. The second, "heteros", means "another" *of a totally different kind.*—see Mark 16:12; Luke 14:31; Acts 7:18; Rom. 7:23. Now the striking thing is that the word used by our Lord in John 5:43 is "allos", another of the *same* genus, not "heteros", another of a different order. Christ, the Son of Abraham, the Son of David, had presented Himself to Israel, and they rejected Him; but "another" of the *same* Abrahamic stock should come to them, and him they would "receive".

If the coming Antichrist were to be a Gentile, the Lord would have employed the word "heteros"; the fact that He used "allos" shows that he will be a *Jew*.

6. The very name "Antichrist" argues strongly his *Jewish* nationality. This title "Antichrist" has a double significance. It means that he will be one who shall be *"opposed"* to Christ, one who will be His enemy. But it also purports that he will be a *mock* Christ, an *imitation* Christ, a *pro*-Christ, a *pseudo* Christ. It intimates that he will ape Christ. He will pose as the real Messiah of Israel. In such case he *must* be a *Jew*.

7. This mock Christ will be "received" by Israel. The Jews will be deceived by Him. They will believe that he is indeed their long-expected Messiah. They will accept him as such. Proofs of this will be furnished in a later chapter. But if this pseudo Christ succeeds in palming himself off on the Jews as their true Messiah he *must* be a *Jew,* for it is unthinkable that they would be deceived by any Gentile.

Ere passing to the next point, we may add, that it was the common belief among Christians during the first four centuries A. D., that the Antichrist would come from the tribe of Dan. Whether this will be the case or no, we do not know. Gen. 49:17, 18 may have ultimate reference to this Son of Perdition. Certainly Dan is the most mysterious of all the twelve tribes.

II. THE ANTICHRIST WILL BE THE SON OF SATAN

That Satan will have a son ought not to surprise us. The Devil is a consummate *imitator* and much of his success in deceiving men is due to his marvelous skill in counterfeiting the things of God. Below we give a list of some of his imitations:—

Do we read of Christ going forth to sow the "good seed" (Matt. 13:24), then we also read of the enemy going forth to sow his "tares"—an imitation wheat (Matt. 13:25). Do we read of "the children of God", then we also read of "the children of the wicked one" (Matt. 13: 38). Do we read of God *working in* His children "both to will and to do of His good pleasure" (Phil. 2:13), then we are also told that the Prince of the power of the air is "the spirit that now *worketh in* the children of disobedience" (Eph. 2:2). Do we read of the Gospel of God, then we also read that Satan has a gospel—"Another gospel, which is not another" (Gal. 1:6, 7). Did Christ appoint "apostles", then Satan has *his* "apostles" too (2 Cor. 11: 13). Are we told that "the Spirit searcheth all things, yea, the *deep things* of God" (1 Cor. 2:10), then Satan also provides *his* "deep things" (see Greek of Rev. 2:24). Are we told that God, by His angel, will "seal" His servants in their foreheads (Rev. 7:3), so also we read that Satan, by his angels, will set a "mark" in the "foreheads" of his devotees (Rev. 13:16). Does the Father seek "worshippers" (John 4:23), so also does Satan (Rev. 13:4). Did Christ quote scripture, so also did Satan (Matt. 4:6). Is Christ the Light of the world, then Satan also is transformed as an "angel of light" (2 Cor. 11:14). Is Christ denominated *"the Lion of the tribe of Judah"* (Rev. 5: 5), then the Devil is also referred to as "a roaring *lion*" (1 Peter 5:6). Do we read of Christ and "His angels" (Matt. 24:31), then we also read of the Devil and *"his* angels" (Matt. 25:41). Did Christ work miracles, so also will Satan (2 Thess. 2:9). Is Christ seated upon a "Throne", so also will Satan be (Rev. 2:13, Gk.). Has Christ a Church, then Satan has his "synagogue" (Rev. 2:9). Has Christ a "bride", then Satan has his "whore" (Rev. 17:

16). Has God His "Vine", so has Satan (Rev. 14:19). Does God have a city, the new Jerusalem, then Satan has a city, Babylon (Rev. 17:5; 18:2). Is there a "mystery of godliness" (1 Tim. 3:16), so also there is a "mystery of iniquity" (2 Thess. 2:7). Does God have an only-begotten Son, so we read of "the Son of Perdition" (2 Thess. 2:3). Is Christ called "the Seed of the woman", then the Antichrist will be "the seed of the serpent" (Gen. 3:15). Is the Son of God also the Son of Man, then the son of Satan will also be the "Man of Sin" (2 Thess. 2:3).

Is there a Holy Trinity, then there is also an Evil Trinity (Rev. 20:10). In this Trinity of Evil Satan himself is supreme, just as in the Blessed Trinity the Father is (governmentally) supreme: note that Satan is several times referred to as a *father* (John 8:44, etc.). Unto his son, the Antichrist, Satan gives his authority and power to represent and act for him (Rev. 13:4) just as God the Son received "all power in heaven and earth" from *His* Father, and uses it for His glory. The Dragon (Satan) and the Beast (Antichrist) are accompanied by a third, the False Prophet, and just as the third person in the Holy Trinity, the Spirit, bears witness to the person and work of Christ and glorifies Him, so shall the third person in the Evil Trinity bear witness to the person and work of the Antichrist and glorify him (see Rev. 13:11-14).

Now the Antichrist will be a man, and yet more than man, just as Christ was Man and yet more than man. The Antichrist will be the 'Superman' of whom the world, even now, is talking, and for whom it is looking. The Wicked One who is to be revealed shortly, will be a supernatural character, he will be the son of Satan. His twofold nature is plainly declared in 2 Thess. 2:3—"That Man of

Sin, the Son of Perdition". In proof of these assertions we ask for a careful attention to what follows.

1. "And I will put enmity between thee and the woman, and between *thy Seed* and her Seed; it shall bruise thy head, and thou shalt bruise his heel" (Gen. 3:15). It is to be noted that there is here a *double* "enmity" spoken of: God says, "I will put enmity between thee and the woman", that is, between Satan and Israel, for Israel was the woman that bore Christ (Rev. 12); *"And* between thy seed and her seed". Observe particularly that *two* "seeds" are here spoken of: "Thy seed" (the antecedent is plainly the "Serpent") and "her seed", the woman's Seed. The woman's "Seed" was Christ, the Serpent's "Seed" will be the Antichrist. The Antichrist, then, will be more than a man, he will be the actual and literal Seed of that old Serpent, the Devil; as Christ was, according to the flesh, the actual and literal Seed of the woman. "Thy seed", Satan's seed, refers to a specific individual, just as "her seed" refers to a specific Individual.

2. "In that day the Lord with His sore and great and strong sword shall punish Leviathan the piercing Serpent, even Leviathan that crooked Serpent; and he shall slay the Dragon that is in the sea" (Isa. 27:1). To appreciate the force of this we need to attend to the context, which is unfortunately broken by the chapter division. In the closing verses of Isa. 26 we hear God saying, "Come, My people, enter thou into thy chambers, and shut thy doors about thee: hide thyself as it were for a little moment, until the indignation be overpast" (26:20). These words are addressed to the elect remnant in Israel. Their ultimate application will be to those on earth at the end of this Age, for it is the time of God's "indignation" (cf. Dan. 8:19 and 11:36). It is the time when "the Lord

cometh out of His place to punish the inhabitants of the earth for their iniquity: the earth also shall disclose her blood, and shall no more cover her slain" (26:21)—notice "iniquity", singular number, not "iniquities". It is their worshipping of Satan's Man which is specifically referred to. Then, immediately following we read, *"In that day the Lord . . . shall punish Leviathan the piercing Serpent"*. The connection, then, makes it plain that it is just before the Millennium when God shall punish the Crooked Serpent, the Antichrist. Now the very fact that the Wicked One is here denominated "the piercing and crooked Serpent" hints strongly that he will be *the son* of "that old Serpent, the Devil".

3. In the first two sections of Ezek. 28 two remarkable characters are brought before us. The second who is described in vv. 12-19 has received considerable attention from Bible students of the last two generations, and since the late Mr. G. H. Pember pointed out that what is there said of "the king of Tyrus" could be true of no earthly king or mere human being, and must outline a character that none but Satan himself (before his fall) could fill*, this view has been adopted by most of the leading Bible teachers. But little attention has been paid to the character described in the first ten verses of this chapter.

Now just as what is said in Ezek. 28 of "the king of Tyrus" can only apply fully to Satan himself, so, what is said of "the prince of Tyrus" manifestly has reference to the Antichrist. The parallelisms between what is said here and what we find in other scriptures which describe the Son of Perdition are so numerous and so evident, that we are obliged to conclude that it is the same person which is

*See also the chapter on Satan's Origin in the writer's "Satan and his Gospel."

here contemplated. We cannot now attempt anything like a complete exposition of the whole passage (though we hope to give one later) but will just call attention to some of the outstanding marks of identification:

First, the Lord God says to this personage, "Because thine heart is lifted up, and thou hast said I am a god, I *sit* in the *seat* of God"—cf. 2 Thess. 2:4. Second, "Behold thou art *wiser* than Daniel"—cf. Dan. 8:23, and 7:8, "Behold, in this horn were *eyes* like the eyes of men, and a mouth speaking great things", which intimates that the Antichrist will be possessed of extraordinary intelligence. Third, it is said of this character, "With thy wisdom and with thine understanding thou hast gotten thee *riches,* and hast gotten gold and silver into *thy treasures*" (v. 4—cf. Psa. 52:7; Dan. 11:38).

Sufficient has been said, we trust, to show that under the figure of this "prince of Tyrus" we may discern clearly the unmistakeable features of the coming Antichrist. But the particular point we would make here, is this, that as Satan is termed "the *king* of Tyre", in the second section of this chapter the Antichrist is referred to as "the *prince* of Tyre". Antichrist, then, is related to Satan as "prince" is to "king", that is, as *son* is to his *father.*

4. In Matt. 12:43 the Antichrist is called "The Unclean Spirit", not merely *an* unclean spirit, but *"the* Unclean Spirit". We cannot now stop and submit the evidence that it *is* the Antichrist who is here in view, for this is another passage which we will consider carefully in a later chapter. But in the writer's mind there is no doubt whatever that none other than the Beast is here in view. If this be the case, then we have further evidence that the coming One will be no mere man indwelt by Satan, but a fallen angel, an evil spirit, the incarnation of the Devil.

5. "Ye are of your father the Devil, and the lusts of your father ye will do. He was a murderer from the beginning, and abode not in the truth, because there is no truth in him. When he speaketh a lie, he speaketh of his own; for he is a liar, and the *father* of it" (John 8:44). Here is still another proof that the Antichrist will be superhuman, the offspring of Satan. In the Greek there is the definite article before the word "lie"—the lie, "the Lie". There is another passage in the New Testament where "the Lie" is mentioned, namely in 2 Thess. 2:11, where again the definite article is found in the Greek, and there the reference is unmistakeable.

A threefold reason may be suggested as to *why* the Antichrist should be termed "the Lie". First, because his fraudulent claim to be the real Christ will be the greatest falsehood palmed off upon humanity. Second, because he is the direct antithesis of the real Christ, who is "the Truth" (John 14:6). Third, because he is the son of Satan who is the *arch* liar. But to return to John 8:44: "When he (the Devil) speaketh (concerning) the Lie, he speaketh of his own". His "own" what? His "own" *son* —the remainder of the verse makes this very plain—"for he (the Devil) is a liar *and the father of it*", i. e., of "the Lie". The Lie, then, is *Satan's "son"!*

6. "That day shall not come, except there come a falling away (the Apostasy) first, and that Man of Sin be revealed, *the Son of Perdition*" (2 Thess. 2:3). Nothing could be plainer than this. Here the Antichrist is expressly declared to be superhuman—"the Son of Perdition". Just as the Christ is the Son of God, so Antichrist will be the son of Satan. Just as in Christ dwelt all the fulness of the Godhead bodily, and just as Christ could say "He that hath seen Me, hath seen the Father", so the Antichrist will

be the full and final embodiment of the Devil. He will not only be the incarnation of the Devil, but the consummation of his wickedness and power.

7. In Rev. 13:1 (R. V.) we read, "And he (the Dragon —see context) stood upon the sand of the sea"—symbolic of taking possession of the Nations: "And I saw a Beast coming up out of the sea, having ten horns and seven heads, and on his horns ten diadems, and upon his heads names of blasphemy". It is deeply significant to mark how these two things are here linked together *as cause and effect*. The coming forth of the Beast (the Antichrist) is immediately connected with the Dragon! But this is not all. Notice the description that is here given of him: he has "ten horns (fulness of power) and seven heads (complete wisdom)" and this is exactly how Satan himself is described in Rev. 12:3—"And behold, a great red Dragon, having *seven heads* and *ten horns, and upon his heads names of blasphemy"!* Does not a linking of these scriptures prove beyond all doubt that the Antichrist will be an *exact replica* of Satan himself!

But one other thing, even more startling, remains to be considered, and that is,

III. The Antichrist will be Judas Reincarnated

1. In Psalm 55 much is said of the Antichrist in his relation to Israel. Among other things we read there, "The words of his mouth were smoother than butter, but war was in his heart: his words were softer than oil, yet were they drawn swords" (v. 21). The occasion for this sad plaint is given in the previous verse—"He hath put forth his hands against such as be at peace with him: he hath *broken his covenant"*. The reference is to Antichrist breaking his seven-year Covenant with the Jews (see Dan.

9:27; 11:21-24). Now if the entire Psalm be read through with these things in mind, it will be seen that it sets forth the sorrows of Israel and the sighings of the godly remnant during the End-time. But the remarkable thing is that when we come to vv. 11-14 we find that which has a *double* application and fulfillment—"wickedness is in the midst thereof: deceit and guile depart not from her streets. For it was not an enemy that reproached me; then I could have borne it: neither was it he that hated me that did magnify himself against me; then I would have hid myself from him: But it was thou, a man mine equal, my guide, and mine acquaintance. We took sweet counsel together, and walked unto the house of God in company". These verses describe not only the base treachery of Judas toward Christ, but they also announce how he shall yet, when reincarnated in the Antichrist, *betray and desert Israel*. The relation of Antichrist to Israel will be precisely the same as that of Judas to Christ of old. He will pose as the friend of the Jews, but later he will come out in his true character. In the Tribulation period, the Nation of Israel shall taste the bitterness of betrayal and desertion by one who masqueraded as a "familiar friend". Hence, we have here the first hint that the Antichrist will be Judas reincarnated.

2. "And your covenant with Death shall be disannulled, and your agreement with Hell shall not stand; when the overflowing scourge shall pass through, then ye shall be trodden down by it" (Isa. 28:18). The "Covenant" referred to is that seven-year one which is mentioned in Dan. 9:27. But here the one with whom this Covenant is made is termed "Death" and "Hell". This is a title of the Antichrist, as "the Resurrection and the Life" is of the true Christ. Nor is this verse in Isa. 28 the only one where

the Son of Perdition is so denominated. In Rev. 6 a four-fold picture of him is given—the antithesis of the four-fold portrayal of the Lord Jesus in the Gospels. Here he is seen as the rider on differently colored horses, which bring before us four stages in his awful career, and when we come to the last of them the Holy Spirit exposes his true identity by telling us, "and his name that sat on him was Death, and Hell followed with him" (Rev. 6:8). Now "Hell" or "hades" is the place which receives the souls of the dead, and the fact that this awful name is here applied to Antichrist intimates that he has *come from there*.

3. Above, we referred to Matt. 12:41-43 to prove that Antichrist will be a super-human being, a fallen and un-clean "spirit"; we turn to it again in order to show that this coming Incarnation of Satan has previously been upon earth. The history of this "Unclean Spirit" is di-vided into three stages. First, as having dwelt in "a man"; second, as having gone out of a man, and walking through dry places, seeking rest and finding none—this has refer-ence to his present condition during the interval between his two appearances on earth. Third, he says, "I will *re-turn* to my house". This Unclean Spirit, then, who has already been here, who is now away in a place where rest is not to be found, is to come back again!

4. In John 17:12 we have a word which, more plainly still, shows that the Antichrist will be Judas reincarnated, for here he is termed by Christ "The Son of Perdition". But first, let us consider the teaching of Scripture concern-ing Judas Iscariot. Who was he? He was a "man" (Matt. 26:24). But was he *more* than a man? Let Scripture make answer. In John 6:70 we read, "Have not I chosen you twelve, and one of you *is a Devil?*" It is hardly necessary to say that in the Greek there are two

different words for "Devil" and "demon". There are
many demons, but only *one* Devil. Further, in no other
passage is the word "devil" applied to any one but to Satan himself. Judas then was the Devil incarnate, just as
the Lord Jesus was God incarnate. Christ Himself *said so,*
and we dare not doubt His word.

As we have seen, in John 17:12 Christ termed Judas
"the Son of Perdition", and 2 Thess. 2:3 we find that the
Antichrist is *similarly designated*—"That Man of Sin be
revealed, *the Son of Perdition".* These are the only two
places in all the Bible where his name occurs, and the fact
that Judas was termed by Christ not *a* "son of perdition",
but *"the* Son of Perdition", and the fact that the Man of
Sin is so named prove that they are *one and the same person.* What other conclusion can a simple and unprejudiced reader of the Bible come to?

5. In Rev. 11:7 we have the first reference to "the Beast"
in the Apocalypse: "The Beast that ascendeth out of the
bottomless pit". Here the Antichrist is seen issuing forth
from the Abyss. What is the Abyss? It is the abode of
lost spirits, the place of their incarceration and torment—
see Rev. 20:1-3, and Luke 8:31, "deep" is "abyss" and cf.
Matt. 9:28. The question naturally arises, How did he
get there? and *when* was he sent there? We answer, When
Judas Iscariot died! *The Antichrist will be Judas Iscariot
reincarnated.* In proof of this we appeal to Acts 1:25
where we are told, "that he may take part of this ministry
and apostleship from which Judas by transgression fell,
that he might go *to his own place".* Of no one else in all
the Bible is it said that at death he went "to his own
place". Put these two scriptures together: Judas went "to
his own place", the Beast *ascends* out of the Abyss.

6. In Rev. 17:8 we read, "The Beast that thou sawest

was, and is not; and shall ascend out of the Bottomless Pit, and go into perdition". This verse is generally understood to refer to the revived Roman Empire, and while allowing that such an application is warrantable, yet we are persuaded it is a mistake to *limit* it to this. In the Apocalypse, the Roman Empire and its final and satanic Head are very closely connected, so much so, that at times it is difficult to distinguish between them. But in Rev. 17 they are distinguishable.

In v. 8 we are told that the Beast "shall ascend out of the Bottomless Pit", and that he shall go into perdition". In v. 11 we are told, "And the Beast that was, and is not, even he is the eighth, and is of the seventh, and goeth into perdition". Now nearly all expositors are agreed that the Beast of v. 11—the "eighth" (head, and form of government of the Roman Empire)—is the Antichrist himself; then why not admit the same of v. 8? In both, the designation is the same—"the Beast"; and in both, we are told he "goeth into perdition."

We take it, then, that what is predicated of "the Beast" in 17:8 is true of *both* the Roman Empire and its last head, the Antichrist: of the former, in the sense that it is infernal in its character. Viewing it now as a declaration of the Antichrist, what does it tell us about him? Four things. First, he "was". Second, he "is not". Third, he shall "ascend out of the Bottomless Pit". Fourth, he shall "go into perdition". The various time-marks here concern the Beast in his relation to *the earth*. First, he "was", i. e., on the earth. Second, he "is not", i. e. now on the earth (cf. Gen. 5:24, "Enoch *was not* for God took him"; that is, "was not" any longer *on the earth*). Third, he shall "ascend out of the Bottomless Pit," where he now is, which agrees with 11:7. Fourth, he shall "go into perdition". We learn then from this scripture that at the time the Apocalypse was written the Beast "was not" then on the earth, but that *he had been on it formerly.* Further, we learn that in John's day the Beast was then in the Bottomless Pit but should yet ascend out of it. Here then is further evidence that the Antichrist who is yet to appear *has been on earth before.*

7. "And the Beast was taken, and with him the False Prophet that wrought miracles before him, with which he deceived them that had received the mark of the Beast, and them that worshipped his image. These both were cast alive into the lake of fire burning with brimstone" (Rev. 19:20). This gives the last word concerning the Antichrist. It makes known the terrible fate which awaits him. He, together with his ally, will be cast alive into the Lake of Fire. This is very striking, and confirms what has been said above, namely, that the Antichrist will be one who has already appeared on earth, and *has been* in "the Abyss" during the interval which precedes his return to the earth. And how remarkably Rev. 19:20 corroborates this. The Antichrist will not be cast, eventually into the Abyss, as Satan will be at the end of the Millennium (Rev. 20:1-3), but into the Lake of Fire which is the *final* abode of the damned. Why is it that he shall not be cast into the Abyss at the return of Christ? It must be because he has *already* been there. Hence, the judgment meted out to him is final and irrevocable, as will be that of the Devil a thousand years later, see Rev. 20:10.

Our next chapter will be devoted to an examination and consideration of the many Names and Titles which are given to the Antichrist in the Word of God, and we would urge the student to diligently search the Scriptures for himself to see how many of these he can find—there are over twenty.

3

NAMES AND TITLES OF THE ANTICHRIST

THERE is a distinct science of nomenclature, a system of names, in the Word of God. Probably every name found in Scripture has either a historic, a symbolic, or a spiritual significance. The names are inseparably bound up with the narrative, and it frequently happens that the meaning of a proper noun is a key to an important passage. Names are not employed by the Holy Spirit in a loose and careless manner—of course not!—but with definite design. A variety of names for the same individual are not given in order to prevent monotonous repetition, but because the significance of each separate appellation is best fitted to express what is recorded in any given instance. "Devil" and "Satan" are not synonyms, nor are they used at haphazard, but with Divine discrimination. Upon the meaning of names found in Holy Writ rests a whole scheme of interpretation; even the order in which names occur is not fortuitous but designed, and constitutes a part of each lesson taught, or each truth presented.

There is here a wide field opened for study, a field which few have made serious effort to explore. It is strange that it has been so neglected, for again and again the Holy Spirit calls attention to the importance and meaning of names. In the first book of the Bible we find that children and places were given meaningful names, which called to remembrance incidents, experiences, characteristics of interest and importance. Examples are given where names were changed to harmonize with a change in the person, place, experience, or situation where it occurred. Abram and Sarai will at once occur to mind. For a place, take Luz, which was changed to Bethel—"House of God"—because by reason of a vision he received there it became *that* to Jacob. Jacob's name is changed to Israel; and in the New Testament an example is furnished in Simeon being re-named Peter. In Heb. 7:1, 2 the Holy Spirit calls attention to the significance of the names Melchizedek and Salem (Jerusalem). These are sufficient to show the importance of this line of study.

Names are used in Scripture with marvelous discrimination, and it was this fact which first demonstrated to the writer the *verbal* inspiration of Scripture. The precision with which names are used in the Bible is especially noticeable in connection with the Divine titles. The names Elohim and Jehovah are found on the pages of the Old Testament several thousand times, but they are never used loosely or interchangeably. Over three hundred names and titles are given to the Lord Jesus Christ, and each has its own distinctive significance, and to substitute any other for the one used would destroy the beauty and perfections of every passage where they are found.

Names are employed to express character; titles are used to denote relationships. It is only as we make a careful study of the various and numerous names and titles of the Lord Jesus Christ, that we are in a position to appreciate His infinite excellencies and the manifold relationships which He sustains. From an opposite standpoint the same is equally true of the Antichrist. As we pay careful attention to the different names and titles which are given to him, we then discover what a marvelously complete delineation the Holy Spirit has furnished us with of the person, the character, and career of this monster of wickedness. It is unfortunate that the great variety of names bestowed upon him has led some brethren to the conclusion that they must belong to separate persons, and has caused them to apportion these out to different individuals; only confusion can result from this. There is almost as much ground to make the Devil and Satan different persons, as there is to regard (as some do) the Beast and the Antichrist as separate entities. That the Devil and Satan are names belonging to *the same* person, and that the Beast and the Antichrist is *the selfsame* individual, is proven by the fact that identically the same characteristics under each is found belonging to the one as to the other. Instead of apportioning these names to different persons, we must see that they denominate the same individual, only in different relationships, or as giving us various phases of his character.

An old writer has said the name Devil is most suggestive of his character. If "d" is taken away *evil* is left. If "e" is taken away *vile* is left. If "v" is taken away *ill* is left. And if "i" is taken away and the next letter be aspirated, it tells of *hell*. It is equally true of the Antichrist: his names reveal his character, expose his vileness, and forcast his career and doom.

The names and titles given to the Antichrist are far more numerous than is commonly supposed. We propose to give as complete a list as possible, and offer a few comments on their significations. We shall not expatiate on them at equal length, for that is not necessary; instead, we shall say the most on those cognomens which are of the greater importance, or, which because of their ambiguity call for a more detailed elucidation.

1. THE ANTICHRIST

"Who is a liar but he that denieth that Jesus is the

Christ? He is *Antichrist,* that denieth the Father and the Son" (1 John 2:22). This name introduces to us one of the most solemn and foreboding subjects in the Word of God. It brings before us one of the persons in the Trinity of Evil. At every point he is the antithesis of Christ. The word "Antichrist" has a double significance. Its primary meaning is one who is *opposed* to Christ; but its secondary meaning is one who is *instead of* Christ. Let not this be thought strange, for it accords with the two stages in his career. At first he will pose as the true Christ, masquerading in the livery of religion. But, later, he will throw off his disguise, stand forth in his true character, and set himself up as one who is against God and His Christ.

Not only does *anti*-christ denote the antagonist of Christ, but it tells of one who is instead of Christ. The word signifies another Christ, a pro-Christ, an *alter christus,* a pretender to the name of Christ. He will seem to be and will set himself up as the true Christ. He will be the Devil's counterfeit. Just as the Devil is an *Anti-theos*— not only the adversary of God, but the *usurper* of the place and prerogatives of God, demanding worship; so the Son of Perdition will be *anti-christ*—not only the antagonist and opponent of Christ, but His rival: assuming the very position and prerogatives of Christ; passing himself off as the rightful claimant to all the rights and honors of the Son of God.

2. THE MAN OF SIN, THE SON OF PERDITION

"Let no man deceive you by any means: for that day shall not come, except there come a falling away first, and that *Man of Sin* be revealed, *the Son of Perdition*" (2 Thess. 2:3). This double appellation is probably the most awful, the most important, and the most revealing title given to the Antichrist in all the Bible. It diagnoses his personality and exposes his awful character. It tells us he will be possessed of a twofold nature: he will be a man, and yet more than a man. He will be Satan's parody of the God-Man. He will be an incarnation of the Devil. The world today is talking of and looking for the Superman. This is exactly what the Antichrist will be. He will be the Serpent's masterpiece.

"That Man of Sin". What a frightful name! The sin of man will culminate in the Man of Sin. The Christ of God was sinless; the Christ of Satan will not only be sinful, but the Man *of Sin*. "Man of Sin" intimates that he will be the living and active embodiment of every form and character of evil. "Man of Sin" signifies that he will be sin itself personified. "Man of Sin" denotes there will be no lengths of wickedness to which he will not go, no forms of evil to which he will be a stranger, no depths of corruption that he will not bottom.

"The Son of Perdition". And again we are forced to exclaim, what a frightful name! Not only a human degenerate, but the offspring of the Dragon. Not only the worst of human kind, but the incarnation of the Devil. Not only the most depraved of all sinners, but an emanation from the Pit itself. "Son of Perdition" denotes that he will be the culmination and consummation of satanic craft and power. All the evil, malignity, cunning, and power of the Serpent will be embodied in this terrible monster.

3. THE LAWLESS ONE

"And then shall be revealed *the Lawless One,* whom the Lord Jesus shall slay with the breath of His mouth, and bring to nought by the manifestation of His coming" (2

Thess. 2:8 R. V.). This is another name of the Antichrist which makes manifest his awful character. Each of his names exhibits him as the antithesis of the true Christ. The Lord Jesus was the Righteous One; the Man of Sin will be the Lawless One. The Lord Jesus was "made under the law" (Gal. 4:4); the Antichrist will oppose all law, being a law unto himself. When the Saviour entered this world, He came saying, "Lo I come to do Thy will, O God" (Heb. 10:9); but of the Antichrist it is written "And the king shall do according to *his* will" (Dan. 11: 36). The Antichrist will set himself up in direct opposition to all authority, both Divine and human.

4. THE BEAST

"And when they shall have finished their testimony *the Beast* that ascendeth out of the bottomless pit shall make war against them, and shall overcome them, and kill them" (Rev. 11:7). This is another name which reveals the terrible nature and character of the Antichrist and which places him in sharp antithesis from the true Christ. "The Beast" is the title by which he is most frequently designated in the Revelation: there are at least thirty references to him under this name in the last book of the Bible. The Greek word signifies a wild beast. This name "the Beast" contrasts the Antichrist from the true Christ as "the Lamb"; and it is a significant fact that by far the great majority of passages where the Lord Jesus is so designated are also found here in the Apocalypse. The "Lamb" is the Saviour of sinners; the "Beast" is the persecutor and slayer of the saints. The "Lamb" calls attention to the gentleness of Christ; the "Beast" tells of the ferocity of the Antichrist. The "Lamb" reveals Christ as the "harmless" One (Heb. 7:26); the "Beast" manifests the Antichrist as the cruel and heartless one.   Under the Law lambs were ceremonially clean and used in sacrifice, but beasts were unclean and unfit for sacrifices.

It is a point of interest to note that there is one other very striking contrast between the persons in the Holy Trinity, and the persons in the trinity of evil.   At our Lord's baptism the Holy Spirit descended upon Him in the form of a *dove,* and the first mention of the Holy Spirit in Scripture represents Him as "brooding" like a dove over the waters which covered the pre-Adamic earth (Gen. 1:2).   How remarkable are these symbols—a "Lamb" and a "Dove"!   A Dove, not a hawk or an eagle.   The gentle, harmless, cooing "dove".   Over against this the Devil is termed "the *Dragon*".   What a contrast—the Dove and the Lamb, the Dragon and the Beast!

5. The Bloody and Deceitful Man

"Thou shalt destroy them that speak leasing: the Lord will abhor the *Bloody and Deceitful Man*" (Psa. 5:6). The Psalm from which this verse is quoted contains a prayer of the godly Jewish remnant, offered during the Tribulation period.   In proof of this assertion observe that in v. 2 God is owned and addressed as "King".   In v. 7 intimation is given that the Temple has been rebuilt in Jerusalem, for turning away from it when it has been defiled by "the Abomination of Desolation", the remnant say, "But as for me I will come into *Thy* House in the multitude of Thy mercy: and in Thy fear will I worship toward *Thy* Holy Temple".   While in v. 10 we find them praying for the destruction of their enemies, which is parallel with Rev. 6:10.   It is during that time the faithful remnant will exclaim, "Thou shalt destroy them that speak leasing: the Lord will abhor the Bloody and Deceitful Man".

The Bloody and Deceitful Man views the Antichrist in relation to the Jews. In the earlier stages of his public career he poses as their friend and benefactor. He recognizes their rights as a separate State and appears anxious to protect their autonomy. He makes a formal covenant with them (Dan. 9:27) and their peace and security seem assured. But a few years later he comes out in his true character. His fair speeches and professions of friendship are seen to be false. He breaks his covenant (Psa. 55:20) and turns upon the Jews in fury. Their benefactor is now their worst enemy. The protector of their interests now aims to cut them off from being a nation in the earth (Psa. 83:4). Thus is he rightfully denominated by them "the Bloody and Deceitful Man".

6. THE WICKED ONE

"The Wicked (One) in his pride doth persecute the poor: the *Wicked* (One), through the pride of his countenance, will not seek after God" (Psa. 10:2, 4). This entire Psalm is about the Wicked One. The opening verse gives the key to its dispensational scope. It contains the cry of the Jewish remnant during the Tribulation period, here denominated "Times of Trouble" (cf. Jer. 30:7). So desperate is the situation of the true Israel, it seems as though Jehovah must have deserted them—"Why standest Thou afar off, O Lord? Why hidest Thou Thyself in times of trouble?" (v. 1). Then follows a remarkably full description of their arch-enemy, the Wicked One. His pride (v. 2), his depravity: "He abhorreth the Lord" (v. 3 margin); his blasphemy: "All his thoughts are, There is no God" (v. 4 margin); his grievous ways, (v. 5); his consuming egotism, (v. 6); his deceitfulness, (v. 7); his treachery, (v. 8); his cruelty, (vv. 9, 10); his complacent

pride, (v. 11), is each described. Then the Remnant cry, "Arise, O Lord; O God, lift up Thine hand: forget not the humble. Break Thou the arm of the Wicked and Evil One" (vv. 12 and 15). The whole Psalm should be carefully studied.

7. THE MAN OF THE EARTH

"To judge the fatherless and the oppressed, that *the Man of the Earth* may no more oppress" (Psa. 10:18). The "Wicked One" describes his character; the "Man of the Earth" defines his position. The one speaks of his awful depths of depravity; the other of his vast dominions. The sphere of his operations will be no mere local one. He will become World-emperor. He will be a king of kings and lord of lords (Rev. 13:7). When the true Christ appeared on earth, Satan offered Him "all the kingdoms of the world and the glory of them" if He would fall down and worship him. When the false Christ appears, this offer will be repeated, the conditions will be met, and the tempting gift will be bestowed (Rev. 13:2). In consequence of this he shall be "the Man of the Earth"; just as later, Christ shall be "King over all the earth" (Zech. 14:7).

8. THE MIGHTY MAN

"Why boasteth thou thyself in mischief, O *Mighty Man*" (Psa. 52:1). This is another Psalm which is devoted to a description of this fearful character. Here again we have mention of his boastfulness (v. 1), his deceitfulness (v. 2), his depravity (v. 3), his egotism (v. 4), his riches (v. 7). His doom is also announced (v. 5). This title, the Mighty Man, refers to his immense wealth and possessions, and the power which they confer upon their possessor. It also points a striking contrast: Christ was the Lowly Man, not having where to lay His head; the Antichrist will be the Mighty Man, of whom it is said, "Lo, this is the man that made not God his strength; but trusted in the abundance of his riches, and strengthened himself in his substance" (Psa. 52:7).

9. THE ENEMY

"Because of the voice of *the Enemy,* because of the oppression of the Wicked: for they cast iniquity upon me, and in wrath they hate me" (Psa. 55:3). This is another title used of the Antichrist in connection with Israel, a title which recurs several times both in the Psalms and the Prophets. It points a designed contrast from that *Friend* that "sticketh closer than a brother". This Enemy of Israel oppresses them sorely. His duplicity and treachery are here referred to. Concerning him Israel shall exclaim, "The words of his mouth were smoother than butter, but war was in his heart: his words were softer than oil, yet were they drawn swords" (Psa. 52:21). Let the student be on the lookout for passages in the Old Testament which make mention of the Enemy.

10. THE ADVERSARY

"They said in their hearts, Let us destroy them together: they have burned up all the synagogues of God in the land. We see not our signs: there is no more any profit: neither is there any among us that knoweth how long. O God, how long shall *the Adversary* reproach? Shall the Enemy blaspheme Thy name forever?" (Psa. 74:8-10). This title occurs in several important passages. In Isa. 59:19 we read, "So shall they fear the name of the Lord from the west, and His glory from the rising of the sun. When the Adversary shall come in like a flood, the Spirit

of the Lord shall lift up a standard against him". Lam. 4:
11, 12 is another scripture which obviously speaks of the
End-time. "The Lord hath accomplished His fury; He
hath poured out His fierce anger, and hath kindled a fire
in Zion, and it hath devoured the foundations thereof.
The kings of the earth, and all the inhabitants of the
world, would not have believed that the Adversary and the
Enemy should have entered into the gates of Jerusalem".
In Amos 3:11 we read, "Therefore thus saith the Lord
God; an Adversary there shall be even round about the
land; and he shall bring down thy strength from thee,
and thy palaces shall be spoiled". This is a title which
intimates his satanic origin, for the Greek word for Devil
means adversary.

11. THE HEAD OVER MANY COUNTRIES

"He shall judge among the heathen, he shall fill the
places with the dead bodies; he shall wound *the Head over
many countries*" (Psa. 110:6). The context here shows
that it must be the Antichrist which is in view. The
Psalm opens by the Father inviting the Son to sit at His
right hand until His enemies shall be made His footstool.
Then follows the affirmation that Jehovah will display
His strength out of Jerusalem, and make His people Israel
willing in the day of His power. Then, following Jehovah's oath that Christ is a Priest forever after the order of
Melchizedek (which contemplates the exercise of His millennial and royal priesthood), we read, "The Lord at thy
right hand shall strike through kings in the day of His
wrath. He shall judge among the heathen, He shall fill
the places with the dead bodies; He shall wound the Head
over many countries". The "Day of His wrath" is the
closing portion of the Tribulation period, and in the Day

of His wrath He wounds this Head over many countries. The Head over many countries refers to the Man of Sin as the Cæsar of the last world-empire, prior to the establishment of the Messianic Kingdom.

12. THE VIOLENT MAN

"Deliver me, O Lord, from the Evil Man: preserve me from *the Violent Man*" (Ps. 140:1). This is another Psalm which expresses the plaintive supplications of the godly remnant in the "time of Jacob's trouble". Three times over the Antichrist is denominated the Violent Man. In v. 1 the remnant pray to be delivered from him. In v. 4 the petition is repeated. In v. 11 his doom is foretold. Cry is made for God to take vengeance upon this bloody persecutor: "Let burning coals fall upon them: let them be cast into the fire; into deep pits, that they rise not up again. Let not an evil speaker be established in the earth: evil shall hunt the Violent Man to overthrow him" (Psa. 140:10, 11). The Violent Man is a name which fully accords with his Beast-like character. It tells of his ferocity and rapacity.

13. THE ASSYRIAN

"*O Assyrian,* the rod of Mine anger, and the staff in their hand is Mine indignation . . . Wherefore it shall come to pass, that when the Lord hath performed His whole work upon mount Zion and on Jerusalem, I will punish the fruit of the stout heart of *the King of Assyria,* and the glory of his high looks" (Isa. 10:5, 12). We cannot here attempt an exposition of the important passage in which these verses occur—that, in subsequent chapters, we shall treat in detail of the Antichrist in the Psalms, and the Antichrist in the Prophets—suffice it now to point out that it treats of the End-time (see vv. 12, 20), and that the leading characteristics of the Man of Sin can be clearly discerned in what is here said of the Assyrian. Almost all pre-millennial students of prophecy are agreed that "the King" of Isa. 30:33 is the Antichrist, and yet in the two verses which precede, this "King" is identified with "the Assyrian".

14. THE KING OF BABYLON

"Thou shalt take up this proverb against *the King of Babylon,* and say, How hath the oppressor ceased! the golden city ceased!" (Isa. 14:4). We do not wish to anticipate what we shall discuss at length in our future studies, enough now to state it is our firm conviction that Scripture plainly teaches that there will be another Babylon which will eclipse the importance and glories of the one of the past, and that Babylon will be one of the headquarters of the Antichrist. He will have three: Jerusalem will be his *religious* headquarters, Rome his *political,* and Babylon his *commercial.* For those who desire to anticipate our future expositions, we recommend them to make a minute study of Isa. 10, 11, 13, 14; Jer. 49-51; Zech. 5, and Rev. 18.

15. SON OF THE MORNING

"How art thou fallen from heaven O Lucifer, *Son of the Morning!* How art thou cut down to the ground, which didst weaken the nations" (Isa. 14:12). "Lucifer" is a Latin word which signifies the "morning star". "All the ancient versions and all the Rabbins make the word a noun denoting the *bright one,* or, more specifically, *bright star,* or according to the ancients more specifically still, the *Morning Star* or harbinger of daylight" (Dr. J. A. Alexander). This term "Lucifer" has been commonly regarded as one of the names of Satan, and what is here said of the Morning Star is viewed as describing his apostasy. Against this interpretation we have nothing to say, except to remark that we are satisfied it does not exhaust this remarkable scripture. A detailed exposition must be reserved for a later chapter. Sufficient now to point out that however Isa. 14 may look back to the distant past when, through pride, Satan fell from his original estate, it most evidently looks forward to a coming day and gives another picture of the Antichrist. In this same passage "Lucifer" is termed "the *Man* that did make the earth to tremble" (v. 16), and in his blasphemous boast "I will be like the Most High" (v. 14), we have no difficulty in identifying him with the Man of Sin of 2 Thess. 2:3, 4. The force of this particular title "Morning Star" is seen by comparing it with Rev. 22:16, where we learn that this is one of the titles of the God-man. The "Morning Star" speaks of Christ coming to usher in the great Day of rest for the earth. In blasphemous travesty of this Satan will send forth the mock messiah to usher in a false millennium.

16. THE SPOILER

"Let mine outcasts dwell with thee, Moab; be thou a covert to them from the face of *the Spoiler:* for the Extortioner is at an end, *the Spoiler* ceaseth, the oppressors are consumed out of the land. And in mercy shall the throne be established: and He shall sit upon it in truth in the tabernacle of David, judging, and seeking judgment, and hasting righteousness" (Isa. 16:4, 5). It will be observed that the verse in which the Antichrist is spoken of as the Spoiler comes immediately before the one where we read of the throne being established, a reference, of course, to the setting up of the Messianic Kingdom. These two things synchronize: the destruction of Antichrist, and the beginning of the real Messiah's reign; hence we read here "the Spoiler ceaseth". A further reference to the Man of Sin under this title of the Spoiler is found in Jer. 6:26: "O daughter of My people, gird thee with sackcloth, and wallow thyself in ashes: make thee mournings, as for an only son, most bitter lamentation: for *the Spoiler* shall suddenly come upon thee". This is another title which views the Antichrist in connection with Israel. After the return of many of the Jews to Palestine, and after their rights have been owned by the Powers, and their security and success seem assured; their enemy, filled with satanic malice, will seek their extermination. "The Spoiler" contrasts him with the Lord Jesus who is the great Restorer (see Psa. 69:4).

17. THE NAIL

"In that day, saith the Lord of hosts, shall *the Nail* that is fastened in the sure place be removed, and be cut down, and fall; and the burden that was upon it shall be cut off: for the Lord hath spoken it" (Isa. 22:25). The last ten verses of this chapter should be read carefully. They furnish a striking foreshadowment of the End-time. Shebna was holding some office *over* (note "government" in v. 21) Israel. Apparently he was a usurper. God announced that he should be set aside in shame, and the man of His choice—Eliakim—should take his place. These historical figures merge into prophetic characters. In v. 22 we read that God says, "And the key of the house of David will I lay upon His shoulder, so He shall open, and none shall shut; and He shall shut, and none shall open". As we know from Rev. 3:7 this refers to none other than the Lord Jesus, and of Him it is here said, "And I will fasten Him as a Nail in a sure place; and He shall be for a glorious throne to His father's house" (v. 23). Then, in the closing verse of the chapter we read, "In that day, saith the Lord of hosts, shall the Nail that is fastened in a sure place be removed, and be cut down, and fall". Just as Eliakim foreshadowed Christ, so Shebna pointed forward to the Antichrist; and just as in v. 23 we have a prophecy announcing the establishment of Messiah's Kingdom, so in v. 25 we have foretold the overthrow of the false messiah's kingdom.

18. The Branch of the Terrible Ones

"Thou shalt bring down the noise of strangers, as the heat in a dry place; even the heat with the shadow of a cloud; *the Branch of the terrible ones* shall be brought low" (Isa. 25:5). The first five verses of this chapter contemplate the Enemy's stronghold—Babylon—and the remainder of the chapter pictures the blessedness of the millennial era. In the fifth verse the Antichrist's overthrow is announced: "The Branch of the terrible ones shall be brought low". With this should be compared Isa. 14:19, where of Lucifer it is said, "Thou art cast out of thy grave like an abominable Branch". This points another contrast. The "Branch" is one of the Messianic names: "Behold, I will bring forth My Servant, the Branch" (Zech. 3:8); "Behold the man whose name is the Branch" (Zech. 6:12). By placing together Isa. 4:2 and Isa. 14:19 the anthithesis will be more evident. Of Christ it is said, "The Branch of the Lord shall be *beautiful and glorious"*; Antichrist is called "an *abominable* Branch": Christ is "the Branch *of the Lord"*; Antichrist is "the Branch *of the terrible ones"*.

19. The Profane and Wicked Prince of Israel

"And thou, *profane wicked Prince of Israel,* whose day is come, when iniquity shall have an end, thus saith the

Lord God; remove the diadem, and take off the crown; this shall not be the same: exalt him that is low, and abase him that is high. I will overturn, overturn, overturn it: and it shall be no more, until He come whose right it is; and I will give it Him" (Ezek. 21:25-27). The Profane and Wicked Prince of Israel here can be none other than the Antichrist, for we are expressly told that his day shall be "when iniquity shall have an end". The reference is, of course, to Israel's "iniquity", and their iniquity shall *end* at the appearing of the Messiah (see Dan. 9:24) when "He shall be a priest upon His throne" (Zech. 6:13). Here in Ezekiel we see how the Son of Perdition shall ape the Christ of God, for he, too, will be a priest-king: "Remove the *diadem*" refers to the insignia of his priesthood (in every other place in the O. T. where occurs the Hebrew word here translated "diadem" it is rendered "mitre"— worn only by the high priest of Israel); "take off the crown" is the symbol of his kingship.

20. THE LITTLE HORN

"I considered the horns, and, behold, there came up among them another *Little Horn,* before whom there were three of the first horns plucked up by the roots: and, behold, in this Horn were eyes like the eyes of man, and a mouth speaking great things" (Dan. 7:8). For a full description of the Antichrist under this title see Dan. 7:8-11, 21-26; 8:9-12, 23-25. We must reserve our comments on these verses till a later chapter. *"Little* Horn" refers to the lowly political origin of the Antichrist, and describes him as he is before he attains governmental supremacy.

21. THE PRINCE THAT SHALL COME

"And after threescore and two weeks shall Messiah be cut off, but not for Himself: and the people of *the Prince that shall come* shall destroy the city and the sanctuary" (Dan. 9:26). This title connects the Antichrist with the Roman Empire in its final form, and presents him as the last of the Cæsars.

22. THE VILE PERSON

"And in his estate shall stand up *a Vile Person,* to whom they shall not give the honor of the kingdom: but he shall come in peaceably, and obtain the kingdom by flatteries" (Dan. 11:21). This contrasts the Antichrist from "the *Holy* One of Israel". His identity is established by noting what is predicated of him.

23. THE WILFUL KING

"And *the King* shall do according *to his will;* and he shall exalt himself, and magnify himself above every god, and shall speak marvelous things against the God of gods, and shall prosper till the indignation be accomplished: for that that is determined shall be done" (Dan. 11:36). The Antichrist will not only be the High Priest of the world's religion, but he will be King supreme at the head of its government.

24. THE IDOL SHEPHERD

"For, lo, I will raise up a *Shepherd* in the land, which shall not visit those that be cut off, neither shall seek the young ones, nor heal that that is broken, nor feed that that standeth still: but he shall eat the flesh of the fat, and tear their claws in pieces. Woe to *the Idol Shepherd* that leaveth the flock! The sword shall be upon his arm, and upon his right eye: his arm shall be clean dried up, and his right eye shall be utterly darkened" (Zech. 11:16, 17). This is in evident contrast from the Good Shepherd who gave His life for His sheep. The Idol Shepherd of deluded Israel will prove himself the monster Desolator, who shall bring upon that people the severest tribulations ever experienced by that race.

25. THE ANGEL OF THE BOTTOMLESS PIT

"And they had a king over them, which is *the Angel of the bottomless pit,* whose name in the Hebrew tongue is Abaddon, but in the Greek tongue hath his name Apollyon" (Rev. 9:11). "Abaddon" and "Apollyon" mean *Destroyer.* It is the "Spoiler" of Isa. 16:4 rendered "Destroyer" in Jer. 4:7. That his name is here given in the Hebrew and the Greek shows that he will be connected with both the Jews and the Gentiles.

Other names of the Antichrist which the student may look up are, "The Rod of God's anger" (Isa. 10:12); "The Unclean Spirit" (Matt. 12:43); "The Lie" (2 Thess. 2:11); "A Star" (Rev. 8:10 and 9:1); and "The Vine of the Earth" (Rev. 14:18).

In our next chapter we shall deal with the *genius* of the Antichrist, and point out the many striking *comparisons and contrasts* between him and the Christ of God. Let the student see how many points of resemblance and opposition he can find.

4

THE GENIUS AND CHARACTER OF THE ANTICHRIST

FOR six thousand years Satan has had full opportunity afforded him to study fallen human nature, to discover its weakest points, and to learn how best to make men do his bidding. The Devil knows full well how to dazzle men by the attraction of power, and how to make them quail before its terrors. He knows how to gratify the craving for knowledge and how to satisfy the taste for refinement and culture: he can delight the ear with melodious music and the eye with entrancing beauty. If he could transport the Saviour from the wilderness to a mountain, in a moment of time, and show Him all the kingdoms of the world and their glory, he is no novice in the art of presenting alluring objects before his victims today. He knows how to stimulate energy and direct inquiry, and how to appease the craving for the occult. He knows how to exalt men to dizzy heights of worldly greatness and fame, and how to control that greatness when attained, so that it may be employed against God and His people.

It is true that up to now Satan's power has been restrained, and his activities have been checked and often counteracted by the Spirit of God. The brightest fires of the Devil's kindling can burn but dimly whilever God sheds around them the power of heavenly light. They require *the full darkness of night* in order to shine in the full strength of their deceiving brightness; and that time is coming. The Word of God reveals the fact that a day is not far distant when Divine restraint will be removed;

the light of God will be withdrawn; and then shall "darkness cover the earth and gross darkness the people" (Isa. 60:2). Not only will that which has hindered the full development of the Mystery of Iniquity be removed, but God will "send them strong delusion, that they should believe the Lie" (2 Thess. 2:13), and Satan will take advantage of this; he will then make full use of all the knowledge which he has acquired during the last six thousand years.

Satan will become incarnate and appear on earth in human form. As we have shown in previous chapters, the Antichrist will not only be the Man of Sin, but also "the Son of Perdition", the Seed of the Serpent. The Antichrist will be the Devil's masterpiece. In him shall dwell all the fulness of the Devil bodily. He will be the culmination and consummation of Satan's workings. The world is now talking of and looking for the Superman; and the Devil is soon to supply him. The Antichrist will be no ordinary person, but one possessed of extraordinary talents. He will be endowed with superhuman powers. With the one exception of the God-man he will be the most remarkable personage who has ever appeared upon the stage of human history. But to particularize:

1. HE WILL BE AN INTELLECTUAL GENIUS

He will be possessed of extraordinary intelligence. He will be the Devil's imitation of that blessed One "in whom are hid all the treasures of wisdom and knowledge" (Col. 2:3). This Son of Perdition will surpass Solomon in wisdom. In Dan. 7:20 he is represented as "A horn that had eyes". It is a double symbol. The "horn" prefigures strength; "eyes" speak of intelligence. Again, in Dan. 8:23 he is referred to as "A King of fierce countenance", who shall "understand dark sentences". That which baffles others shall be simple to him.   The Hebrew word here translated "dark sentences" is the same as the one rendered "hard questions" in 1 Kings 10:1, where we read of the Queen of Sheba coming to Solomon with her "hard questions" in order to test his wisdom.   It is also the word that is used of Samson's riddle in Judges 14.   It indicates that the Antichrist will be master of all the secrets of occult science.   Ezek. 28:3 declares of him, "Behold, thou art wiser than Daniel; there is *no secret* that they can hide from thee".   This will be one of his most alluring attractions.   His master mind will captivate the educated world. His marvelous store of knowledge, his acquaintance with the secrets of nature, his superhuman powers of perception, will stamp him as an intellectual genius of the first magnitude.

2. HE WILL BE AN ORATORICAL GENIUS

In Dan. 7:20 we are told that he has "a mouth that spake very great things".   As a wizard of words he will surpass Demosthenes.   Here also will the Devil imitate that One "who spake as never man spake".   The people were "astonished" at Christ's doctrine (Matt. 7:28), and said "Whence hath this man this wisdom?" (Matt. 13: 54).   So will it be with this daring counterfeiter: he will have a mouth speaking very great things.   He will have a perfect command and flow of language.   His oratory will not only gain attention but command respect.   Rev. 13:2 declares that his mouth is "as the mouth of a lion" which is a symbolic expression telling of the majesty and awe-producing effects of his voice.   The voice of the lion excels that of any other beast.   So the Antichrist will outrival orators ancient and modern.

3. He will be a Political Genius.

He will emerge from obscurity, but by dint of his diplomatic skill he will win the admiration and compel the co-operation of the political world. In the early stages of his career he appears as "a *little* horn" (or power), but it is not long before he climbs the ladder of fame, and by means of brilliant statesmanship, ascends its topmost rung. Like the majority of politicians, he will not scruple to employ questionable methods; in fact it will be by diplomatic chicanery and intrigue that he will win his early successes. Dan. 11:21 tells us that at first they will not give to him the honor of the kingdom, but "he shall come in peaceably, and obtain the kingdom by flatteries". Once he gains the ascendancy none will dare to challenge his authority. Kings will be his pawns and princes his playthings.

4. He will be a Commercial Genius

"And through his policy also he shall cause craft to prosper in his hand" (Dan. 8:25). Under his regime everything will be nationalized, and none will be able to buy or sell without his permission (Rev. 13:17). All commerce will be under his personal control, and this will be used for his own aggrandizement. The wealth of the world will be at his disposal. There are several scriptures which call attention to this. For example in Psa. 52:7 we read, "Lo, this is the man that made not God his strength; but trusted *in the abundance of his riches;* and strengthened himself in his substance". Again in Dan. 11:38 we are told, "But in his estate shall he honor the god of forces (Satan): and a god whom his fathers knew not shall he honor with gold, and silver, and with precious stones, and pleasant things". Even plainer is Dan. 11:

43, "But he shall have power over *the treasures of gold and of silver,* and over *all* the precious things of Egypt". In the last verse of Dan. 11 mention is made of his "palace". He will be wealthier than Croesus. Ezek. 28:4, 5 speaks of him thus, "With thy wisdom and with thine understanding thou hast gotten thee riches, and hast gotten gold and silver into thy treasures: By thy great wisdom and by thy traffic hast thou increased thy riches, and thine heart is lifted up because of thy riches". Thus will he be able to wield the sceptre of financial power and outdo Solomon in all his glory.

5. HE WILL BE A MILITARY GENIUS

He will be endowed with the most extraordinary powers, so that "he shall destroy wonderfully, and shall prosper, and practice, and shall destroy the mighty and the holy people" (Dan. 8:24). Before his exploits the fame of Alexander and Napoleon will be forgotten. None will be able to stand before him. He will go "forth conquering and to conquer" (Rev. 6:2). He will sweep everything before him so that the world will exclaim, "Who is like unto the beast? who is able to make war with him?" (Rev. 13:4). His military exploits will not be confined to a corner, but carried out on a vast scale. He is spoken of as the man who will "shake kingdoms" and "make the earth to tremble" (Isa. 14:16).

6. HE WILL BE A GOVERNMENTAL GENIUS

He will weld together opposing forces. He will unify conflicting agencies. Under the compelling power of his skill the world Powers will be united. The dream of a League of Nations will then be realized. The Orient and the Occident shall no longer be divided. A marvelous symbolic picture of this is given us in Rev. 13:1, 2: "And

I stood upon the sand of the sea, and saw a Beast rise up out of the sea, having seven heads and ten horns, and upon his horns ten crowns, and upon his heads the name of blasphemy. And the Beast which I saw was like unto a leopard, and his feet were as the feet of a bear, and his mouth as the mouth of a lion: and the Dragon gave him his power, and his seat, and great authority". Here we find the forces of the Roman, the Grecian, the Medo-Persian, and the Babylonian empires coalesced. He will be the personal embodiment of the world's political authority in its final form. So completely will the world be swayed by the hypnotic spell cast over it by the Beast that the ten kings of the Roman empire in its ultimate form shall "give their kingdoms unto him" (Rev. 17:17). He will be the last great Caesar.

7. HE WILL BE A RELIGIOUS GENIUS

He will proclaim himself God, demanding that Divine honors should be rendered to him and sitting in the Temple shall show himself forth that he is God (2 Thess. 2: 4). Such wonders will he perform, such prodigious marvels will he work, the very elect would be deceived by him did not God directly protect them. The Man of Sin will combine in himself all the varied genius of the human race, and what is more, he will be invested with all the wisdom and power of Satan. He will be a master of science, acquainted with all of nature's forces, compelling her to give up for him her long held secrets. "In this master-piece of Satan", says one, "will be concentrated intellectual greatness, sovereign power and human glory, combined with every species of iniquity, pride, tyranny, wilfulness, deceit, and blasphemy, such as Antiochus Epiphanes, Mohammed, the whole line of popes, atheists, and deists of every age of the world have failed to unite in any individual person".

"All the world wondered after the Beast" (Rev. 13:3). His final triumph shall be that, wounded by a sword, he shall live again (Rev. 13:3). He shall raise himself from the dead, and so wonder-struck will men be at this stupendous marvel they will readily pay him Divine homage, yea, so great will be his dazzling power over men, they will worship his very image (Rev. 13:14, 15).

Having contemplated something of the *genius* of Satan's prodigy, let us now consider his *character*. In doing so we shall view him in the light of the Character of the Lord Jesus. Christ is the Divine plumb-line and standard of measurement by which all character must be tested.

In our last chapter we pointed out how that the distinguishing title of the coming Super-man—*the Antichrist* —has a double significance, inasmuch as it points to him as the imitator of Christ and the opponent of Christ. Hence, in studying his character, we find a series of comparisons and a series of contrasts drawn between the false christ and the true Christ; and these we now propose to set before the reader.

Comparisons between Christ and the Antichrist

Satan is the master-counterfeiter, and in nothing will this appear more conspicuously than in his next great move. He is now preparing the stage for his climactic production, which will issue in a blasphemous imitation of the Divine incarnation. When the Son of Perdition appears he will pose as the Christ of God, and so perfect will be his disguise, the very elect would be deceived, were it not that God will grant them special illumination. It is this disguise, this simulation of the true Christ which we shall now examine, pointing out the various parallelisms which Scripture furnishes:

1. Christ was the subject of Old Testament prophecy: so also is the Antichrist; many are the predictions which describe this coming one, see especially Dan. 11:21-45.

2. The Lord Jesus was typified by many Old Testament characters such as Abel, Joseph, Moses, David, etc. So also will the Antichrist be: such characters as Cain, Pharaoh, Absalom, Saul, etc., foreshadow the Man of Sin. We shall devote a separate chapter to this most fascinating and totally neglected branch of our subject.

3. Christ was revealed only at God's appointed time: such will also be the case with the Antichrist. Of the one we read, "But when *the fulness of time was come,* God sent forth His Son" (Gal. 4:4); of the other it is said, "And now we know what withholdeth that he might be *revealed in his time"* (2 Thess. 2:6).

4. Christ was a Man, a real Man, "the Man Christ Jesus" (1 Tim. 2:5); so also will the Antichrist be—"that Man of Sin" (2 Thess. 2:3).

5. But Christ was more than a man: He was the God-Man; so also will the Antichrist be more than a man: the Super-man.

6. Christ was, according to the flesh, a Jew (Rom. 1:3); so also will the Antichrist be—for proofs see chapter three, section one.

7. Christ will make a covenant with Israel (Heb. 8:8); so also will the Antichrist (Dan. 9:27).

8. Christ is our "Great High Priest"; so Antichrist will yet be Israel's great high priest (Ezek. 21:26).

9. Christ was and will be the King of the Jews (Matt. 2:1); so also will the Antichrist be (Dan. 11:36).

10. Christ will be the King of kings (Rev. 17:14); so also will the Antichrist be (Rev. 17:12, 13).

11. Christ wrought miracles: of Him it is said "approved of God among you by miracles and wonders and signs" (Acts 2:22); so also will the Antichrist, concerning whom it is written, "whose coming is after the working of Satan with all power and signs and lying wonders" (2 Thess. 2:9).

12. Christ's public ministry was limited to three years and a half; so also will the Antichrist's final ministry be (Rev. 13:5).

13. Christ is shown to us riding a "white horse" (Rev. 19:11); so also is the Antichrist (Rev. 6:2).

14. Christ will return to the earth as Prince of Peace (Isa. 9:6, 7); so also will the Antichrist introduce an era of peace (Dan. 11:21); it is to this that 1 Thess. 5:3 directly refers.

15. Christ is entitled "the Morning Star" (Rev. 22:16); so also is the Antichrist (Isa. 14:12).

16. Christ is referred to as Him "which was, and is, and is to come" (Rev. 4:8); the Antichrist is referred to as him that "was, and is not; and shall ascend out of the bottomless pit" (Rev. 17:8).

17. Christ died and rose again; so also will the Antichrist (Rev. 13:3).

18. Christ will be the object of universal worship (Phil. 2:10); so also will the Antichrist (Rev. 13:4).

19. The followers of the Lamb will be sealed in their foreheads (Rev. 7:3; 14:1); so also will the followers of the Beast (Rev. 13:16, 17).

20. Christ has been followed by the Holy Spirit who causes men to worship Him; so the Antichrist will be fol-

lowed by the Anti-spirit—the False Prophet—who will cause men to worship the Beast (Rev. 13:12).

There is no need for us to make any comments on these striking correspondences: they speak for themselves. They show the incredible lengths to which God will permit Satan to go in mimicking the Lord Jesus. We turn now to consider:

Contrasts between Christ and the Antichrist

I. In their respective Designations.

1. One is called the Christ (Matt. 16:16) ; the other the Antichrist (1 John 4:3).

2. One is called the Man of Sorrows (Isa. 53:3) ; the other the Man of Sin (2 Thess. 2:3).

3. One is called the Son of God (John 1:34) ; the other the Son of Perdition (2 Thess. 2:3).

4. One is called the Seed of the woman (Gen. 3:15) ; the other the seed of the Serpent (Gen. 3:15).

5. One is called the Lamb (Isa. 53:7) ; the other the Beast (Rev. 11:7).

6. One is called the Holy One (Mark 1:24) ; the other the Wicked One (2 Thess. 2:8).

7. One is called the Truth (John 14:6) ; the other the Lie (John 8:44).

8. One is called the Prince of Peace (Isa. 9:6) ; the other the wicked, profane Prince (Ezek. 21:25).

9. One is called the glorious Branch (Isa. 4:2) ; the other the abominable Branch (Isa. 14:19).

10. One is called the Mighty Angel (Rev. 10:1) ; the other is called the Angel of the Bottomless Pit (Rev. 9:11).

11. One is called the Good Shepherd (John 10:11); the other is called the Idol Shepherd (Zech. 11:17).

12. One has for the number of His name (the gematria of "Jesus") 888; the other has for the number of his name 666 (Rev. 13:18).

II. In their respective Careers.

1. Christ came down from heaven (John 3:13); Antichrist comes up out of the bottomless pit (Rev. 11:7).

2. Christ came in Another's Name (John 5:43); Antichrist will come in his own name (John 5:43).

3. Christ came to do the Father's will (John 6:38); Antichrist will do his own will (Dan. 11:36).

4. Christ was energized by the Holy Spirit (Luke 4:14); Antichrist will be energized by Satan (Rev. 13:4).

5. Christ submitted Himself to God (John 5:30); Antichrist defies God (2 Thess. 2:4).

6. Christ humbled Himself (Phil. 2:8); Antichrist exalts himself (Dan. 11:36).

7. Christ honored the God of His fathers (Luke 4:16); Antichrist refuses to (Dan. 11:37).

8. Christ cleansed the temple (John 2:14, 16); Antichrist defiles the temple (Matt. 24:15).

9. Christ ministered to the needy (Luke 4:18); the Antichrist robs the poor (Psa. 10:8, 9).

10. Christ was rejected of men (Isa. 53:7); Antichrist will be accepted by men (Rev. 13:4).

11. Christ leadeth the flock (John 10:3); Antichrist leaveth the flock (Zech. 11:17).

12. Christ was slain for the people (John 11:51); Antichrist slays the people (Isa. 14:20).

13. Christ glorified God on earth (John 17:4); Antichrist blasphemes the name of God in heaven (Rev. 13:6).

14. Christ was received up into heaven (Luke 24:51); Antichrist goes down into the Lake of Fire (Rev. 19:20).

5

THE CAREER OF THE ANTICHRIST

WE now come to the most interesting and yet the most difficult part of our subject. When will the Antichrist be manifested? where will he appear? what will he do? are questions which readily occur to all who have given any thought to the matter. It is not our purpose to seek to satisfy the idly curious, still less is it to gratify those who love the sensational. We are well aware that our present theme is one that appeals strongly to the curiously inclined, and were it not for the importance of our inquiry we would leave it alone. But without due regard to the person and place of the coming Superman, it is impossible to understand the eschatology of either the Old or New Testaments.

The chief difficulty is to arrange in chronological sequence the many passages which treat of the Antichrist. It is by no means easy to discover the precise order in which the prophecies which deal with the Man of Sin will receive their fulfillment. There is great need for much prayerful study along this line. We can only write according to the light we now have, and our readers must examine for themselves what we say in the light of the Scriptures. It ill becomes any one to be dogmatic where the Word itself does not plainly state the exact time when certain prophecies are to be fulfilled.

In this chapter we are placed somewhat at a disadvantage, because we shall be obliged to give brief expositions of many scriptures where it will be impossible for us to pause and furnish proofs or reasons for each interpretation. For example, it is our firm conviction that the Assyrian of

Isa. 10, the King of Babylon of Isa. 14, the Little Horn of
Dan. 7, the Little Horn of Dan. 8, and the first Beast of
Rev. 13, each and all view the Antichrist himself in different relationships. There are some Bible students who
may take issue with us on these points, and complain because that in this chapter we make assertions without en-
deavoring to prove them. We regret this, but would ask
all to bear with us patiently. In the later chapters of this
book we shall devote separate studies to the Antichrist in
the Psalms, in the Prophets, in the Gospels and Epistles,
and in the Apocalypse; when we shall endeavor to examine
each passage separately and attempt to give scriptural
proofs for every interpretation adopted.

While it is admittedly difficult, and perhaps impossible,
to fit each prophecy concerning the Antichrist into its
proper chronological place, *we are* able to determine the
relative position of most of them. The career of the Antichrist is divided into two distinct parts, and there is a
clearly defined dividing line between them. In previous
chapters we have pointed out how that the name "Antichrist" has a double meaning, signifying one who imitates
Christ, and one who is opposed to Christ. This double
meaning to his name corresponds exactly with the two
chief parts in his career. In the first, he poses as the true
Christ, claiming to be indeed the Messiah of Israel. This
claim will be backed up with the most imposing credentials, and all excepting God's elect will be deceived. He
will sit in the Temple (a rebuilt temple in Jerusalem)
showing himself forth to be God, and Divine honors will
be paid him. But at a later stage he will throw off his
mask, and appear in his true character as the opponent of
Christ and the defier of God. Then, instead of befriending
the Jews, he will turn against them and seek to extermi-

nate them from the earth. Thus, with many of the scriptures which describe the person and career of the Antichrist it is a comparatively easy matter to decide whether they belong to the first or to the second stage of his history. But beyond this it is difficult, with some scriptures at least to go.

We shall now consider, first the *time* of Antichrist's appearing. It is hardly necessary for us to enter into a lengthy argument to show that the Antichrist (as such) has not already appeared. Many antichrists have already come and gone, and some are in the world even now; the same is equally true of the many false prophets foretold in. Scripture; but all of these are but the forecasts and foreshadowings of *the* Antichrist and *the* False Prophet, who are yet to be revealed, and who will receive their final overthrow by the Lord Jesus at His return to the earth. Before *the* Antichrist can appear the Holy Spirit must be "taken out of the way" (2 Thess. 2:7); the old Roman Empire must be revived and assume its final form—divided under "ten kings"—*before* the "Little horn" comes into prominence (Dan. 7:24—he rises *"after* them") : Israel must be restored to their land and the Temple be rebuilt, etc., etc.

At the present time the ultimate development of "the Mystery of Iniquity" is being hindered. God's people are the salt of the earth, and their presence here stays the corruption of the "carcase" (Matt. 24:28—The "Carcase" is the antithesis of the "Body" of Christ). The saints are the light of the world, and while they remain in it it is impossible for darkness to *cover* the earth and gross darkness the people (Isa. 60:2). The Spirit of God is here, indwelling believers, and His holy presence checks the final outworking of Satan's plans. But when all believers of this dispensation have been "caught up to meet the Lord in the air" (1 Thess. 4:16), and the Holy Spirit has departed from the earth, all restraint will be removed, and Satan will be allowed to bring forth his false christ, who will be "revealed in his time" (2 Thess. 2:6), and it would seem that even now signs are not wanting to show that God has already given permission to Satan to prepare the stage of action for the ghastly consummation of his evil efforts. There can be no doubt but that the Devil has desired to reveal the Son of Perdition long before this, so that by means of him he may reduce the whole world to submission. But the restraining hand of God, now so soon to be removed, has held him back.

The time, then, when the Antichrist will be revealed is after this present Dispensation of Grace has run its course; after the Mystical Body of Christ has been completed; after the whole company of God's people have been caught up to meet the Lord in the air; after the Holy Spirit has departed from the world. How soon after we cannot say for certain. The majority of prophetic students seem to think that the last great Caesar will come into prominence almost immediately after the rapture of the saints. Personally, we believe there will be an interval, long or short, between the two. As there was a period of thirty years after the birth of the Lord Jesus—a period of silence—before His public ministry commenced, so there may be a similar interval between the Rapture and the Revelation of Antichrist.

The Antichrist will enter the arena of public affairs sometime *before* the beginning of Daniel's seventieth week, for at the beginning of it he makes a seven-years' covenant with the Jews, then in their land. But at that point he will be the Dictator of the world's policies, and as he begins in comparative obscurity (at least from a governmental standpoint), some time—probably years—must be allowed for his gradual rise to political supremacy. His meteoric course will not be terminated until the Lord Himself descends to earth to usher in the Millennium. Just as the reign of Saul preceded that of David, so shall that of Antichrist antedate that of the true Christ.

We turn now to consider the *place* of Antichrist's appearing. So far as the writer is aware there are only two scriptures which give direct information upon this point, and they are each found in the prophecy of Daniel. We refer to the passages which speak of "the Little Horn". In Dan. 7:7,8 we read, "After this I saw in the night visions, and, behold, a fourth beast, dreadful and terrible, and strong exceedingly; and it had great iron teeth: it devoured and break in pieces, and stamped the residue with the feet of it: and it was diverse from all the beasts that were before it; and it had ten horns. I considered the horns, and, behold, there came up among them another little horn". This "fourth Beast" is the last world-empire, prior to the setting up of the Messianic kingdom. This empire will, at first, be ruled over by ten kings—the "ten horns" of v. 7 are defined as "ten kings" in v. 24. After them arises another, the "Little Horn," which signifies another "king", see v. 24. He is termed "little" because at that stage his kingdom is but small compared with that of the others, and the power he then wields is insignificant when contrasted from the ten kings. But not for long will he remain weak and insignificant. Soon the ten kings will themselves own allegiance to this eleventh—see Rev. 17: 12, 13. We reserve for a later chapter the proofs that this "Little Horn" *is* the Antichrist, asking our readers to

study carefully the description furnished of him in Dan.
7:8, 20-27; 8:9-12, 23-25.

Taking it for granted (at the moment) that the Little
Horn of Dan. 7 is the Antichrist let us see how what is
there said of him helps us to determine the quarter from
which he will arise. In Dan. 7:7 the "fourth Beast" is described, and in 7:23 we are told, "the fourth beast shall be
the fourth *kingdom* upon earth, which shall be diverse
from all kingdoms, and shall devour the whole earth, and
shall tread it down, and break it in pieces". This Kingdom will be divided into ten parts, over which will be the
ten kings (7:24). This kingdom will be, we believe, the
old Roman Empire revived in its final form, and divided
into two great halves—the Eastern and the Western. This
fourth kingdom will include within itself all the territory
and will perpetuate all the dominant characteristics of the
other three which have preceded it, i. e., the Babylonian,
the Medo-Persian, and Grecian. Turning now to Dan. 7:
8 we are told, "I considered the horns, and, behold, there
came up *among them* another little horn". The Antichrist, then, will have his rise within the limits of the old
Roman Empire. This narrows considerably our circle of
inquiry. The next question is, Can we determine from
which part of the empire he will arise—the Eastern or the
Western? Dan. 8 furnishes light upon this point.

In Dan. 8:8, 9 we read, "Therefore the he-goat waxed
very great: and when he was strong, the great horn was
broken; and for it came up four notable ones toward the
four winds of heaven. And out of one of them came forth
a little horn, which waxed exceeding great, toward the
south, and toward the east, and toward the pleasant land."
Now v. 21 of this same chapter tells us, "The rough goat is
the king (kingdom) of Grecia", and v. 22 informs us

"and the great horn that is between his eyes is the first king. Now that being broken, whereas four stood up for it, four kingdoms (or kings) shall stand up out of the nation". This, of course, refers to the act of Alexander the Great who divided his kingdom into four parts—Greece, Egypt, Syria, and the rest of the domains of Turkey—under his four great generals: Ptolemy, Cassander, Lysimachus, and Seleucus. This, again, very appreciably narrows our circle of inquiry. Dan. 7 tells us the Little Horn is to arise in a part of the territory covered by the old Roman Empire, which Empire gradually included within its domains that of the preceding empires. Now here in Dan. 8 we learn that the Little Horn will spring from that part of the revived Roman Empire which was included in the Grecian Empire. But this is not all that Dan. 8 tells us. The Grecian Empire is here viewed as disintegrated into four parts or kingdoms, from which of *these* parts, then, may we expect him to issue—Macedonia, Egypt, Syria, or Thrace? This question, we believe, receives answer in Dan. 8:9 where we are told, that the Little Horn "waxed exceeding great toward the south, and toward the east, and toward the pleasant land". Practically all students are agreed that "the south" here refers to Egypt, the "east" to Persia and Greece, and "the pleasant land" to Palestine, hence it would seem that the country from which Antichrist will first be manifested is *Syria.* It will be noted that nothing is said in Dan. 8:9 about the Little Horn "waxing great" toward *the north,* and we believe the reason for this is because *that* is the quarter from whence he shall arise. This is confirmed by the fact that "the king of Assyria" in Isa. 10:12 is clearly none other than the Antichrist. We may say this was the current view of Christian writers on prophecy through the first ten centuries A. D. The late Mr. W. B. Newton in his splendid "Aids to the Study of Prophetic Inquiry" has succinctly summarized the various arguments of the ancients in the following language:

"In the first place, as Nimrod—the founder of Babel, that is, the Tower of Babylon—a savage tyrant and cruel oppressor of men, was the first person who declared open war against God; so it is meet that there should arise from the selfsame Babylon, the last and most atrocious persecutor of the saints—the Antichrist. Moreover, seeing that Nebuchadnezzar and Antiochus Epiphanes—two monsters who bore down upon the people of God with an overwhelming power of destruction, and who were the antichrists of the Old Testament and remarkable types of the Antichrist which is to come; seeing, I say, that these monarchs reigned in Babylon, it is fitting that the true Antichrist of the New Testament should arise from the same Babylon.

"Besides, no place can be pointed out more meet for the nativity of Antichrist than Babylon, for it is the City of the Devil—always diametrically opposed to Jerusalem, which is deemed the City of God; the former city, that is, Babylon, being the mother and disseminator of every kind of confusion, idolatry, impiety—a vast sink of every foul pollution, crime, and iniquity—the first city in the world which cut itself off from the worship of the true God—which reared the city of universal vice,—which perpetually (according to the record of Holy Writ) carries on the mystery of iniquity, and bears imprinted on her brow the inscription of blasphemy against the name of God. The consummation, therefore, of impiety, which is to have its recapitulation in Antichrist, could not break forth from a more fitting place than Babylon".

Having dwelt at some length on the *time* and the *place* of the Antichrist's appearing, we shall attempt to give now a brief outline of the leading events in his *career*. We have seen that the scriptures which help us to determine the direction from which he will arise, speak of him under the title of the "Little Horn". Now the first thing this title denotes is that he is a *king,* king of Assyria. Some, no doubt, will wonder how a Jew will succeed in obtaining the throne of Syria. Several answers might be suggested, such, for example, as heading a successful rebellion—the spectacle of an obscure plebian speedily rising to the rank of national Dictator, has been forcibly exhibited before our own eyes in Russia. But on this point we are not left to speculation. Dan. 11:21 tells us that the "Vile Person" will "come in peaceably, and obtain the kingdom by flatteries". With this agrees Rev. 6:2, where the Antichrist is seen riding a white war-horse, and with bow in hand, but with no arrow fitted to it. The symbol suggests bloodless victories.

As soon as this Jew acquires the crown of Syria he will speedily enlarge his dominions. As Rev. 6:2 tells us, he will go forth "conquering, and to conquer", and as we are told further in Hab. 2:5, "He is a proud man, neither keepeth at home, who enlargeth his desire as hell, and is as death, and cannot be satisfied, but gathereth unto him all nations, and heapeth unto him all people". The first thing which is predicated of him (as "the Little Horn") is that "he shall subdue three kings" (Dan. 7:24). As to what "kings" these may be, appears to be intimated in Dan. 8:9 where we are told, "And out of one of them came forth a little horn, which waxed exceeding great toward the south, and toward the east, and toward the pleasant land". He "waxes great" first toward the south, that is, most probably, by a victorious expedition into Egypt. Next, he is seen moving "toward the east", reducing, to what extent we are not told, the dominions of Persia and Greece; finally he turns his face "toward the pleasant land", which is Palestine. Without being dogmatic, we would suggest that the three kings he subdues are those of Egypt, Persia, and Greece.

Having subdued the three kings by his military prowess a "league" is made with him (see Dan. 11:23). Probably it is the remaining seven kings of the revived Roman Empire, plus the three vassals of the Antichrist who take the place of the kings he had deposed, that enter into this League with the Little Horn, or king of Assyria; but he "shall work deceitfully, and shall become strong with a small people" (Dan. 11:23). So strong does he become that in a short time he rises to political supremacy, and the whole of the ten kings shall "give their kingdom unto the Beast" (Rev. 17:17), and he will then be recognized as the imperial Emperor. Thus as King of kings he will dictate the policies of Europe and Asia.

"The Little Horn will revive in himself all the personified glory of Babylon, Medo-Persia, Greece and Rome. And let not this be regarded as an event incredible. We are to remember that Antichrist will be Satan's masterpiece; furnished with every auxiliary of influence and wealth, for wresting the sceptre from the hands of Him who won it by His humiliation on the Cross. Thus it is said he will 'resist the God of gods'. The accumulated and restored honors of each royal successor are thus to crown the brow of this last and greatest of Gentile monarchs. And so shall he stand in his unrivalled magnificence till the Stone shall smite him and his power, and grind all to powder" *(Mrs. G. Needham)*.

After the Antichrist has acquired the political sovereignty of the prophetic earth he will then enter upon his religious role, claiming to be the Christ of God and demanding Divine honors. At first sight it appears strange, if not incongruous, that a military despot should be found filling the character of a religious impostor. But history shows that there is a point at which one character readily merges into the other. Political ambition, intoxicated by success, finds it an easy step from self-glorification to self-deification, and the popular infatuation as easily passes from the abject adulation of the tyrant to the adoration of the god. Or again; a religious impostor, encouraged by the ascendancy he has acquired over the minds of men, grasps the sceptre of secular power and becomes the most arbitrary of despots. Rev. 13:4 makes it plain that the military prowess of the Antichrist first induces men to render him Divine homage: "And they worshipped the Dragon which gave power unto the Beast: and they worshipped the Beast, saying, Who is like unto the Beast? who is able to make war with him?" But no ordinary honors will suffice him. His religious ambitions are as insatiable as his political, for he will "oppose and exalt himself above all that is called God, or that is worshipped; so that he as God sitteth in the temple of God, showing himself that he is God" (2 Thess. 2:4). This claim to be God Himself, incarnate, will be backed up by imposing credentials, for his coming will be, "after the working of Satan, with all power and signs and lying wonders" (2 Thess. 2:9). These miracles will be no mere pretenses, but prodigies of power.

The Jews, previously returned to Palestine, and with temple in Jerusalem rebuilt, will receive this Son of Perdition as their long-promised Messiah" (John 5:43). In imitation of the true Christ who will, at His return to the earth, "make a new covenant with the House of Israel and with the House of Judah" (Heb. 8:8, compare Jer. 31 and Ezek. 36), the Antichrist will make a covenant with the Jews (see Dan. 9:27 and 11:22). Under a seven years' treaty, and in the guise of friendship, he will gain ascendancy in Jerusalem, only later to throw off the mask and break the covenant.

About seven months after the Antichrist, the "Prince" (i. e. of the Roman Empire) of Dan. 9:27 has made the Covenant with the Jews he will begin to "practice" in Jerusalem (Dan. 8:24). This we believe is the explanation of the two thousand three hundred days of Dan. 8:14 which has puzzled so many of the commentators. This two thousand three hundred days is the whole period during which the false messiah will practice in Jerusalem and have power over the "sanctuary": two thousand three hundred days is seven years less seven months and ten days.

There, in Jerusalem, he will pose as the Christ of God, the Prince of Peace. The world will suppose that the long looked-for Millennium has arrived. There will be every indication that the eagerly desired Golden Age has, at last, dawned. The great Powers of Europe and Asia will have been united under the ten-kingdomed Empire. It will be expected that the League of Nations guarantees the peace of the earth. For a season quietness and amity will prevail. None will dare to oppose the mighty Emperor. But not for long will the hideous war-spectre hide himself. Soon will the "white horse" of Rev. 6 be found to change his hue. A "red horse" will go forth, and then "peace shall be taken from the earth" (Rev. 6). At the very time the world is congratulating itself that all is well, and the slogan of the hour is "Peace and Safety", *then* "sudden destruction cometh upon them" (1 Thess. 5:3).

In the midst of the seven years the Antichrist will throw off his mask, break his covenant with Israel, and stand forth as the most daring idolater who has ever trodden this earth. After he has "practiced" in Jerusalem for two years and five months, he will "take away the daily sacrifice" (Dan. 8:11; 9:27) from the Temple, and in its place rear an image to himself in the holy place, which is the "abomination of desolation" referred to by Christ (see Matt. 24:15).

This brings us to the great dividing line in his career, to which reference was made near the beginning of this chapter. It is a point not only of interest but of considerable importance to ascertain what it is that causes this startling change of front, from posing as the true Christ to that of the open defier of God. There are several scriptures which throw light on this point. Satan will cause the Man of Sin to crown his daring imitation of the Christ of God by being slain and rising again from the dead.

Both the Old and the New Testaments refer to the death of the Antichrist, and attribute it to the *sword*. In Rev. 13:14 we read that the false Prophet shall say to them that dwell on the earth "that they should make an image to the Beast, which had the wound by the *sword* and did live". In harmony with this we read in Zech. 11:17, "Woe to the Idol Shepherd that leaveth the flock! The *sword* shall be upon his arm, and upon his right eye". It is to be noted that before we read that "the sword shall be" upon him, we are told that he "leaveth the flock", and the previous verse tells us that he was raised up "in *the* Land", which can only mean that he was ruling in Palestine. Hence it is clear that he leaves the Land before he receives his death wound by the sword. In perfect accord with this is what we read in Isa. 37:6, 7 (in a later chapter we shall treat at length of the future Babylon, restored; the connection of Antichrist with it, and the typical and prophetical significance of Isa. 37 and 38): "Behold, I will send a blast upon him, and he shall hear a rumour, and return to his own land; and I will cause him to fall *by the sword* in his own land".

Leaving Palestine, the Antichrist will "return to *his own* land", that is, the land of his nativity—Assyria—which confirms what we have said previously about Assyria being the country where Antichrist will first be manifested. There, in his own land, he will fall by the sword. Most probably he will be slain there by his political enemies, envious of his power and chafing under his haughty autocracy. In death he will be hated and dishonored, and burial will be refused him. It is to this that Isa. 14 (speaking of the King of Babylon, see v. 4) refers: "But thou art cast out of thy grave like an abominable branch, and as the raiment of those that are slain, thrust through *with a sword,* that go down to the stones of the pit. As a carcase trodden under feet, thou shalt not be joined with them in burial, because thou hast destroyed thy land, and slain thy people" (vv. 19, 20). But his enemies will suddenly be filled with consternation and then admiration, for to their amazement this one slain by the sword shall rise from the dead, and his deadly wound will be healed—note how this is implied in Isa. 14, for v. 25 shows him once more in the land of the living, only to meet his final doom at the hands of the Lord Himself. It is to this amazing resurrection of the Antichrist that Rev. 13:3, 4 refers: "And I saw one of his heads as it were wounded to death; and his deadly wound was healed: and all the world wondered after the Beast. And they worshipped the Dragon which gave power unto the Beast: and they worshipped the Beast, saying, Who is like unto the Beast? who is able to make war with him?" Details of his resurrection are supplied in Rev. 9, from which we gather that just as Christ was raised from the dead by God the Father, so the Antichrist will be raised from the dead by his father the Devil, see v. 1 where the fallen "Star", which refers to Satan, is given the "key of the bottomless pit", and when this is opened there comes out of it the mysterious "locusts" whose king is the Destroyer (v. 11), the Antichrist.

A further reference to the resurrection of the Antichrist, his coming forth from the Bottomless Pit, is found in Rev. 17:8: "The Beast that thou sawest was, and is not; and shall ascend out of the Bottomless Pit, and go into Perdition: and they that dwell on the earth shall wonder, whose names were not written in the book of life from the foundation of the world, when they behold the Beast that was, and is not, and yet is". It is to be noted that the earth-dwellers wonder *when they behold* the Beast that was (alive), and is not (now alive), and yet is (raised again). The world will then be presented with the spectacle of a man raised from the dead. All know him, for his career and amazing progress were eagerly watched; his wonderful achievements and military campaigns were the subjects of daily interest; his transcendent genius elicited their admiration. They had witnessed his death. They stood awe-struck, no doubt, at the downfall of this King of kings. And now he is made alive; his wound of death is healed; and the whole world wonders, and worships him.

It is about this time, apparently, that the "False Prophet" (Rev. 13:11-16), the third person in the Trinity of Evil will appear on the scene. From a number of scrip-

tures it is evident that the Antichrist will not spend all his
time in Palestine during the last three and a half years
of his career. It seems that shortly after the middle of the
"week" the Beast will turn his face again toward Babylon, leaving the False Prophet to act as his vicegerent,
compelling all in Jerusalem to worship the image of the
Beast under pain of death (Rev. 13:15). It is to be noted
that Hab. 2:5 tells us that the Antichrist is "a proud man,
neither keepeth at home, who enlargeth his desire as hell,
and is as death, and cannot be satisfied, but gathereth unto
him all nations, and heapeth unto him all people".

The reason for the Antichrist's return to Babylon is not
far to seek. Having thrown off his mask of religious pretension, he now stands forth as the Defier of God. His
first move now will be to blot out from the earth everything that bears His name. To accomplish this the Jewish race must be utterly exterminated, and to this end he
will put forth all his power to banish Israel from the earth.
He will make war with the saints (the Jewish saints) and
prevail against them (Dan. 7:21; 8:24): this is the going
forth of the "red horse" of Rev. 6:4.

Those of the godly remnant who are left will "flee to the
mountains" (Matt. 24:16), and there they will be hunted
like partridges. It is then they will cry, "Keep not Thou
silence, O God: hold not Thy peace, and be not still, O
God. For, lo, Thine enemies make a tumult: and they
that hate Thee have lifted up the head. They have taken
crafty counsel against Thy people, and consulted against
Thy hidden ones. They have said, Come, and let us *cut
them off from being a nation;* that the name of Israel may
be no more in remembrance" (Psa. 83:1-4). Then, because many of the Jews will be found in that day dwelling
in Babylon (see Jer. 50:8; 51:6, 45; Rev. 18:4) the Anti-

christ will go thither to wreak his vengeance upon them. But not for long will he be suffered to continue his blasphemous and bloody course. Soon will heaven respond to the cries of the faithful remnant of Israel, and terrible shall be the punishment meted out on their last enemy. This, however, must be left for consideration in our next chapter, when we shall treat of the last days and doom of the Antichrist.

6

THE DOOM OF THE ANTICHRIST

I F there is a measure of difficulty attending the placing and elucidation of some of the prophecies which depict the various phases and stages of the Antichrist's career, the cloud lifts as the end is neared. And this is in full accord with many other things which pertain to the closing days of the Age. The nearer we come to the blessed event of our Lord's return to this earth, the more light has God seemed to cast on those things which immediately precede the Second Advent. It is as though, at first, God furnishes only a bare outline, but ultimately He fills in the details for us. It is thus with the end of the Antichrist. The Holy Spirit has been pleased to supply us with a most comprehensive and vivid description of the closing scenes in the career of the Son of Perdition. It is with mingled feelings that we turn and ponder what has thus been recorded for our learning.

The awful course which is followed by the Man of Sin cannot but shock us. The frightful hypocrisy, the shocking duplicity and treachery, the terrible cruelty, and the amazing impiety of this Monster of wickedness, make us marvel at the forbearance of God, who endures "with much long-suffering the vessels of wrath fitted to destruction". But when we come to the final scenes, and behold the Antichrist openly challenging heaven, publicly defying God, and making a deliberate and determined effort to prevent the Lord Jesus returning to this earth, we are wellnigh rendered speechless by the unthinkable lengths to which sin will go. On the other hand, as we learn that all of this is the ending of that long dismal night which precedes the Day of Christ, the Millennium, we see that it is but the dark background to bring into more vivid relief the glories of the God-Man. The destruction of the Antichrist will be followed at once by the setting up of the Messianic Kingdom which shall bring peace and blessing to all the earth. And the contemplation of this cannot but fill us with joy and thanksgiving.

"The end of the Man of Sin marks an era of sublimest interest to the believing children of God. It shall be the day of our triumphant manifestation, and the Jubilee of all creation. The day, Oh, Hallelujah! when Satan's crown of pride shall be smitten, and his glory trailed in the dust; when his long-continued and persistent temptations shall have an end; and his power receive the wounding from which it shall never recover itself. That blessed, blessed day, when He whose right it is, shall reign, and the kingdom of Israel be no more overturned and dishonored. The sweet, sweet day, when the mockings, the scourgings, the bonds, the imprisonments, the afflictions, and the torments of the great multitude 'of whom the world was not worthy,' shall cease to annoy forever, and the whole earth be at rest, and break forth into gladness" *(Mrs. G. Needham)*.

But before that blessed Day arrives, the last hour of the night of Christ's absence has to run its course, and as the darkest hour precedes the dawn, so the last hour of this "night" shall be the most foreboding of all. The period which immediately precedes the return of Christ to the earth will witness the most awful events ever chronicled. It was of this period that Daniel spoke when he said, "There shall be a time of trouble, such as never was since there was a nation even to that same time" (12:1). It was to this same time that Christ referred when He declared,

"For in those days shall be affliction, such as was not from the beginning of the creation which God created unto this time, neither shall be. And except that the Lord had shortened those days, no flesh should be saved: but for the elect's sake, whom He hath chosen, He hath shortened the days" (Mark 13:19, 20). This is "the hour of temptation which shall come upon all the world" (Rev. 3:10). It will be a time of unparalleled wickedness, and a time of unprecedented suffering. It is the time when God shall avenge the murder of His Son, when He shall take to task a world that has so long despised His Word, and trampled His commandments under foot. The very Antichrist will be one of the instruments of His vengeance—"the rod of His anger" (Isa. 10:5).

It is because men received not the love of God's truth He shall send them strong delusion that they should believe the Devil's lie. It is because men had "pleasure in unrighteousness" they shall be deceived by the Lawless One. It is because Israel refused that blessed One who came in His Father's name that they shall receive the one who comes in his own name. This is why the Antichrist will, for a season, be suffered to prosper, and apparently to defy God with impugnity. But when God has used him to perform His own pleasure, then shall He empty upon his kingdom and upon his subjects the vials of His wrath. Just as God has set the bounds of the sea, saying thus far shalt thou go and no further, so has He fixed the limits to which He will allow the Antichrist to go. And when that limit is reached the Son of Perdition will find himself as helpless to pass beyond what God has decreed as a worm would be beneath the foot of an elephant. This will be made evident as we proceed.

At the close of our last chapter we followed the career of

the Antichrist to the point where he turns upon the Jewish people and seeks to cut them off from being a nation. Fearful will be his assaults upon them, and bitter will be their wailings. It is at that time the Remnant will cry, "O God; why hast Thou cast us off forever? why doth Thine anger smoke against the sheep of Thy pasture? Remember Thy congregation, which Thou hast purchased of old; the rod of Thine inheritance, which Thou hast redeemed; this mount Zion, wherein Thou hast dwelt. Lift up Thy feet unto the perpetual desolations; even all that the Enemy hath done wickedly in the sanctuary. Thine enemies roar in the midst of Thy congregations; they set up their ensigns for signs. A man was famous according as he had lifted up axes upon the thick trees. But now they break down the carved work thereof at once with axes and hammers. They have cast fire into Thy sanctuary, they have defiled by casting down the dwelling-place of Thy name to the ground. They said in their hearts, Let us destroy them together; they have *burned up all the synagogues of God in the land.* We see not our signs: there is no more any profit neither is there any among us which knoweth how long. O God, how long shall the Adversary reproach? Shall the Enemy blaspheme Thy name forever? Why withdrawest Thou Thy hand, even Thy right hand? Pluck it out of Thy bosom" (Psa. 74:1-11).

It is at this same time that the prophecy of Amos 8 will receive its final fulfillment: "The Lord hath sworn by the excellency of Jacob, Surely I will never forget any of their works. Shall not the land tremble for this, and every one mourn that dwelleth therein? and it shall rise wholly as a flood; and it shall be cast out and drowned, as by the flood of Egypt. And it shall come to pass in that day, saith the Lord God, that I will cause the sun to go down at noon, and I will darken the earth in the clear day: And I will turn your feasts into mourning, and all your songs into lamentation; and I will bring up sackcloth upon all loins, and baldness upon every head; and I will make it as the mourning of an only son, and the end thereof as a bitter day. Behold, the days come, saith the Lord God, that I will send a famine in the land, not a famine of bread, nor a thirst for water, but of hearing the words of the Lord: And they shall wander from sea to sea, and from the north even to the east, they shall run to and fro *to seek the word of the Lord, and shall not find it.* In that day shall the fair virgins and the young men faint for thirst" (Amos 8:7-13). How remarkably does Psa. 74 interpret this prophecy of Amos! The reason why the godly Remnant shall run to and fro to "seek the word of the Lord" and shall not find it, and the meaning of the "famine of *hearing* the words of the Lord" is that "all the synagogues in the land" shall have been burned up.

But not for long will this frightful persecution continue: "Therefore thus saith the Lord God of hosts, O My people that dwellest in Zion, be not afraid of the Assyrian: he shall smite thee with a rod, and shall lift up his staff against thee, after the manner of Egypt. For yet *a very little while,* and the indignation shall cease, and Mine anger in their destruction" (Isa. 10:24, 25). Once the Antichrist turns upon Israel his days are numbered, for to touch that nation is to touch the apple of God's eye (Zech. 2:8). God shall respond to the cries of the faithful Remnant and shall "stir up a scourge for him" (Isa. 10: 26). What this "scourge" is we learn from Dan. 11:40: "And at the time of the end shall the king of the south push at him; and the king of the north (the Antichrist) shall come against him (i. e. the king of the south) like a whirlwind, with chariots, and with horsemen, and with many ships; and he shall enter into the countries, and shall overflow, and pass over" (Dan. 11:40).

The king of the south who pushes at—assails—the Antichrist is the king of Egypt. The Antichrist, here termed "the king of the north", i. e. Assyria, shall leave Babylon, and marshalling his imperial forces, which he has ready for immediate action, shall lead them against him (the king of Egypt) like a whirlwind. The rapidity of his movements and the immensity of his armies, is intimated by the words, "He shall enter into the countries, and shall overflow and pass over". His progress will be as the rushing of an overwhelming torrent from the mountains, that spreads over the land, and carries everything before it. "He shall enter also into the glorious land, and many countries shall be overthrown" (Dan. 11:41). His route from Babylon to Egypt will take him through Palestine, the land which is soon to be the glory of all lands; and, although we are not told here what he will do there at that time, his hand will, no doubt, be heavy upon it, as also upon the many other countries which he will overthrow. "But these shall escape out of his hand, even Edom, and Moab, and the chief of the children of Ammon" (Dan. 11:41). These three peoples will escape his fury. The reason for *their* escape seems to be a double one. In Ps. 83, which describes an event at a little earlier period, we are told, "they have taken crafty counsel against Thy people, and consulted against Thy hidden ones. They have said, Come, and let us cut them off from being a nation; that the name of Israel may be no more in remembrance. For they have consulted together with one consent, they are confederate against Thee: the tabernacles of *Edom,* and the Ishmaelites; of *Moab,* and the

Hagarenes; Gebal, and *Ammon,* and Amalek; the Philistines with the inhabitants of Tyre; Assur (the Assyrian) also is joined with them" (Psa. 83:3-8). Thus we see that these three peoples acted in concert with the Antichrist, when a determined effort was made to utterly exterminate the Jewish people. The Antichrist, therefore, spares these submissive allies of his when he goes forth to overthrow the other countries.

So much for the human side as to why "these shall escape out of his hand, even Edom, and Moab, and the chief of the children of Ammon". But there is a Divine side, too. These peoples are spared at that time in order that they may be dealt with later by God Himself. Thus did Jehovah declare of old through Balaam the heathen prophet: "There shall come a Star out of Jacob, and a Sceptre shall rise out of Israel, and shall smite the corners of Moab, and destroy all the children of Sheth. And Edom shall be a possession, Seir also shall be a possession for his enemies" (Num. 24:17, 18). This will be right at the beginning of the Millennium. Israel, too, shall be used by God in this work of judgment upon their ancient enemies: "But they shall fly upon the shoulders of the Philistines toward the west; they shall spoil them of the east together: they shall lay their hand upon Edom and Moab; and the children of Ammon shall obey them" (Isa. 11:14).

"He shall stretch forth his hand also upon the countries: and the land of Egypt shall not escape. But he shall have power over the treasures of gold and of silver, and over all the precious things of Egypt: and the Libyans and the Ethiopians shall be at his steps" (Dan. 11:42, 43). The victorious King will then take possession of those countries which were overthrown by him during his march from Babylon to Egypt. Having now reached this land which dared to "push at him"—the land never completely subjugated by the previous kings of the north referred to in the earlier part of Dan. 11—its king and subjects must now bow before his iron sceptre. He becomes master of its treasures of gold, silver, and precious things. The Libyans and Ethiopians, who were the allies of Egypt, will be compelled to follow in his train. Thus will he crush this Egyptian rebellion, and demonstrate once more his military prowess. Yet not for long will he be permitted to defy Heaven with impugnity.

"But tidings out of the east and out of the north shall trouble him: therefore he shall go forth with great fury to destroy, and utterly to make away many" (Dan. 11:44). What these troublous tidings are we learn from Jer. 51. A serious attack will be made upon his Babylonian headquarters, and during his absence from there, the kings of Ararat, Minni, and Ashchenaz—no doubt emboldened by the insubordination of Egypt—will besiege and capture one end of the Capital. The time is nigh at hand when God shall utterly destroy that City of the Devil, and a preliminary warning of this is now given: "And I will render unto Babylon and to all the inhabitants of Chaldea all their evil that they have done in Zion in your sight, saith the Lord. Behold, I am against thee, O destroying mountain, saith the Lord, which destroyeth all the earth: and I will stretch out Mine hand upon thee, and roll thee down from the rocks, and will make thee a burnt mountain. And they shall not take of thee a stone for a corner, nor a stone for foundations; but thou shalt be desolate forever, saith the Lord" (Jer. 51:24-26).

As a beginning to this end, the Lord says, "Set ye up a standard in the land, blow the trumpet among the nations, prepare the nations against her, call together against her the kingdoms of Ararat, Minni, and Ashchenaz (all situated in the vicinity of Armenia); appoint a captain against her; cause the horses to come up as the rough caterpillers. Prepare against her the nations with the kings of the Medes, the captains thereof, and all the rulers thereof, and all the land of his dominion. And the land shall tremble and sorrow: for every purpose of the Lord shall be performed against Babylon, to make the land of Babylon a desolation without an inhabitant. The mighty man of Babylon hath forborn to fight, they have remained in their holds: their might hath failed; they became as women: they have burned their dwelling places; her bars are broken" (Jer. 51:27-30).

It is this ominous news—the "tidings" which "trouble him" of Dan. 11:44—which reaches the ears of Babylon's King, then absent in Egypt. The alarming tidings that part of the city has already been destroyed arouses him to fierce anger, for we are told, "therefore he shall go forth with great fury to destroy, and utterly to make away many" (Dan. 11:44). As he nears the capital, "one post shall run to meet another, and one messenger to meet another, to show the King of Babylon that his city is taken at one end, and that the passages are stopped, and the reeds they have burned with fire, and the men of war are affrighted" (Jer. 51:31, 32). The end is not far distant: "For thus saith the Lord of hosts, the God of Israel; the daughter of Babylon is like a threshing floor, it is time to thresh her: yet a little while, and the time of her harvest shall come" (Jer. 51:33). God now calls on the Jews who are found dwelling within that city to leave at once, lest they be caught in the storm of His fierce anger: "My people, go ye out of the midst of her, and deliver you every man his soul from the fierce anger of the Lord" (Jer. 51: 45). A graphic description of Babylon's destruction is found at the end of Jer. 51 and also in Rev. 18.

The fury of the Antichrist at the destruction of Babylon will know no bounds. Enraged at his loss, and incensed against God, he will now turn his face toward Palestine, and at the head of his vast forces will bear down upon the glorious land. Even so, it is *God* who is directing him and his blinded dupes—directing him to finish the work of judgment upon Israel, and directing him to his awful doom. Habakkuk gives a fearful description of the spirit in which the King of Babylon and his hosts shall fall upon the dwellers of Palestine:—"For, lo, I raise up the Chaldeans, that bitter and hasty nation, which shall march through the breadth of the land, to possess the dwelling places that are not theirs. They are terrible and dreadful: their judgment and their dignity shall proceed of themselves. Their horses also are swifter than the leopards, and are more fierce than the evening wolves: and their horsemen shall spread themselves, and their horsemen shall come from far; they shall *fly* as the eagle that hasteth to eat. (How this verse anticipates the cruel aerial war-weapons!). They shall come all for violence: their faces shall sup up as the east wind, and they shall gather the captivity as the sand. And they shall scoff at the kings, and the princes shall be a scorn unto them: they shall deride every stronghold; for they shall heap dust, and take it. Then shall his mind change, and he shall pass over, and offend, imputing this his power unto his god" (Note how this last verse serves to identify the "Chaldean" with the "King" of Dan. 11:38, 39). So terrible will be this onslaught that we are told, "And it shall come to pass, that in all the land, saith the Lord, two parts therein shall be cut off and die; but the third shall be left there-in" (Zech. 13:8).

His course is vividly sketched by Isaiah in the tenth chapter of his prophecy: "He is come to Aiath, he is passed to Migron; at Mickmash he hath laid up his carriages: They are gone over the passage: they have taken up their lodging at Geba; Ramah is afraid; Gibeah of Saul is fled. Lift up thy voice, O daughter of Galim: cause it to be heard unto Laish, O poor Anathoth. Madmena is removed; the inhabitants of Gebim gather themselves to flee. As yet shall he remain at Nob that day" (Isa. 10: 28-32). Nob is his camping-ground for that day, and it is there he will "plant the tabernacles of his palace between the seas in the goodly holy mountain" (Dan. 11: 45). Nob must be some elevation commanding a distant view of Jerusalem from the west. As he stands on the hill that night and looks at the Holy City, he "shall shake his hand against the mount of the daughter of Zion, the hill of Jerusalem" (Isa. 10:32).

We now come to the closing scene. The following morning the Man of Sin leads his forces to the famous Armageddon, there awaiting his final re-inforcements before attacking Jerusalem. It is of this that Joel speaks: "Proclaim ye this among the Gentiles; Prepare war, wake up the mighty men, let all the men of war draw near; let them come up: Beat your plowshares into swords, and your pruning hooks into spears: let the weak say, I am strong. Assemble yourselves, and come all ye heathen, and gather yourselves together round about: thither cause Thy mighty ones to come down, O Lord. Let the heathen be wakened, and come up to the valley of Jehoshaphat; for there will I sit to judge all the heathen round about. Put ye in the sickle, for the harvest is ripe: come, get you

down; for the press is full, the fats overflow; for their
wickedness is great. Multitudes, multitudes in the valley
of decision: for the day of the Lord is near in the valley of
decision" (Joel 3:9-14).

It is to this that Micah refers: "Now also many nations
are gathered against thee, that say, Let her be defiled, and
let our eye look upon Zion. But they know not the
thoughts of the Lord, neither understand they His counsel: for *He* shall gather them as the sheaves into the floor"
(4:10, 11). But it is not in the valley that the battle is
fought, but around Jerusalem, where the Beast and his
armies deliver the final blow of God's judgment on that
city ere the Deliverer appears. It is then that God will
say, "O Assyrian, the rod of Mine anger, and the staff in
their hands is Mine indignation. I will send him against
an hypocritical nation, and against the people of My wrath
will I give him a charge, to take the spoil, and to take the
prey, and to tread them down like the mire of the streets.
Howbeit he meaneth not so, neither doth his heart think
so; but it is in his heart to destroy and cut off nations not
a few. For he saith, Are not my princes altogether kings?
Is not Calno as Carchemish? Is not Hamath as Arpad?
Is not Samaria as Damascus? As my hand hath found
the kingdoms of the idols, and whose graven images did
excel them of Jerusalem and of Samaria; Shall I not, as
I have done unto Samaria and her idols, so do to Jerusalem and her idols? Wherefore it shall come to pass, that
when the Lord hath performed His whole work upon
mount Zion and on Jerusalem, I will punish the fruit of
the stout heart of the King of Assyria, and the glory of his
high looks" (Isa. 10:5-12). The Antichrist is but the
Lord's instrument after all. Just as Moses picked up and
held in his hand the rod which became a serpent, so shall

this offspring of the Serpent be wielded by the hand of God to accomplish His predetermined counsels.

Once again, though, the Beast appears to be successful. Jerusalem falls before his onslaught as Jehovah had foretold that it should—"For I will gather all nations against Jerusalem to battle; and the city shall be taken, and the houses rifled, and the women ravished; and half of the city shall go forth into captivity, and the residue of the people shall not be cut off from the city" (Zech. 14:2). Intoxicated by their success, it is then that the heathen shall rage and the people imagine a vain thing: "The kings of the earth set themselves, and the rulers take counsel together, against the Lord, and against His anointed, saying, Let us brake their bands asunder, and cast away their cords from us" (Psa. 2:2, 3).

And then comes the grand finale. The heaven will open and from it will descend the King of kings and Lord of lords, seated on a white horse, with His eyes "as a flame of fire" (Rev. 19:11, 12). Attending Him will be the armies of heaven, also seated on white horses (Rev. 19:14). Far from being appalled at this awe-inspiring spectacle, the Beast and the kings of the earth and their armies shall gather together to "make war against Him that sat on the horse, and against His armies" (Rev. 19:19). *"Then* shall the Lord go forth, and fight against those nations, as when He fought in the day of battle" (Zech. 14:3). At last the Christ of God and the christ of Satan will confront each other. But the instant the conflict begins, it is ended. The Foe will be paralyzed, and all resistance cease.

Scripture has solemnly recorded the end of various august evil personages. Some were overwhelmed by waters: some devoured by flames; some engulfed in the jaws of the earth; some stricken by a loathsome disease; some ignominiously slaughtered; some hanged; some eaten up of dogs; some consumed by worms. But to no sinful dweller on earth, save the Man of Sin, "the Wicked One", has been appointed the terrible distinction of being consumed by the brightness of the personal appearing of the Lord Jesus Himself. Such shall be his unprecedented doom, an end that shall fittingly climax his ignoble origin, his amazing career, and his unparalleled wickedness.

"Hitherto proud boastings have issued from the lips of Satan's king; but now he falls helplessly to the ground, blasted by the lightening which streams from the King of kings; and together with the False Prophet and in the full sight of his countless armies, he is seized by the angels of the Lord, to be hurled alive into the lake which burneth with fire and brimstone" *(G. H. Pember)*.

The overthrow of the Antichrist is described as follows: —"But with righteousness shall He judge the poor, and reprove with equity for the meek of the earth: and He shall smite the earth with the rod of His mouth and *with the breath of His lips shall He slay the Wicked"* (Isa. 11: 14).

"And through his policy also he shall cause craft to prosper in his hand; and he shall magnify himself in his heart, and by peace shall destroy many: he shall also stand up against the Prince of princes; but *he shall be broken without hand"*—an expression which always refers to that which is supernatural (Dan. 8:25).

"And he shall plant the tabernacles of his palace between the seas in the glorious holy mountain; yet shall he *come to his end, and none shall help him"* (Dan. 11:45).

"And then shall that Wicked (One) be revealed, whom the Lord *shall consume with the spirit of His mouth, and shall destroy with the brightness of His coming"* (2 Thess. 2:8).

"And the Beast was taken, and with him the False Prophet that wrought miracles before him, with which he deceived them that had received the mark of the Beast, and them that worshipped his image. These both were *cast alive into a lake of fire burning with brimstone"* (Rev. 19:20).

"For Tophet is ordained of old; yea, *for the King it is prepared;* he hath made it deep and large: the pile thereof is fire and much wood; *the breath of the Lord, like a stream of brimstone, doth kindle it"* (Isa. 30:33).

"And the Devil that deceived them was cast into the lake of fire and brimstone, where the Beast and the False Prophet are, and (they) *shall be tormented day and night for ever and ever"* (Rev. 20:10).

Frightful, too, shall be the doom meted out to the followers of the Antichrist. Zech. 14 tells us, "And this shall be the plague wherewith the Lord will smite all the people that have fought against Jerusalem; Their flesh shall consume away while they stand upon their feet, and their eyes shall consume away in their holes, and their tongues shall consume away in their mouth. And it shall come to pass in that day, that a great tumult from the Lord shall be among them; and they shall lay hold every one on the hand of his neighbour, and his hand shall rise up against the hand of his neighbour" (vv. 12, 13). So, also Rev. 19:21 declares, "And the remnant were slain with the sword of Him that sat upon the horse, which sword proceeded out of His mouth: and all the fowls were filled with their flesh".

7

ANTICHRIST IN THE PSALMS

THE references to the Man of Sin in the book of Psalms are, for the most part, more or less incidental ones. With rare exceptions he comes into view only as he is related to Israel, or as he affects their fortunes. One cannot appreciate the force of what is there said of him except as that is examined in the light of its prophetic setting. The time when the Antichrist will be in full power is during the Tribulation period, and it is not until we discover, by careful searching, which of the Psalms describe the Time of Jacob's trouble, that we know where to look for their last great Troubler.

Politically and ecclesiastically the Antichrist may be viewed in a threefold connection: first, as he is related to the Gentiles; second, as he is related to the apostate Jewish nation; third, as he is related to the godly Jewish Remnant, who separate themselves from their unbelieving brethren. More details are furnished us in the Psalms upon this third relationship than upon the other two, though we have occasional allusions to Antichrist's connections with the Gentiles and the Jewish nation as a whole.

The second Psalm gives us a brief but vivid picture of that which will wind up the Tribulation period, and while the Antichrist is not directly named, yet the light which other scriptures throw upon it reveals the dreadful personality who heads the rebellion there described. This second Psalm is prophetic in its character and has, like most (if not all) prophecy, a *double* fulfillment.

"Why do the heathen rage, and the people imagine a

vain thing? The kings of the earth set themselves, and the rulers take counsel together, against the Lord, and against His anointed, saying, Let us break their bands asunder, and cast away their cords from us" (Psa. 2:1-3). A part of this passage is found quoted in Acts 4, but it is striking to note where the quotation ceases. Peter and John had been arraigned before the religious authorities of Israel, because that in the name of Jesus Christ they had healed an impotent man. The apostles boldly and faithfully vindicated themselves, and after being admonished and threatened were allowed to depart to their own company. Then it was that they "lifted up their voice to God with one accord, and said, Lord, Thou art God, which hast made heaven, and earth, and the sea, and all that in them is: Who by the mouth of Thy servant David hath said, Why did the heathen rage, and the people imagine vain things? The kings of the earth stood up, and the rulers were gathered together against the Lord, and against His Christ" (Acts 4:24-26). Notice they quoted only the first two verses of Psalm 2, and *this* they did not say was now "fulfilled". What they did say was, "For of a truth against Thy holy child Jesus, whom Thou hast anointed, both Herod, and Pontius Pilate, with the Gentiles, and the people of Israel, were gathered together, for to do whatsoever Thy hand and Thy counsel determined before to be done" (v. 28). In the apprehension of Christ and in His trials before the Jewish and Gentilish authorities, this prophecy through David had received a partial fulfillment, but its final one is yet future. The time when Psalm 2 is to receive its complete accomplishment is intimated in the middle section—it is just prior to the time when Christ returns to the earth as "King", and receives the heathen for His inheritance and the uttermost parts of

the earth for His possession; in other words, it is just before the dawn of the Millennium, namely, the end of the
Tribulation period.

As we re-read this second Psalm in the light of Rev. 16:
14 and 19:19 we find that it depicts the final act in the
blatant and defiant career of the last great Caesar. It is an
act of insane desperation. The Son of Perdition will gather his forces and make a concerted effort to prevent the
Christ of God entering into His earthly inheritance. This
we believe is evident from the terms of the Psalm itself.

The Psalm opens with an interrogation: *"Why* do the
heathen (the Gentiles) rage (better, "tumultuously assemble"), and the people (Israel) imagine (meditate) a
vain thing?" The fact that this is put in the form of a
question is to arrest more quickly the reader's attention,
and to emphasize the unthinkable impiety of what follows.
"The kings of the earth set themselves, and the rulers take
counsel together, against the Lord, and against His Anointed." Notice that this rebellion is staged not only against
the Lord but also against His "Anointed", that is, His
Christ. The madness of this effort (headed by Antichrist)
is intimated in v. 4: "He that sitteth in the heavens shall
laugh: the Lord shall have them in derision". The futili-
ty of this movement is seen in v. 6: "Yet have I set My
King upon My holy hill of Zion". The "yet" here has
the force of "notwithstanding ": it shows the aim and the
object which the insurrectionists had in view, namely, an
attempt to *prevent* Christ returning to earth to set up His
millennial kingdom. The response of heaven is noted in
v. 5: "Then shall He speak unto them in His wrath, and
vex them in His sore displeasure". This is enlarged upon
in Rev. 19:20, 21. Psalm 2, then, brings us to the *end* of
the Antichrist's history and treats only of the closing

events in his awful career. In the other Psalms where he is in view earlier incidents are noted and his dealings with the Jews are described.

The next Psalm in which the Antichrist appears is the fifth. This Psalm sets forth the petitions which the faithful Remnant of Israel will make to God during the Tribulation period. It would carry us beyond our present bounds to attempt anything like a complete exposition of this Psalm in the light of its prophetic application. We shall do little more than generalize.

The Tribulation period is the time when Satan is given the freest rein, when lawlessness abounds, and when to the unbelieving heart it would seem that God had vacated His throne. But the eye of faith recognizes the fact that Jehovah is still ruling amid the armies of the heavens and among the inhabitants of the earth. Hence the force of the Divine title in v. 2—the remnant address Jehovah as "My *King* and my God". The most awful wickedness and rebellion is going on around them, but they are fully assured that God is quite able to cope with the situation. "The Wicked shall not stand in Thy sight: Thou hatest all workers of iniquity. Thou shalt destroy them that speak leasing: the Lord will abhor the bloody and deceitful man" (vv. 5, 6).

The "Bloody and Deceitful Man" is plainly the Man of Sin. He is denominated "bloody" by virtue of his military ferocity; he is called "deceitful" because of his political duplicity. One after another of his opponents will fall before him: through a sea of blood will he advance to his imperial throne. Utterly unreliable will be his word, worthless his promises. A manifest incarnation of that one who is the father of the Lie will he be. Most completely will he deceive the Jews. At first, posing as their friend;

later, standing forth as their arch-enemy. All doubt as to the identity of this "Bloody and Deceitful Man" is removed by what is said of him in v. 9, "for there is no faithfulness in his mouth".

From Psalm 5 we turn to Psalm 7 where we find the godly Jewish Remnant crying unto the Lord against their persecutors, chief of which is the Antichrist. This is clear from the first two verses, where the change from the plural to the singular number is very significant—"O Lord my God, in Thee do I put my trust: save me from all *them* that persecute me, and deliver me: Lest *he* tear my soul like a lion, rending it in pieces, while there is none to deliver". The Remnant plead their innocency before God and call down upon themselves the Enemy's curse if they have acted unjustly—"O Lord my God, If I have done this; if there be iniquity in my hands; if I have requited him that did evil unto me, or spoiled mine adversary unto emptiness; Let the Enemy pursue my soul, and overtake it" (vv. 4-6, Jewish translation). This at once serves to identify the individual of v. 2 who would tear their souls like a lion" (not "like a *bear*")—showing his kinship with that awful one who "goeth about as a roaring lion, seeking whom he may devour". Observe, too, the word he *"was* at peace," but now "without cause *is* mine enemy". Clearly it is the Antichrist that is here in view, and, as manifested in the second half of Daniel's seventieth week, when he shall have thrown off his mask and stood forth revealed in all his dreadfulness. The twelfth verse goes on to say, "If he turn not, he will whet his sword; he hath bent his bow and made it ready". It is this which causes the Remnant to cry, "O Lord my God, in Thee do I put my trust: save me from all them that persecute me, and deliver me" (v. 1). The fourteenth verse unmistakeably identifies this end-time Enemy of Israel, and again stamps him as a worthy son of the father of the Lie—"Behold, he travaileth with iniquity, and hath conceived mischief, and brought forth falsehood". In the sixteenth verse the Remnant express their assurance of the certain fate of their Foe: "His mischief shall return upon his own head, and his violent dealing shall come down upon his own pate".

The eighth Psalm is closely connected with the seventh. In the last verse of the seventh we hear the Remnant saying, "I will praise the Lord according to His righteousness: and will sing praise to the name of the Lord most high". This anticipates the time when they shall be delivered from their awful Enemy, and when the glorious Millennium shall have dawned—"The Lord *most high*" is His distinctive millennial title. Psalm 8 follows this with a lovely millennial picture, when Jehovah will be worshipped because His name is then "excellent in *all* the earth". Then shall the Remnant say, "Out of the mouth of babes and sucklings hast Thou ordained strength because of Thine enemies, that Thou mightest still *the Enemy and the Avenger*" (v. 2). The "Enemy and the Avenger", more literally "the Foe and the Revenger", are two of the many names of the Antichrist.

Much in the ninth Psalm also anticipates millennial conditions and celebrates the overthrow of the Man of Sin. Sings the Remnant, "For Thou hast maintained my right and my cause; Thou satest in the throne judging right. Thou hast rebuked the heathen, Thou hast destroyed the Wicked" (vv. 4, 5). That the Wicked, or Lawless One, is the Antichrist, is clear from the next verse: "The destructions of the Enemy are come to a perpetual end: and their cities hast Thou destroyed". We hope to show in a later chapter that "their cities" which God will destroy are the cities of Antichrist and the False Prophet, namely, Babylon and Rome. Again; in vv. 15, 16 of this Psalm we read, "The heathen are sunk down in the pit that they made: in the net which they hid is their own foot taken. The Lord is known by the judgment which He executeth: the Wicked is snared in the work of his own hands!" This refers to the destruction of the Antichrist and his forces at Armageddon.

In the tenth Psalm we have the fullest description of the Antichrist found in any of the Psalms. This Psalm is divided into four sections: first, the Cry of the Remnant (v. 1); second, the Character of the Antichrist (vv. 2-11); third, the Cry of the Remnant renewed (vv. 12-15); fourth, the Confidence of the Remnant (vv. 16-18). In its opening verse we discover its dispensational key—the "Times of Trouble" (cf. Jer. 30:7) being the great Tribulation. Observe now what is here said of the Wicked One. In v. 2 we read, "The Wicked in his pride doth persecute (R. V. "hotly pursue") the poor". The "poor" (referred to in this Psalm seven times—vv. 2, 8, 9, 9, 10, 14, and "humble" in v. 17 should be "poor"—emphasizing the *completeness* of their poverty) are the faithful Remnant who have refused to receive the mark of the Beast, and as the result are suffered to neither "buy nor sell" (see Rev. 13:17). In vv. 3, 4 we are told, "For the Wicked (One) boasteth of his heart's desire, and curseth, yea, abhorreth the Lord (see Hebrew). The Wicked, through the pride of his countenance, will not seek after God: all his thoughts are—no God". This tells of his frightful impiety and reveals his satanic origin. In v. 6 his consuming egotism is depicted: "He hath said in his heart, I shall not be moved: for I shall never be in adversity". Then follows a description of his awful wickedness: "His mouth is full of cursing and deceit and fraud: under his tongue is mischief and vanity. He sitteth in the lurking places of the villages: in the secret places doth he murder the innocent: his eyes are privily set against the poor". Notice in this last verse the mention of "the secret places". It was to them our Lord referred in His Olivet Discourse, when He said, "Wherefore if they shall say unto you, Behold, he is in the desert; go not forth: Behold, he is in the *secret chambers;* believe it not". This whole Psalm will well repay the most minute study.

In the opening verse of the fourteenth Psalm we have what we doubt not is another reference to the Antichrist, here called *"The* Fool". He is the arch-fool, who, in his blatant defiance, says in his heart—"no God". The mark of identification is found in the marginal reading of Psalm 10:4: "All his thoughts are—no God". Does not this title point out another contrast between Christ and the Antichrist: One is "the wonderful Counseller", the other is "the Fool"!

In the seventeenth Psalm, which contains the confession of the Remnant (pleading their innocency before God), reference is again made to the Antichrist. "By the word of God's lips" will the believing Jews be "kept from the paths of the Destroyer". This is another of his titles which points a contrast: Christ is the Saviour; Antichrist the Destroyer. That it is the Antichrist who is here in view is clear from what follows in vv. 12 and 13, where we read, "Like as a lion that is greedy of his prey, and as it were a young lion lurking in secret places. Arise, O Lord, disappoint him, cast him down: deliver my soul from the Wicked, by Thy sword". The "Wicked" is here in the singular number. Note again the reference to the "secret places", about which we shall have something to say, in our exposition of Matt. 24, vv. 25 and 26 when we treat of the Antichrist in the Gospels.

We pass over several Psalms which contain incidental allusions to the Wicked One and turn now to the thirty-sixth. The wording of the first verse is somewhat ambiguous, and we believe its force comes out better by rendering it, with the Sept., Syriac and Vulgate, "the transgression of the Wicked saith within his heart, that there is no fear of God before his eyes". He defies Jehovah and fears not Elohim. "For he flattereth himself in his own eyes, until his iniquity be found to be hateful" (v. 2). Haughty conceit fills him, but in the end he shall reap as he has sown. "The words of his mouth are iniquity and deceit; he hath left off to be wise, and to do good" (v. 3). This refers to his treacherous dealings with the Jews, and takes note of the two great stages in his career; first, when he poses as Israel's friend, later when he comes out in his true character as their enemy. Verse 4 describes his moral character: "he deviseth mischief upon his bed; he setteth himself in a way that is not good; he abhorreth not evil".

The thirty-seventh Psalm, which in its ultimate application has to do with the godly Remnant in the Tribulation period, contains a number of references to the Antichrist. In the seventh verse the Remnant is exhorted to "rest in the Lord and wait patiently for Him" (i. e. for His personal appearing) and to "fret not because of him who prospereth in his way, because of the Man who bringeth wicked devices to pass"—a manifest allusion to the Man of Sin. In the tenth verse they are assured, "for yet a little while, and the Wicked shall not be: yea, thou shalt diligently consider his place, and it shall not be". In vv. 12 and 13 we read, "the Wicked plotteth against the just, and gnasheth upon him with his teeth. The Lord shall laugh at Him: for He seeth that his day is coming". This brings out the satanic malice of Antichrist against the people of God, and also marks the Lord's contempt for him as He beholds the swiftly-approaching doom of this one who has so daringly defied Him. The end of the Wicked is noticed in v. 35. "I have seen the Wicked in great power, and spreading himself like a green bay tree. Yet he passed away, and, lo, he was not: yea, I sought him, but he could not be found". The whole of this wondrous Psalm calls for close study. It throws a flood of light on the experiences of the Remnant amid the awful trials of the end of the age.

"I said, I will take heed to my ways, that I sin not with my tongue: I will keep my mouth with a bridle, while the Wicked is before me" (Psa. 39:1). This sets forth the resolutions of the Remnant in view of the troublesome presence of the Wicked One; while in v. 8 they are seen praying that they may not be made the reproach of the Foolish One—"Deliver me from all my transgressions: make me not the reproach of the Foolish".

The forty-third Psalm opens with the plaintive supplications of the Remnant in view of the contempt and opposition of the Jewish nation as a whole, at the head of which will be the false Messiah: "Judge me, O God, and plead my cause against an ungodly nation: O deliver me from the deceitful and unjust Man. For Thou art the God of my strength: why dost Thou cast me off? Why go I mourning because of the oppression of the Enemy?" The allusion to the deceit and injustice of the Man of Sin views, of course, his breaking of the covenant.

In the forty-fourth Psalm we are given to hear more of the bitter lamentations of the Remnant, betrayed as they have been by the one who posed as their benefactor, and scorned as they are by their fellow-Jews: "Thou makest us a byword among the heathen, a shaking of the head among the people (Israel). My confusion is continually before me, and the shame of my face covered me, For the voice of him that reproacheth and blasphemeth; by reason of the Enemy and Avenger".

The fiftieth Psalm is one of deep interest in this connection. It announces the response of Jehovah to the cries of His faithful people. It declares that "God shall come, and shall not keep silence: a fire shall devour before Him, and it shall be tempestuous round about Him" (v. 3). It promises that He will gather His saints together unto Him (v. 5). It contains an expostulation with Israel as a whole (see vv. 7-14). And then, after bidding His people call upon Him "in the Day of Trouble" and assuring them He will deliver them, God addresses their Enemy as follows: —"But unto the Wicked God saith, What hast thou to do to declare My statutes, or that thou shouldest take My covenant in thy mouth? Seeing thou hatest instruction, and casteth My words behind thee. When thou sawest.a thief, then thou consentedst with him, and hast been partaker with adulterers. Thou givest thy mouth to evil, and thy tongue frameth deceit. Thou sittest and speakest against thy brother; thou slanderest thine own mother's son" (vv. 16-22). First, God rebukes the Antichrist for his hypocrisy, referring to the time when, at the beginning of his career, he had (like Satan in tempting the Saviour) come declaring God's statutes and taking the Divine Covenant in his mouth (v. 16). Second, He charges him with his treachery when, at the midst of the seventieth week, he had cast God's words behind him (v. 17). Third, He exposes his depravity and shows that he is altogether destitute of any moral sensibility (vv. 18-20).

Fourth, He reminds him of how he had congratulated himself that he should continue on his vile course with impugnity and escape the due reward of his wickedness (v. 21). Finally, He announces the certainty of retribution and the fearful doom which awaits him (v. 22).

The fifty-second continues and amplifies what has just been before us from the closing verses of the fiftieth Psalm. Here again the Antichrist is indicted by God—no doubt through the Remnant. "Why boastest thou thyself in mischief, O mighty man? The goodness of God endureth continually. Thy tongue deviseth mischiefs; like a sharp razor, working deceitfully. Thou lovest evil more than good; and lying rather than to speak righteousness. Selah. Thou lovest all devouring words, O thou deceitful tongue. God shall likewise destroy thee forever, and pluck thee out of thy dwelling place, and root thee out of the land of the living. Selah. The righteous also shall see, and fear, and shall laugh at him: Lo, this is the Man that made not God his strength; but trusted in the abundance of his riches, and strengthened himself in his wickedness" (vv. 1-7). The pride, the enmity, the treachery, the moral corruption, and the vaunting of the incarnate Son of Perdition are all noticed and charged against him. The certainty of his doom, and his degradation before those he had persecuted, is graphically depicted.

The prophetic application of the fifty-fifth Psalm first found its tragic realization in the treachery of Judas against the Lord Jesus, but its final accomplishment yet awaits a coming day. In it we may see a pathetic description of the heart-pangs of the Remnant, mourning over the duplicity of the mock Messiah. Driven out of Jerusalem, they bewail the awful wickedness now holding high carnival in the holy city: "Wickedness is in the midst thereof: deceit and guile depart not from her streets. For it was not an enemy that reproached me; then I could have borne it: neither was it he that hated me that did magnify himself against me; then I would have hid myself from him: But it was thou, a man mine equal (i. e. a Jew), my guide, and mine acquaintance" (vv. 11-13). Thus will the Jews in a coming day be called upon to endure the bitter experience of betrayal and desertion by one whom they regarded as their friend. Concerning their Enemy the Remnant exclaim, "He hath put forth his hand against such as be at peace with him: he hath broken his covenant. The words of his mouth were smoother than butter, but war was in his heart: his words were softer than oil, yet were they drawn swords" (vv. 20, 21). The reference is to the seven-year Treaty which the final Cæsar makes with Palestine, and which after three and one half years is treated as 'a scrap of paper'. But such treachery will not go unpunished. In the end Antichrist and his abettors will be summarily dealt with by the Judge of all the earth: "But Thou, O God, shalt bring them down into the pit of destruction: bloody and deceitful men shall not live out half their days" (v. 23).

Psalm seventy-one contains another of the Remnant's prayers during the End-time. "Deliver me, O my God, out of the hand of the Wicked, out of the hand of the unrighteous and cruel Man" (v. 4). The reference is, again, to the Man of Sin who has acted unjustly, and whose fiendish delight it will be to persecute the people of God.

In Psalm seventy-two we find expressed the confidence of the Remnant. They are there seen anticipating that joyful time when God's King shall reign in righteousness. With glad assurance they exclaim: "He shall judge Thy people with righteousness, and Thy poor with judgments.

The mountains shall bring peace to the people, and the little hills Thy righteousness. He shall judge the poor of the people, He shall save the children of the needy, and shall break in pieces the Oppressor" (vv. 2-4). Mighty as their Enemy appeared in the eyes of men, and invincible as he was in his own estimation, when God's appointed time comes he shall be broken in pieces as easily as the chaff is removed by the on-blowing wind.

The seventy-fourth Psalm makes reference to the violence of the Antichrist against the believing Remnant: "They said in their hearts, Let us destroy them together: they have burned up all the synagogues of God in the land. We see not our signs: there is no more any profit: neither is there any among us that knoweth how long. O God, how long shall the Adversary reproach? Shall the Enemy blaspheme Thy name forever?" (vv. 8-10). This contemplates the time when the Man of Sin and his lieutenants will make a desperate effort to cut off Israel from the earth and abolish everything which bears the name of God. Note it does not say "all the synagogues" will be burned up, but the "synagogues *of God*", that is, where the true and living God is owned and worshipped.

The eighty-third Psalm carries us to a point a little nearer the end. Not only will the synagogues of God be all destroyed, but an attempt will be made to exterminate those who still worship God in secret. Listen to the tragic pleadings of this Satan-hunted company, "Keep not Thou silence, O God: hold not Thy peace, and be not still, O God. For, lo, Thine enemies make a tumult: and they that hate Thee have lifted up the head. They have taken crafty counsel against Thy people, and consulted against Thy *hidden ones*. They have said, Come, and let us cut them off from being a nation; that the name of Israel may be no more in remembrance" (vv. 1-4). As to who is responsible for this the verses following show. In v. 5 we read, "For they have consulted together with one consent; they are confederate against Thee". The word "confederate" means "leagued together". Then will be realized man's dream of a League of Nations. It is remarkable that just *ten* nations are here named—see vv. 6-8. "Assur" in v. 8 is "the Assyrian"—the Antichrist in his king-of-Babylon character. This verse is one of the few passages in the Psalms which shows the Antichrist in connection with the Gentiles. Psalm 110:6 also contains a reference to him as related to the Gentiles—"He hath stricken the Head over many countries" (R. V.).

The one hundred and fortieth appears to be the last of the Psalms that takes note of the Antichrist. There we hear once more the piteous cries of the Remnant to God: "Deliver me, O Lord, from the Evil Man: preserve me from the Violent Man: Keep me, O Lord, from the hands of the Wicked; preserve me from the Violent Man; who hath purposed to overthrow my goings . . . . Grant not, O Lord, the desires of the Wicked: further not his wicked device" (vv. 1, 4, 8).

Thus we have glanced at no less than *twenty* Psalms in which allusion is made to the Antichrist. This by no means exhausts the list; but sufficient has been noted to show what a prominent place is there given to this dreadful monster. Let it not be supposed that we are denying the *present* value and application of the Psalms to ourselves. Nothing is more foreign to our desire. We not only firmly believe that *all* Scripture is given by inspiration of God and is "profitable for doctrine," but we readily and gladly unite with the saints of all ages in turning to this precious portion of God's Word to provide us with language suited to express to God the varying emotions of our hearts. But while allowing fully the experimental and doctrinal value of the Psalmter for us today, it needs to be pointed out that many of the Psalms have a prophetic significance, and will be used by another company of believers after the Church which is the body of Christ has been removed from these scenes of sin and suffering. We would urge those of our readers who are interested in dispensational truth to re-study these lyrics of David with a view of discovering how much they reveal of things to come.

8

ANTICHRIST IN THE PROPHETS

THE references to the Antichrist in the Prophets are numerous; nor is this to be wondered at. It is there, more than anywhere else in Scripture, that we learn of the future of both Israel and the Gentiles. It is there we have the fullest information concerning End-time conditions, and the completest description of the varied parts which the leading characters shall play in those days. It would carry us beyond the scope designed for these articles were we to examine *every* passage in the Prophets which makes mention of the Man of Sin and the numerous roles he will fill. Yet we do not desire to pass by any of the more important allusions to him. We shall, therefore, make a selection, and yet such a selection that we trust a complete outline at least will be supplied. Certain scriptures, notably those which view the Antichrist in connection with Babylon, will be waived now, because they will receive separate consideration in a later chapter.

One other introductory remark needs to be made. We are conscious that this chapter will probably be somewhat unsatisfactory to a few of our readers, inasmuch as we shall be obliged to take a good deal for granted. It is manifest that we cannot here attempt to give a complete analysis of the passages where the different allusions to the Antichrist occur, nor should this be necessary. We are writing to Bible students, therefore we shall ask *them* to turn to the different places from which we quote and examine the contexts so as to satisfy themselves that they treat of End-time conditions. While in most instances the context will show that we are not reading into the Scriptures what is not

there, yet in a few cases they may fail us. This is some-
times true with passages which contain prophecies concerning Christ. It is often the case in the prophets that
the Holy Spirit is treating of something near at hand and
then, without any warning, projects the view into the distant future. But just as the New Testament enables us to
determine *which* Old Testament passages speak of Christ,
so other scriptures help us to identify the person of the
Antichrist in verses where there is but an indefinite and
passing allusion to him.

1. ANTICHRIST IN ISAIAH

A brief notice is taken of the Man of Sin in chapter 16.
The opening verses make it clear that conditions in the
Tribulation period are being described. They intimate
how that the persecuted Jews flee to the land of Moab for
refuge—"Hide the outcasts; bewray not him that wander-
eth", makes this clear. These "outcasts" are definitely
identified in v. 4, where Jehovah terms them *"Mine* outcasts". The same verse goes on to tell *why* they were "outcasts", outcasts from Palestine: "Let Mine outcasts dwell
with thee, Moab; be thou a covert to them from the face
of the Spoiler: for the Extortioner is at an end, the Spoiler
ceaseth, the oppressors are consumed out of the land".
Here the destruction of the Antichrist is noted. A further
proof that these verses describe what immediately precedes
the Millennium is found in the next verse, which conducts
us to the beginning of the Millennium itself: "And in
mercy shall the throne be established: and He shall sit
upon it in truth in the tabernacle of David, judging, and
seeking judgment, and hasting righteousness". Thus, in
the light of other scriptures, there is little room for doubt

that *the* Spoiler and *the* Extortioner refer to none other than the Son of Perdition.

In 22:25 we have another incidental reference to the Antichrist. For our comments on this verse we refer the reader to chapter 4, section 17.

"In that day the Lord with His sore and great and strong sword shall punish Leviathan the piercing Serpent, even Leviathan that crooked Serpent; and He shall slay the Dragon that is in the sea" (Isa. 27:1). This chapter is by no means easy to analyze: its structure seems complex. That its contents point to a yet future date is intimated by its opening words—compare other verses in Isaiah where "in that day" occur. As one reads the chapter through it will be found that there is a peculiar alternation between references to the Tribulation period and conditions in the Millennium. The closing verse clearly refers to the end of the Tribulation period. So, also, does the first verse with which we are now chiefly concerned.

Leviathan, the piercing Serpent, is, we believe, one of the names of the Antichrist, compare chapter 3, section II, 2. A comparison with a passage in Job confirms this conclusion. It is generally agreed that "leviathan" in Job 41 refers to the crocodile, yet the commentators do not appear to have seen in it anything more than a description of that creature. But surely a whole chapter of Scripture would scarcely be devoted to describing a reptile! Personally, we are satisfied that under the figure of that treacherous and cruel monster we have a remarkable silhouette of the Prince of darkness. Note the following striking points:

In verses 1 and 2 (of Job 41) the strength of Leviathan is referred to. In v. 3 the question is asked "will he speak *soft words* unto thee?": this is meaningless if only a crocodile is in view; but it is very pertinent if we have here a symbolic description of Antichrist. In v. 4 the question is put, "Will he *make a covenant* with thee?": this, too, is pointless if nothing but a reptile is the subject of the passage; but if it looks to some Monster more dreadful, it serves to identify. "None is so fierce that dare stir him up" (v. 10) : how closely this corresponds with Rev. 13:4 —"Who is able to make war with the Beast?" "His teeth are terrible round about" (v. 14) : how aptly this pictures the fierceness and cruelty of the Antichrist! "His heart is as firm as a stone; yea, as hard as a piece of the nether millstone" (v. 24) : how accurately this portrays the moral depravity of the Antichrist! "When he raiseth up himself the mighty are afraid . . . . the sword of him that layeth at him cannot hold . . . . the arrow cannot make him flee" (vv. 25, 26, 28) : how these words suggest the invincibility of Antichrist so far as human power is concerned. "Upon earth there is not his like, who is made without fear. He beholdeth all high things: he is a king over all the children of pride" (vv. 33, 34). Surely these last verses remove all doubt as to *who* is really before us here! The whole of Job 41 should be studied carefully, for we are assured that it contains a remarkable but veiled amplification of Isa. 27:1.

In Isa. 33 there is another reference to the Antichrist. This chapter, like so many in Isaiah, passes from a notice of Tribulation conditions to the Millennial state and back again. The opening verse reads, "Woe to thee that spoileth, and thou wast not spoiled; and dealest treacherously, and they dealt not treacherously with thee! When thou shalt cease to spoil, thou shalt be spoiled; and when thou shalt make an end to deal treacherously, they shall deal treacherously with thee". This is evidently a judgment

pronounced upon the head of the false messiah. Two
things serve to identify him: he is the great Spoiler, and
the one who shall deal treacherously with Israel. It is in
view of the perfidy and rapacity of their Enemy that the
godly remnant cry, "O Lord, be gracious unto us; we have
waited for Thee: be Thou their arm every morning, our
salvation also in *the time of trouble*" (v. 2). A further
word concerning the Antichrist is found in v. 8: "The
highways lie waste, the wayfaring man ceaseth: he hath
broken the covenant, he hath despised the cities, he regard-
eth no man". The last three statements in this verse make
it certain who is there in view. It is the Antichrist displayed in his true colors; the one who breaks his covenant
with Israel, sacks their cities, and defies all human government to resist him.

A brief notice must be taken of 57: 9 ere we turn from
Isaiah. In this chapter we find God arraigning Israel for
their horrid idolatries and wickedness. The opening verse
again makes it clear that it is the Tribulation period which
is in view: "The righteous perisheth, and no man layeth it
to heart", etc. Following this we have the various indict-
ments which God makes against the unfaithful Jews—
"But draw near hither, ye sons of the sorceress, the seed of
the adulterer and the whore" (v. 3, etc.). The remainder
of the chapter continues in the same strain. Among the
many charges which God brings against Israel is this:
"And thou wentest to the King with ointment, and didst
increase thy perfumes, and didst send thy messengers far
off, and didst debase thyself even unto hell" (v. 9). It is
evident that as this chapter is describing the sins of Israel
committed in the End-time that "the King" here must be
the false messiah. Incidentally this verse furnishes one of

the many proofs that the Antichrist will be king over the Jews.

2. ANTICHRIST IN JEREMIAH

In the 4th chapter of this prophet there is a vivid description of the fearful afflictions which shall come upon the inhabitants of Palestine. Doubtless, what is there said received a tragic fulfillment in the past. But like most, if not all prophecy, this one will receive a later and final accomplishment. There are several statements found in it which indicate that it treats of the End-time. The plainest of these is found in the closing verse, where we read, "For I have heard a voice as of a woman in travail, and the anguish as of her which bringeth forth her first child, the voice of the daughter of Zion". It is the "birth-pangs" of Matt. 24:8 (see Greek) which is in view. The sore trials which Israel shall then undergo are tragically depicted: "Blow ye the trumpet in the land: cry, gather together, and say, Assemble yourselves, and let us go into the defenced cities. Set up the standard toward Zion: retire, stay not: for I will bring evil from the north, and a great destruction. The Lion is come up from his thicket, and the Destroyer of the Gentiles is on his way; he is gone forth from his place to make thy land desolate; and thy cities shall be laid waste, without an inhabitant" (vv. 5-7). The Destroyer of the Gentiles now turns to vent his fiendish malignity upon the holy land. Destruction is in his heart. Terrible shall be his onslaught: "Behold, he shall come up as clouds, and his chariots shall be as a whirlwind: his horses are swifter than eagles. Woe unto us! for we are spoiled" (v. 13). Fearful will be the devastations his fury shall accomplish: The whole city shall flee for the noise of the horsemen and bowmen: They shall go into thickets, and climb up upon the rocks: every city shall be forsaken, and not a man dwell therein" (v. 29).

In 6:26, 27 there is a remarkable statement made concerning the Antichrist: "O daughter of My people, gird thee with sackcloth, and wallow thyself in ashes: make thee mourning, as for an only son, most bitter lamentation: for the Spoiler (*Destroyer,* as in 4:7) shall suddenly come upon us". This Spoiler is "the Destroyer of the Gentiles". But it is what follows in the next verse which is so striking: *"I have set thee* for a tower and a fortress among My people, that thou mayest know and try their way"*. Here we learn that, after all, the Antichrist is but a tool in the hands of Jehovah. It is *He* who sets him in the midst of Israel to "try" them. A parallel statement is found in Isa. 10:5, 6, where the Lord says of the Assyrian *"I will send him* against a hypocritical nation". It reminds us very much of what we read concerning Pharaoh in Rom. 9:17. He was "raised up" by God to accomplish *His* purpose. Even so shall it be with this one whom Pharaoh foreshadowed. He shall be an instrument in God's hand to chastise recreant Israel.

Chap. 15 contains brief allusions to the Antichrist. In v. 8 we have a statement similar to what was before us in the last passage. Speaking to Israel God says, "I have brought upon them against the mother of the young men a Spoiler at noonday: I have caused him to fall upon it suddenly, and terrors upon the city". It is the Lord, then, (behind Satan) who brings this Spoiler against them. After His purpose has been accomplished, after the Antichrist has done what (unknown to himself) God has appointed, we read how that the Lord assures His people, "I will deliver thee out of the hand of the Wicked, and I will redeem thee out of the hand of the Terrible" (v. 21). Thus will God demonstrate His supremacy over the Son of Perdition.

25:38 takes us back a little and notices the awful desolation which the Antichrist brings upon the land of Israel: "He hath forsaken his covert, as the lion: for their land is desolate because of the fierceness of the Oppressor, and because of his fierce anger".

3. ANTICHRIST IN EZEKIEL

We shall notice here but two passages in this prophet. First, in 21:25-27—"And thou, profane wicked Prince of Israel, whose day is come, when iniquity shall have an end, Thus saith the Lord God; Remove the diadem, and take off the crown: this shall not be the same: exalt him that is low, and abase him that is high. I will overturn, overturn, overturn it; and it shall be no more, until He come whose right it is; and I will give it Him".

So far as we are aware, all pre-millennial students regard this passage as a description of the Antichrist. It pictures him as Satan's parody of the Son of Man seated upon "the throne of His glory". It sets him forth as the priest-king. Just as in the Millennium the Lord Jesus will "be a *Priest upon His throne*" (Zech. 6:13), so will the Antichrist *combine* in his person the headships of both the civil and religious realms. He will be what the popes have long aspired to be—head of the World-State, and head of the World-Church.

"And thou, O deadly wounded Wicked One, the Prince of Israel, whose day is come, in the time of the iniquity of the end; thus saith the Lord: remove the mitre, and take off the crown" (R. V.). This is clearly Israel's last king, ere the King of kings and Lord of lords returns to the earth. He is here termed "the Prince of Israel" as the true Christ is denominated "Messiah the Prince" in Dan.

9:25. The description "O *deadly wounded* Wicked One" looks forward to Rev. 13:12, where we read, "The first Beast whose *deadly wound* was healed"! "Remove the *mitre* and take off the *crown*" point to his assumption of both priestly and kingly honors. The Heb. word for "mitre" here is in every other passage used of the head-dress of Israel's high priest! Finally, the statement that his "day is come . . . . in the time of the iniquity of the end" establishes, beyond a doubt, the identity of this person.

In the opening verses of Ezek. 28 we have a striking view of the Man of Sin under the title of "the Prince of Tyre", just as what is said of "the King of Tyre" in the second half of the chapter is an esoteric allusion to Satan. First, we are told his "heart is lifted up" (v. 2), which is precisely what is said to his father, the Devil, in v. 17. Second, he makes the boast "I am God" and "I sit in the seat of God" (v. 2), which is parallel with 2 Thess. 2:4. Third, it is here said of him, "Behold, thou art wiser than Daniel; there is no secret that they can hide from thee" (v. 3), which intimates he will be endowed with superhuman wisdom by that one of whom this same chapter declares, "Thou sealest up the sum, full of wisdom" (v. 12). Fourth, it is said of him, "By thy wisdom and by thine understanding thou hast gotten thee riches, and hast gotten gold and silver into thy treasures" (v. 4). Thus will he be able to dazzle the worshippers of Mammon by his Croesus-like wealth, and out-do Solomon in the glory of his kingdom. Finally, his death by the sword is here noted, see vv. 7, 8.

4. ANTICHRIST IN DANIEL

It is here that we find the fullest description of the Man of Sin. First, he is looked at under the figure of "the little horn". As there has been some dispute whether this expression really applies to him, we propose to examine the more carefully what is here said of "the little horn". Personally, we have long been convinced that this expression refers to none other than the Antichrist. There are a number of plain marks which make it comparatively easy to recognize his person, whenever Scripture brings him before us. For example: his insolent and blasphemous pride; his exalting himself against and above God; his impious and cruel warfare against the people of God; his sudden, terrible, and supernatural end. Let us compare these features with what is said of "the little horn" in Dan. 7 and 8.

We turn first to Dan. 7. In vv. 7 and 8 we read, "After this I saw in the night visions, and behold a fourth beast, dreadful and terrible, and strong exceedingly; and it had great iron teeth: it devoured and brake in pieces, and stamped the residue with the feet of it: and it was diverse from all the beasts which were before it; and it had ten horns. I considered the horns, and, behold, there came up among them another *little horn,* before whom there were three of the first horns plucked up by the roots: and, behold, in this horn were eyes like the eyes of man, and a mouth speaking great things". This refers to the *rise* of "the little horn" within the bounds of the Roman Empire, for that is what is represented by the "fourth beast". The first thing said of the little horn is that he has "eyes like the eyes of man", which speak of intelligence, and "a mouth speaking great things"—the Heb. word signifies "very great", and the reference is, no doubt, to his lofty pretensions and his daring blasphemies.

In 7:21 it is further said of him that he "made war with the saints, and prevailed against them". This contemplates his persecution of the godly Jews, and agrees perfectly with Rev. 13:7: "And it was given unto him to make war with the saints, and to overcome them". In v. 25 we are told, "He shall speak great words against the Most High". Surely this serves to *identify* this "little horn" as the first beast of Rev. 13: "And there was given unto him a mouth speaking great things and blasphemies" (v. 5). If further proof be needed, it is supplied by the remainder of verse 25: "And shall wear out the saints of the Most High . . . . and they shall be given into his hand until a time and times and the dividing of time". A "time" equals a year (see Dan. 4:23 and Rev. 12:14, and cf. 12:6), so that a "time and times and the dividing of time" would be three and one-half years during which the saints are given into his hand. This corresponds exactly with Rev. 13:5, where of the first Beast, the Antichrist, it is said, "And power was given unto him to continue forty and two months"—in a later chapter we shall give a number of proofs to show that the first Beast of Rev. 13 *is* the Antichrist.

In Dan. 8 the Little Horn is before us again, and that it is *the same* dread personage as in chapter 7 appears from what is predicted of him. First, he is referred to as "a king of fierce countenance" (8:23), which agrees with "whose *look* was *more stout* than his fellows" (7:20). Second, it is said of him that he "waxed exceeding great (first) towards the south, and (second) towards the east, and (third) toward the pleasant land" (8:9), which agrees with "there came up among them another little horn, before whom there were *three* of the first horns plucked up" (7:8). Third, it is said that he "shall destroy the mighty and the holy people" (8:24), which agrees with "and the same horn made war with the saints and prevailed against them" (7:21). There should, then, be no doubt whatever that the "little horn" of Dan. 7 and the "little horn" of Dan. 8 refer to one and the same person. Their moral features co-incide: both, from an insignificant beginning, become great in the end: both persecute the people of God: both are stricken down by direct interposition of God. We may add that Messrs. B. W. Newton, James Inglis, G. H. Pember, Sir Robert Anderson, Drs. Tregelles, J. H. Brookes, Haldeman, and a host of other devout scholars and students, take the same view, namely, that the "little horn" of Dan. 7 and 8 and the Man of Sin is one and the same person.

Let us now consider briefly what is revealed concerning the Antichrist under this title of his, the "little horn". We confine ourself to Dan. 8:23-25.

First, he is "a king of fierce countenance". This we believe is a literal description of his facial expression, though we are satisfied that it also has a moral significance. In Deut. 28:50 we read of "a nation of fierce countenance, which shall not regard the person of the old nor show favor to the young". In the light of this scripture it seems clear that when the Antichrist is denominated the "King of fierce countenance" the reference is not only to his actual features, but that it also intimates he will be empowered to face the most perplexing and frightful dangers and the most appalling scenes of horror without flinching or blanching. It is significant that the reference in Deut. 28:50 is to the *Romans,* while what is said of the Antichrist in Dan. 8:23 relates, specially, to his connections with *Greece.* The two dominant characteristics of these Powers will be combined in the Man of Sin. There will be concentrated in him the irresistible will of the Romans and the brilliant intellect of the Greeks.

Second, we are told that he shall be able to "understand

dark sentences". The Heb. noun for "dark sentences" is used of Samson's *riddle* (Judges 14:12), of the Queen of Sheba's "hard questions" (1 Kings 10:1), and of the *dark sayings* of the wise (Prov. 1:6), which are too profound to be understood by the simple. This characteristic of the King of fierce countenance, that he shall be able to "understand dark sentences", suggests an attempted rivalry of Christ as the Revealer of secret things. This is one of the fascinations by which the Antichrist will dazzle humanity. He will present himself as one in whom are hidden treasures of wisdom and knowledge. He will bewitch the world by his solutions of the enigmas of life, and most probably by his revelation of occult powers implanted in men hitherto unsuspected by most, and of forces and secrets of nature previously undiscovered.

Third, it is said "And his power shall be mighty, but not by his own power" (8:24). This is explained in Rev. 13:2, where we are told, "And the Dragon *gave him his* power, and his throne, and great authority". Just as we read of the Lord Jesus, "The Father that dwelleth in Me, He doeth the works" (John 14:10), so shall the Son of Perdition perform his prodigies by power from his father, the Devil. This is exactly what 2 Thess. 2:9 declares, "Whose coming is after the working of Satan with all power and signs and lying wonders". Thus will men be deceived by the miracles he performs.

Fourth, he will "destroy wonderfully, and shall prosper, and practise, and shall destroy the mighty and the holy people" (8:24). This has received enlargement in the previous chapter, where we have given several illustrations from the Psalms of the Antichrist persecuting Israel.

Fifth, "And through his policy also he shall cause craft to prosper in his hand" (8:25). The Heb. word for "pol-

icy" denotes wisdom and understanding. It was the word
used by David to Solomon, when he said, "Only the Lord
give thee *wisdom*" (1 Chron. 22:12), as it is also employed
by Huram when writing to Solomon: "Blessed be the Lord
God of Israel, that made heaven and earth, who hath giv-
en to David the king a wise son, endued with *prudence*"
(2 Chron. 2:12). The Heb. word for "craft"—"He shall
cause craft to prosper"—is the one employed by Isaac
when speaking to Esau concerning Jacob: "Thy brother
came with *subtilty*" (Gen. 27:35). It has in view the chicanery and treacherous methods the Antichrist will employ. "By peace shall destroy many" (v. 25) refers to
the fact that he will pose as the Prince of peace, and after
gaining men's confidence—particularly that of the Jews—
will take advantage of this to spring his bloody schemes
upon them.

Sixth, it is said "He shall also stand up against the
Prince of princes" (8:25). This unmistakably identifies
him with the Beast of Rev. 19:19, where we are told,
"And I saw the Beast, and the kings of the earth, and their
armies, gathered together to make war *against Him* that
sat on the horse, and against His army".

Seventh, "But he shall be broken without hand" (8:
25). This expression means that he shall come to his doom
without *human* intervention or instrumentality—see Dan.
2:45; 2 Cor. 5:1, etc. That the King of fierce countenance
shall be *"broken* without hand" refers to his destruction
by the Lord Himself—"And He shall smite the earth with
the rod of His mouth, and with the breath of His lips shall
He slay the Wicked" (Is. 11:4).

We turn now to Dan. 9:26, 27. This forms a part of
the celebrated prophecy of the seventy "weeks" or hebdomads. We cannot now attempt an exposition of the whole

prophecy: sufficient to point out its principal divisions and examine that part of it which bears on our present theme.

The prophecy begins with v. 24 and concerns the seventy hebdomads, a word signifying "sevens". Each "hebdomad" equals seven years, so that a period of 490 years in all is here comprehended. These seventy "sevens" are divided into three portions: First, seven "sevens" which concerned the re-building of Jerusalem, following the Babylonian captivity. Second, sixty-two "sevens" unto "Messiah the Prince", that is, unto the time when He formally presented Himself to Israel as their King: this receiving its fulfillment in the so-called "Triumphal Entrance into Jerusalem". Third, the last "seven" which is severed from the others. It should be carefully noted that we are expressly told that *"after* threescore and two weeks (which added to the preceding seven would make sixty-nine in all up to this point) shall Messiah be *cut off"*. The reference is to the Cross, when Christ was "cut off" from Israel and from the land of the living. This occurred *after* the sixty-ninth week and before the seventieth began.

The sixty-ninth terminated with the formal presentation of Christ to Israel as their "Prince". This is described by Matthew (the distinctively *Jewish* Gospel) in chapter 21. The rejection of their Prince caused the break between Christ and Israel. It is very striking to note that (following the Rejection) Matthew records three distinct proofs or evidences of this break. The first is found in Matt. 21:19 in the cursing of the "fig tree", which signified the rejection of *the Nation*. The second was His sorrowful announcement from the brow of Olivet that the time of Israel's visitation was past and her overthrow now certain (Matt. 23:37 and cf. Luke 19:41-44). This was the abandonment of *the City*. The third was His solemn pronouncement concerning the Temple: "Behold your House is left unto you desolate. For I say unto you, Ye shall not see Me henceforth, till ye shall say, Blessed is He that cometh in the name of the Lord" (Matt. 23:38, 39). This was the giving up of *the Sanctuary*.

The entire Christian dispensation (which began with the crucifixion of Christ) is passed by unnoticed in this prophecy of the seventy "weeks". It comes in, parenthetically, between the sixty-ninth and the seventieth. What follows in Dan. 9:26, 27 concerns what will happen *after* the Christian dispensation is ended, when God again takes up Israel and accomplishes His purpose concerning them. This purpose will be accomplished by means of sore judgment, which will be God's answer to Israel's rejection of His Son. But let us examine more closely the form this judgment will take.

The judgment of God upon the people who were primarily responsible for the "cutting off" of their Messiah was to issue in the *destruction* of their "city and sanctuary" (9:26). This destruction was to be brought about by the people of a Prince who should subsequently appear, and be himself destroyed. The "Prince" here is the Antichrist, but the Antichrist connected with and at the head of the Roman Empire in its final form.* Now we know that it was the Romans who destroyed Jerusalem and the temple in A. D. 70, but that "the Prince" here does not refer to the one who then headed the Roman armies is clear from the fact that Dan. 9:27 informs us this Prince is to play his part in the yet future seventieth week—further proof is furnished in that v. 26 carries us to "the end" (i. e. of Israel's "desolations") which is to be marked by a "flood," and Isa. 28:14, 15 intimates that this is to be after Israel's

---

* It is the Man of Sin who is to be the last great Cæsar: this will be made clear in our study of the Antichrist in the Revelation.

covenant with Antichrist: "Wherefore hear the word of the Lord, ye scornful men, that rule this people which was in Jerusalem. Because ye have said, We have made a covenant with Death, and with Hell are we at agreement; when the overflowing scourge shall pass through·it, it shall not come unto us: for we have made lies our refuge, and under falsehood have we hid ourselves". To this God replies, "Your covenant with Death shall be disannulled, and your agreement with Hell shall not stand; when the overflowing scourge shall pass through, then ye shall be trodden down by it" (v. 18). The "overflowing scourge" is, literally, "the scourge coming in like *a flood*".

A few words remain to be said on 9:27: "And he shall confirm the covenant with many for one week: and in the midst of the week he shall cause the sacrifice and the oblation to cease, and for the overspreading of abominations he shall make it desolate, even until the consummation, and that determined shall be poured upon the desolate". The subject of this verse is the Antichrist, "the Prince that shall come" of the previous verse. By the time he appears on the scene large numbers of Jews will have been carried back to their land (cf. Isa. 18). With them the Prince makes a covenant, as of old Jehovah made one with Abraham, and as Christ will yet do with Israel, see Jer. 31. This will be regarded by God with indignation, as "a covenant with Death, and an agreement with Sheol". But while this covenant is accepted by the majority of the Jews, God will again reserve to Himself a remnant who will refuse to bow the knee to Baal: hence the qualification, "He shall confirm the covenant with *many*", not all.

"In the midst of the week he shall cause the sacrifice and the oblation to cease". The returned Jews will rebuild their temple and there offer sacrifices. But these, so far from being acceptable to God, will be an offense. There seems a clear reference to this in the opening verses of Isa. 66, which describe conditions just before the Lord's appearing (see v. 15). And here the Lord says, "He that killeth an ox is as if he slew a man; he that sacrificeth a lamb, as if he cut off a dog's neck", etc. (v. 3). But three and a half years before the end, the Prince will issue a decree demanding that the sacrifices must cease, and the worship of Jehovah be transferred to himself, for it is at this point he shall "exalt himself above all that is called God, or that is worshipped" (2 Thess. 2:4). The fact that we are here told that *he* causes the sacrifices and the oblation to cease, at once identifies this Prince of the Romans as the Antichrist—cf. 8:11. The remaining portion of 9: 27 will be considered when we come to Matt. 24:15.

We turn now to Dan. 11, which is undoubtedly the most difficult chapter in the book. It contains a prophecy which is remarkable for its fulness of details. Much of it has already received a most striking fulfillment, but like other prophecies, we are fully satisfied that this one yet awaits its final accomplishment. That Dan. 11 treats of the Antichrist all pre-millennial students are agreed, but as to how much of it refers to him there is considerable difference of opinion. A small minority, from whom we must dissent, confine the first thirty-five verses to the past. Others make the division in the middle of the chapter and regard all from v. 21 onwards as a description of the Man of Sin, and with them the writer is in hearty accord. A few consider the entire chapter, after v. 2, as containing a prediction of the Antichrist under the title of "The King of the North", and while we are not prepared to unreservedly endorse this, yet it is fully allowed that there is not a little to be said in its favor.

We shall here confine ourself to the second half of Dan. 11. Our present limits of space, however, will permit of nothing more than brief notes upon it. Commencing at v. 31 we read, "And in his estate shall stand up a vile person, to whom they shall not give the honor of the kingdom: but he shall come in peaceably, and obtain the kingdom by flatteries". The history of this "vile person" is here divided into three parts: first, the means by which he obtains the kingdom: vv. 21, 22; second, the interval which elapses between the time when he makes a covenant with Israel, the taking away of the daily sacrifice and the setting up of the abomination of desolation: vv. 23—31; third, the brief season when he comes out in his true colors and enters upon his career of open defiance of God, reaching on to his destruction: vv. 32-45. Thus from v. 21 to the end of the chapter we have a continuous history of the Antichrist.

"In his estate shall stand up a vile person . . . . he shall come in peaceably, and obtain the kingdom by flatteries". This epithet "the vile person" is a manifest antithesis from "the *Holy* One of God". This twenty-first verse takes notice of the Man of Sin posing as the Prince of peace. He shall achieve what his antitype, Absalom, tried but failed to do—"Obtain the kingdom by flatteries".

"And with the arms of a flood shall they be overflown from before him, and shall be broken; yea, also the Prince of the Covenant" (v. 22). This "Vile Person" is denominated "the Prince of the Covenant", which, at once, identifies him with the "Prince" of 9:26, 27. Then we are told in v. 23 "And after the league made with him he shall work deceitfully: for he shall come up, and shall become strong with a *small* people". This "league" or "covenant" is doubtless the seven-years-treaty confirmed with Israel, which is made at an early point in the Antichrist's career, and which corresponds with the fact that at the first he appears as a *"little horn"*, the "small people" being the Syrians—cf. our remarks on Dan. 8:8, 9 in chapter six.

Vv. 25 and 26 describe his victory over the king of Egypt. Then, in v. 28 we read, "Then shall he return into his land with great riches". *His* land is Assyria. The mention of "great riches" corresponds with what we are told of the Antichrist in Psa. 52:7; Ezek. 28:4, etc.

"And arms shall stand on his part, and they shall pollute the sanctuary of strength and shall take away the daily sacrifice, and they shall place the abomination that maketh desolate". This is clear evidence that these verses are treating of that which takes place during the seventieth week. The mention of polluting the Sanctuary is an unmistakable reference to "the abomination of desolation", i. e. the setting up of an idol to the Antichrist in the Temple. Note the repeated use of the plural pronoun in this verse; the "they" refer to the Antichrist *and* the False Prophet, cf. Rev. 13. It is significant that in the next verse (v. 32) there is an allusion made to the faithful remnant—"The people that do know their God".

"And the king shall do according to his will; and he shall exalt himself, and magnify himself above every god, and shall speak marvelous things against the God of gods, and shall prosper till the indignation be accomplished: for that that is determined shall be done" (v. 36). That "the King" here is the "Vile Person" is not only indicated by the absence of any break in the prophecy, as also by the connecting "and" with which the verse opens, but is definitely established by the fact that in v. 27 (note context) the Vile Person is expressly termed a "king"! The contents of this thirty-sixth verse clearly connects "the king" with the Man of Sin of 2 Thess. 2:3, 4, and also as definitely identifies him with the "little horn"—cf. 7:23 and 8: 25. The remaining verses of Dan. 11 have been before us in previous chapters and need not detain us now.

5. ANTICHRIST IN THE MINOR PROPHETS

Here a wide field for study is opened, but we must content ourself with but a few selections and brief comments on them. *Hosea* makes several references to the Man of Sin. In 8:10 he is termed "the King of princes", as such he is Satan's imitation of the King of kings. In 10:15 he is named "the King of Israel", which shows his connection with the Jews. In 12:7 he is called a "Merchant" or Trafficker, and of him it is said, "The balances of deceit are in his hands: he loveth to oppress", with this should be compared Rev. 6:5. These words denote his twofold character in connection with the Jews: first he makes them believe he is the true Christ; second, he ultimately stands forth as their great Enemy.

Joel alludes to him as the head of the "northern army", i. e. the Assyrian. And here God declares that He will "drive him into a land barren and desolate, with his face toward the east sea; and his stink shall come up, and his ill savor shall come up, because he has magnified to do great things" (2:20).

Amos speaks of him as "an Adversary" which shall be "even round about the land; and he shall bring down thy strength from thee, and thy palaces shall be spoiled" (3: 11). That this is referring to the End-time is clear from the verses that follow, where we read, "That in the day that I shall visit the transgressions of Israel upon him", etc. (v. 14).

Micah terms him "the Assyrian", and of him it is said,

when he "shall come into our land, and when he shall tread in our palaces, then shall we raise against him seven shepherds, and eight principal men . . . . thus shall he deliver us from the Assyrian" (5:5, 6).

Nahum has this to say of him: "There is one come out of thee, that imagineth evil against the Lord, a wicked counseller. Thus saith the Lord; Though they be quiet, and likewise many, yet thus shall they be cut down, when *he* shall pass through. Though I have afflicted thee, I will afflict thee no more . . . . for the Wicked shall no more pass through thee" (1:11, 12, 15). These verses contain another of the many antitheses between Christ and the Antichrist. The One is the "Wonderful Counseller" (Isa. 9:6); the other, the "Wicked Counseller".

Habakkuk describes him as one whose "soul is lifted up" and "is not upright in him", and as one who "transgresseth by wine", as "a proud man, neither keepeth at home, who enlargeth his desire as hell, and is as death, and cannot be satisfied, but gathereth unto him all nations, and heapeth unto him all people" (2:4, 5).

Zechariah denominates him "the Idol Shepherd that leaveth the flock", and then pronounces judgment upon him—"The sword shall be upon his arm, and upon his right eye" (11:17).

9

ANTICHRIST IN THE GOSPELS AND EPISTLES

THE Old and New Testaments have many things in common—far more than some teachers of "dispensational" truth seem to be aware of—but there are also some noticeable contrasts between them. Speaking generally, the one is principally prophetic; the other mainly didactic. There is far more said in the former about the future of Israel than there is in the latter. Much more space in the Old Testament than in the New is devoted to describing the conditions which shall obtain in the Tribulation period. And far more was revealed through the prophets about the Antichrist than was made known through the apostles. It is in full keeping with this that we find there is one book in the New Testament which is a noticeable exception, and that is the one which is peculiarly prophetic in its character and contents, namely, the Revelation. There, perhaps, more is told us concerning the person and career of the Man of Sin than in all the rest of the New Testament put together.

The passages which refer directly to the Antichrist in the four Gospels are few in number; but in addition to these there are several indirect references to him, and these call for a more careful examination because of their apparent obscurity. The writer believes there may be other passages in the Gospels treating of the Man of Sin in his varied relations, and which contain an *esoteric* view of him, but which the Holy Spirit has not yet been pleased to reveal unto students of prophecy. Let not the reader then regard this chapter as in any-wise a complete or exhaustive treatment of the subject, rather let its brief hints bestir him to make prayerful and patient examination for himself.

The Antichrist receives an even more scant notice in the Epistles than he does in the four Gospels. So far as we have been able to discover he is alluded to only in 2 Thess. 2 and in John's Epistles. The reason for this is not difficult to discover. The Epistles concern those who are members of the Body of Christ, and by the time the Antichrist appears upon the stage of human history, they shall be far above these scenes—with their blessed Lord in the Father's House. Nevertheless "all Scripture" is profitable for our instruction and necessary for our enlightenment. God has been pleased to reveal much concerning those things which must shortly come to pass, and it may be that they who now ignore or neglect the study of the prophetical portions of Scripture will be overtaken by surprise when, in a coming day, they shall behold with wonder the fulfillment of prophecy; and possibly *this* surprise (due to culpable ignorance) is included in what the apostle refers to when he speaks of not being *"ashamed* before Him at His coming" (1 John 2:28). Certainly it is our duty as well as privilege to examine diligently *all* that God has been pleased to make known in His Word.

1. Passing by the typical teaching of Matt. 2, which will come before us in a later chapter, we turn first to Matt. 12 which is one of the most important chapters in that book, supplying as it does one of the principal keys to its dispensational interpretation. In it is recorded the first great break between the Jews and Christ, which eventually terminated in their crucifying Him. In v. 14 we read, "Then the Pharisees went out, and held a council against Him, how they might destroy Him". This is the first

time we read of anything like this in Matthew's Gospel. Following this we read, "Then was brought unto Him one possessed with a demon, blind, and dumb; and He healed him, insomuch that the blind and dumb both spake and saw" (v. 22). Up to that time this was by far the most remarkable miracle our Lord had performed. Its effect upon those who witnessed it was general and deep—"And all the people were amazed, and said, Is not this the Son of David?" (v. 23). It *must be* the long-promised Messiah who now stood in their midst. But the Pharisees were blinded by their hatred of Him, and committed the sin for which there is no forgiveness: "This fellow doth not cast out demons, but by Beelzebub the prince of the demons" (v. 24). Then, following His reply to their awful blasphemy and terming them "a generation of vipers" (v. 34), our Lord uttered a prophetic parable which bears directly on our present theme:

"When the unclean spirit is gone out of a man, he walketh through dry places, seeking rest, and findeth none. Then he saith, I will return into my house from whence I came out; and when he is come, he findeth it empty, swept, and garnished. Then goeth he, and taketh with himself seven other spirits more wicked than himself, and they enter in and dwell there: and the last state of that man is worse than the first. Even so shall it be also unto this wicked generation" (vv. 43-45). The first thing to note concerning this mysterious and remarkable passage is its setting. This, as we have sought to indicate above, has to do with Christ's solemn pronouncement on those who had determined to destroy Him, and who were guilty of the unpardonable sin. In it He declares the judgment which God shall yet send upon apostate Israel.

Our next concern is to ascertain the meaning of this

parabolic utterance. The central figure is "The unclean spirit". This "unclean spirit" is viewed here in three connections: first, as indwelling a man; second, as going out of the man; third, as returning to the man and indwelling him again. In v. 44 the "man" is termed by the unclean spirit "my house". This "man" unquestionably represents Israel, for at the close of the parable Christ says, "Even so shall it be also unto this wicked generation". Who, then, is referred to by "the unclean spirit"? We believe that it is the Son of Perdition. The following reasons lead us to this conclusion: First, mark attentively the use of the definite article: it is not simply *an* unclean spirit, but *"the* unclean spirit". Second, note his threefold relation to Israel. At the time the Saviour uttered these words the Son of Perdition was then present in Israel's midst. But a little later he was no longer so. When he hanged himself he passed out of these scenes into the next world: as Acts 1:25 compared with Rev. 11:7 tells us, into the Pit. His present state in the Abyss is graphically and solemnly depicted—"He walketh through dry places, seeking rest, and findeth none" (v. 43). Then, he says, "I will *return* into *my house* from whence I came out". This, we are satisfied, refers to the re-incarnation of the Son of Perdition, when he appears on earth for the last time as the Man of Sin. Then, in a special sense, will Israel be *his* "house". A third reason why we believe "The Unclean Spirit" is the Son of Perdition is furnished by Zech. 13:2—"And it shall come to pass in that day, saith the Lord of hosts, that I will cut off the names of the idols out of the land, and they shall no more be remembered: and also I will cause the prophets and *the unclean spirit* to pass out of the land". Clearly this verse speaks of the End-time. What follows is very striking. Vv. 3 and 4 concern the prophets who shall prophesy falsely. But in v. 5 there is a noticeable change from the plural to the singular number: "But *he* shall say, I am no prophet", etc. The only antecedent to this pronoun is "The Unclean Spirit" of v. 2, which here in v. 5 is shown to be no mere abstraction but a definite person. And then in v. 6 the question is asked, "What are these wounds in thine hands?" We believe this intimates that God will even permit the Man of Sin to imitate the Saviour to the extent that he will appear with *wounds in his hands:* thus will he be the better able to pose as the true Christ.

When the Son of Perdition returns to Israel, he finds his house "empty, swept, and garnished". This depicts the moral and spiritual state of the Jews at the time the Antichrist is manifested. Though clean from the horrible idolatries which defiled them of old, and though adorned with all that temporal prosperity will bring them, Israel, nevertheless, will be devoid of the Shekinah-glory, and have no Holy Spirit indwelling them. Next, we are told, "Then goeth he, and taketh with himself seven other spirits more wicked than himself, and they enter in and dwell there". We believe that this has a double meaning. One plus seven equals eight; and in Scripture eight signifies *a new beginning.* This is in keeping with the *re*-incarnation of the Son of Perdition. But we think there is also a reference here to Satan's blasphemous imitation of what we are told in Rev. 5:6, where we read of the Lamb having seven eyes, which are *the seven spirits of God".* Just as the Christ of God will come back to earth endued with the Spirit of God in the sevenfold plentitude of His power, so will the Antichrist present himself to Israel in the seven-fold fulness of satanic power and uncleanness. Then, indeed, shall Israel's last state be worse than their first—i. e when they rejected Christ in the days of *Judas*.

2. We turn now to Matt. 24, which contains a lengthy forecast concerning the end of this Age. Here we find our Lord describing the conditions which shall obtain during the Tribulation period. Christ announces with considerable detail those things which are to precede His own return to the earth. The whole chapter sets forth the Master's answers to three questions asked by His disciples, namely, as to when the Temple was to be destroyed, what was to be the sign of His coming, and of the end of the Age (see v. 3). A similar, but by no means identical prophecy, is to be found in Luke 21. The main difference between them being that Luke 21 treats of conditions which obtained *prior* to the destruction of Jerusalem in A. D. 70—it is not until v. 25 that the Tribulation period is reached; whereas *the whole* of Matt. 24 is yet *future*.

It is striking to note that our Lord begins His prophecy by saying, "Take heed that no man deceive you, for many shall come in My name, saying I am Christ; and shall deceive many" (vv. 4, 5). The significance of this appears by comparing v. 11, "And many false prophets shall arise, and shall deceive many". These false christs and false prophets are to head up in *the* Antichrist and *the* False Prophet, who will be the arch-deceivers. When we reach v. 15 a clear allusion is made to the Man of Sin: "When ye therefore shall see the abomination of desolation, spoken of by Daniel the prophet, stand in the holy place, whoso readeth, let him understand". This reference of Christ to "the abomination of desolation" which is to "stand in the holy place", looks back to Dan. 12:11: "And from the time that the daily sacrifice shall be taken away, and the abomination that maketh desolate set up, there shall be a thousand two hundred and ninety days". This, in turn, carries us back to Dan. 9:27: "And in the midst of the week he shall cause the sacrifice and the oblation to cease, and for the overspreading of abominations he shall make it desolate". With these verses should be compared Rev. 13:11-15, where we are told that the False Prophet who shall perform great wonders, will command men that "they should make an image to the beast". The False Prophet will have "power to give life unto the image of the beast, that the image of the beast should both speak, and cause that as many as would not worship the beast should be killed". By linking these scriptures together the following facts are brought out:

First, an "image" is going to be made to the Antichrist (Rev. 13:15). Second, this "image" will "stand in the holy place" (Matt. 24:15), that is, in the re-built Temple at Jerusalem. Third, this "image" will possess supernatural power, for it shall be able to "speak" (Rev. 13:15). Fourth, this "image" unto the beast shall be an object of worship, and those who refuse to worship it shall be killed (Rev. 13:14, 15). Fifth, this "image" is termed by Christ "the abomination of desolation". The term "abomination" is an Old Testament expression connected with idolatry, and signifies some special idol or false god (see Deut. 7:26; 1 Kings 11:5-7). Sixth, this "abomination" or idol-god will be set up during the middle of Daniel's seventieth week, or three and one half years from the end of Antichrist's career. This is clear from Dan. 12:11 and 9:27. The taking away of "the daily sacrifice" occurs when the Antichrist throws off his mask and stands forth as the Defier of heaven. In the re-built Temple of the Jews sacrifices shall once more be offered by them to God. These their King suffers, while he is posing as the Christ. But when he drops his religious pretensions and defies heaven as well as earth, the "sacrifices" will be taken away, and in their place worship to an image of himself will be substituted. Seventh, the setting up of this "image" to the Antichrist will, most probably, be attended with supernatural phenomenon. We gather this from Dan. 9:27, where we read, "And he shall cause the sacrifice and the oblation to cease, and for the overspreading of abominations he shall make it desolate". Now the word here translated "overspreading" is never so rendered elsewhere. Seventy times is this word translated "wing" or "wings". It is the word used of the wings of the cherubim in Ex. 25:20 and Ezek. 10:5, etc. And in Psa. 18:10 we read of Jehovah that "He rode upon a cherub, and did fly: yea, He did fly upon the wings of the wind".

One profound Hebrew scholar has rendered the last clause of Dan. 9:27 as follows, "And upon the wing of abominations he shall come desolating". Remembering that "abomination" has reference to an idol or false god, the force would then be "upon the wing of a false god shall he come desolating". Now in view of Psa. 18:10 it is highly probable that Dan. 9:27 refers to *a satanic imitation* of the Chariot of the Cherubim. This is strengthened by 1 Cor. 10:20—"The things which the Gentiles sacrifice, they sacrifice to *demons,* and not to God"—which shows the demoniacal nature of the "idols" or "abominations" worshipped. If this view be correct, then the Antichrist will be supernaturally borne aloft (by invisible demons), and apparently descending from on high (in blasphemous mimicry of Mal. 3:1) will finally persuade the world to worship him as God. The apostate Jews will, no doubt, believe that their eyes at last behold the long-awaited sign from heaven, and the return of the Glory to the Temple.

For it is thither the false christ will be borne, and there his image set up. We believe that the words of 2 Thess. 2:4, "He as God sitteth in the temple of God, *showing himself that HE IS GOD"* may, most likely, have reference to this same event.

Coming back now to the words of Christ, Matt. 24:15 will, we trust, be much more intelligible. What our Lord there said was designed specially for the godly Jewish remnant who will be in Palestine during the Tribulation period. When the "abomination of desolation" is set up in the holy place, whoso *readeth* should "understand". How wondrously this agrees with other scriptures, and what a value it places upon the written Word! No supernatural revelation will be granted—these all *ceased* when the Canon of Scripture closed. Then, as now, "understanding" is made dependent upon the *reading* of what God *has* revealed.

What, then, is it that those godly Jews should "understand"? Why, that a crisis has been reached. That the Antichrist now stands fully revealed for the impious impostor that he is. And now that his character is clearly manifested, let them beware. Let them turn to Rev. 13: 14, 15, and they will discover that *death* awaits them should they tarry any longer in Jerusalem. Therefore, says Christ, "Let them which be in Judea flee into the mountains: let him that is on the housetop not come down to take anything out of his house . . . . for then shall be great tribulation, such as was not since the beginning of the world to this time, no, nor ever shall be" (Matt. 24:16-21). How marvellously one scripture throws light on another! How clearly does Rev. 13:14, 15 explain the need for this hurried flight of the faithful remnant!

There is one other reference to the Antichrist in this

24th chapter of Matthew, namely, in vv. 23-26: "Then if any man shall say unto you, Lo, here is Christ, or there; believe it not. For there shall arise false christs, and false prophets, and shall show great signs and wonders; insomuch that, if it were possible, they shall deceive the very elect. Behold, I have told you before. Wherefore if they shall say unto you, Behold, *he* is in the desert; go not forth: behold, *he* is in the secret chamber; believe it not". The reference to the "great signs and wonders" is explained, at least in part, in Rev. 13. We have already seen that the False Prophet will have power to give "life" or "breath" unto the image of the Beast, so that the image shall speak (v. 15). In addition, it is recorded how that "He doeth great wonders, so that he maketh fire come down from heaven on the earth in the sight of men, and deceiveth them that dwell on the earth by those miracles which he had power to do in the sight of the beast" (vv. 13, 14).

We had hoped to be able to say something further on the "secret chambers" of Matt. 24:26, but in the absence of any clear light from other scriptures, we refrain from speculations of our own. It seems plain, however, that the reference is to the *occult* powers and activities of the Wicked One, who ever loveth darkness rather than light.

3. Our next passage will be the first eight verses of Luke 18, where in a parable the Lord gives us another view of the Antichrist: "And He spake a parable unto them, that men ought always to pray, and not to faint; Saying, There was in a city a judge, which feared not God, neither regarded man: And there was a widow in that city; and she came unto him, saying, Avenge me of mine adversary. And he would not for awhile: but afterward he said within himself, Though I fear not God, nor regard man: yet

because this woman troubleth me, I will avenge her, lest by her continual coming she weary me. And the Lord said, Hear what the unjust judge saith. And shall not God avenge His own elect, which cry day and night unto Him, though He bear long with them? I tell you that He will avenge them speedily. Nevertheless when the Son of Man cometh, shall He find faith on the earth?"

Like many of Christ's parables, this one is plainly prophetic in its character. It looks forward to a coming day: it treats of conditions which are to obtain during the Tribulation period. This is easily seen from the context. Luke 18 opens with the word "and", and the last eighteen verses of the previous chapter, with which the 18th is thus connected, treat of those things which are to immediately precede the establishing of the Messiah's Kingdom—note particularly v. 26. So, too, the closing words of the parable now before us read, "When the Son of Man *cometh,* shall He find faith on the earth?"

Having thus pointed out the time when this prophetic parable is to receive its fulfillment, our next concern is to ascertain the significance of its terms. The parable revolves around a "widow" and an "unjust judge". Once we discover *who* are represented by these, everything will be simple. Our task ought not to be difficult seeing that we have already learned the time when these characters are to appear.

The "widow" in Scripture is ever the figure of desolation, loneliness, weakness. Dispensationally, *Israel* is the widow, spiritually dead as she now is to her Divine Husband. Here in the parable of Luke 18 it is the new Israel, the "Israel of God", the faithful remnant, which is in view. To quote one scripture is sufficient to establish this: "Fear not; for thou shalt not be ashamed: neither be thou confounded; for thou shalt not be put to shame: for thou shalt forget the shame of thy youth, and shalt not remember the reproach of *thy widowhood* any more. For thy Maker is thine Husband; the Lord of Hosts is His name; and thy Redeemer the Holy One of Israel; the God of the whole earth shall He be called. For the Lord hath called thee as *a widow* forsaken and grieved in spirit, and a wife of youth, when thou wast refused, saith thy God. For a small moment have I forsaken thee; but with great mercy will I gather thee" (Isa. 54:4-7). These are the words which Christ will speak to the remnant right at the beginning of the Millennium, after they have made Isa. 53 their own repentant confession.

In the chapter on the Antichrist in the Psalms attention was repeatedly directed to passages which treat of the condition of the godly Jewish remnant during the Tribulation period. We saw that their lot is to be a bitter one. Severe will be their testings; terrible their sufferings. Not the least painful of their experiences will be the fierce opposition of their unbelieving brethren. Just as the worst enemies of the Saviour were found among His brethren according to the flesh, and just as the most relentless persecutors of the saints during this dispensation have been those who professed to be the followers of Christ, so the most merciless foes of the Jewish remnant will be the unbelieving portion of their own nation. These, too, are noticed in our parable: *they* are the "adversary" against which the "widow" appeals to the "Judge"—"Avenge me of mine adversary" is her plea.

In the light of what has been said above it is easy to discover who is represented by the one to whom the "widow" appeals—appeals no doubt some little time before the end of the Tribulation period is reached. Clearly it is the Antichrist himself, and what is here said of him establishes this beyond a reasonable doubt. First, he is termed "a Judge", so that he is viewed as being in the position of *authority:* we may add, it is the same word as rendered "Judge" in James 5:9 which speaks of the Lord Jesus. Second, he is represented as being located in a certain "city": whether this is Jerusalem or Babylon, we cannot say; but we rather think it is the latter. In the third place, it is said of this Judge that he "feared not God, neither regarded man". We need not tarry to point out how fully this accords with what is elsewhere said of the Man of Sin. Godlessness and lawlessness are the two most prominent elements in his character. In the fourth place, the Lord specifically terms him "the *unjust* Judge" (v. 6). The word signifies "unrighteousness". This word points an antithesis between him and the true Christ who shall reign in righteousness. In the fifth place, his *callousness* is noted in the words "and he would not for awhile" (v. 4). The Greek verb of v. 3 signifies that the widow came to this "Judge" again and again. But in his hard-heartedness he repeatedly turned a deaf ear to her entreaties. Such will be the brutal indifference of the Antichrist to the sufferings of the faithful Jews. In the sixth place, his *untruthfulness* and *treachery* are clearly implied. In v. 5 this unjust Judge is represented as saying, "Because this widow troubleth me, I will avenge her", etc.; but that he fails to keep his word is clear from what we read in the seventh verse—"Shall not *God avenge* His own elect?" etc. The Antichrist does not avenge him, but God will. Finally, his *doom* is hinted at in the words last quoted. When God "avenges" the elect remnant the Antichrist will be destroyed together with those of his followers who had persecuted them.

There is only one difficulty in the way of the above interpretation and that is the appeal of the Jewish remnant *to the Antichrist.* Can it be possible that they should seek help from him! But is there any real difficulty in this? Let us consult our own experience for answer. How often, in the hour of trial, do *we* turn to the arm of flesh for relief! Even the Apostle Paul appealed to Cæsar! But lest this be thought an invention of ours to meet a pertinent objection against the interpretation advanced above, note carefully the wording of the seventh verse: "And shall not God avenge His own elect, which cry day and night unto Him, *though He bear long with them?*" Do not the words "bear long with them" intimate that though they had cried unto God day and night, yet they had *also* sought help from some one else. Even clearer is the testimony of Isa. 10:20—"And it shall come to pass in that day that the remnant of Israel and such as are escaped of the house of Jacob, shall *no more* again *stay upon him that smote them;* but shall stay upon the Lord"!

4. "I am come in My Father's name, and ye receive Me not: if another shall come in his own name, him ye will receive" (John 5:43). This scripture has already been before us (see chapter three I:5) so it need not detain us long. It speaks of the Antichrist in connection with unbelieving Israel. It draws a double contrast between the Son of God and the Son of Perdition. The Christ of God, in lowly condescension, came not in His own name, but in that of His Father—in perfect subjection; but the christ of Satan, in lofty arrogance, shall come in his own name. This will at once appeal to the corrupt hearts of fallen men. The very meekness of the Lord Jesus was an offense to the Jews; but the pride and egotism of the Man of Sin will make him acceptable to them. By the apostate

Nation Christ was not received. As we read in this same Gospel, "He came unto His own, and His own received Him not" (1:11). But the Antichrist shall be welcomed by them—"*him* ye *will* receive", says the Lord. They will receive him as their long-expected Messiah. They will receive him as their King. They will receive him as the promised Deliverer. His yoke will be accepted. Divine honors will be paid him. But bitterly will they rue it; and terrible will be God's judgment upon them.

5. "Ye are of your father the Devil, and the lusts of your father ye will do. He was a murderer from the beginning, and abode not in the truth, because there is no truth in him. When he speaketh the Lie, he speaketh of his own (son): for he is a liar, and the father of it" (John 8:44). The Greek word for "lie" is "pseudos". It occurs in the New Testament just nine times—the number of *judgment*. It always has reference to that which is opposed to the truth. It is a fit appellation for the Antichrist, who is the son of him who is the Arch-liar, the Devil. The Christ of God is "The Truth"; the christ of Satan, "The Lie". That this is one of the many names of the Man of Sin is clear from 2 Thess. 2. There we are told that his coming is "after the working of Satan with all power and signs and lying wonders and with all deceivableness of unrighteousness in them that perish; because they received not the love of the truth, that they might be saved". Then we are told, "And for this cause God shall send them strong delusion that they should believe the Lie (cf. chapter three, II:5).

Upon John 8:44 we cannot do better than quote from Sir Robert Anderson: " 'To speak a lie' is not English. In our language the proper expression is 'to tell a lie'. But no one would so render the Greek words here. It is not the false in the abstract which is in view, but a concrete instance of it. And thus the connection is clear between Satan the liar and Satan the murderer. He is not the instigator of all murders, but of *the* murder, there and then in question, the murder of the Christ; he is not the father of *lies,* but the father of *the* Lie. In 2 Thess. 2:11 it is again *the* Lie of John 8:44. God does not incite men to tell lies or to believe lies. But of those who reject '*the* truth', it is written, 'He shall send them strong delusion that they should believe *the* Lie'. Because they have rejected the Christ of God, a judicial blindness shall fall upon them that they should accept the Christ of humanity, who will be Satan incarnate" (The Silence of God).

6. "While I was with them in the world, I kept them in Thy name: those that Thou gavest Me I have kept, and none of them is lost, but the Son of Perdition; that the Scripture might be fulfilled" (John 17:5). That our Lord was referring to the Antichrist is unequivocally established by 2 Thess. 2:3, where the Man of Sin is denominated "the Son of Perdition". That Judas, here termed the Son of Perdition, was more than a man is clear from John 6:70 where we read, "Have not I chosen you twelve, and one of you is a Devil?" In no other passage is the word "Diabolos" applied to anyone but Satan himself. Just as the Lord Jesus was God incarnate, so will Judas be the Devil incarnate; and, as we have shown in chapter three (third main section) Judas will be re-incarnated in the Antichrist.

Perhaps one other word should be said on John 17:12 before we pass from it. Some have thought that this verse weakens the doctrine of the absolute security of the saints, but in fact it does nothing of the kind. Notice Christ did not say, "Those that Thou gavest Me I have kept, and none of them is lost *except* the Son of Perdition", instead, He said, "None of them is lost *but* the Son of Perdition". The word "but" is used adversatively, not exceptively; that is to say, Judas is here *opposed* to those that were given to Christ (for other scriptures with a similar construction see Matt. 12:4, Acts 27:22, Rev. 21:27). This interpretation is unequivocally established by John 18:9— "Of them which Thou gavest Me have I lost *none*".

7. 2 Thess. 2 contains the chief passage in the Epistles concerning the Antichrist. Here he is denominated "that Man of Sin, the Son of Perdition" (v. 3). It is solemnly true that all men are sinners (Rom. 3:23), but the Antichrist will be more than a sinner, he will be the Man *of Sin*. As such he will be the direct opposite of Christ, who was the *Holy One* of God. Sin in all its terrible satanic treachery, daring blasphemy, and tremendous appeal to the corrupt hearts of men, will be consummated in this frightful monster. For fuller notes on the force of these titles we again refer the reader to chapter three.

Concerning the Man of Sin it is said, "Who opposeth and exalteth himself above all that is called God, or that is worshipped; so that he as God sitteth in the temple of God, showing himself that he is God" (v. 4). Here he reaches the climax of his frightful blasphemy. He will assume Divine honors, and under pain of death (Rev. 13:15) will demand the worship of all. In vindication of his impious claims he will compel men to regard his mandates as transcending all laws and customs, whether of human or Divine origin (Dan. 7:25). For a season the Almighty will suffer his satanic impiety, the Hinderer having been taken out of the way (v. 7). No lightning flash will strike down his blasted form to the dust. The earth will not open her mouth to swallow him up alive. The

Angel of the Lord, who smote Herod with death for a much milder blasphemy, will restrain His hand from the hilt of the sword. For a season Heaven will remain silent while this haughty rebel is doing according to his will. But at the appointed hour "the Lord shall consume (him) with the spirit of His mouth, and shall destroy with the brightness of His coming" (v. 8).

"Even him whose coming is after the working of Satan with all power and signs and lying wonders" (v. 9). The Antichrist will be the culmination and consummation of Satan's craft and genius. He will be endowed with superhuman energy so that he shall perform miracles which will be no mere pretenses, but prodigies of power. By means of these miracles and signs he will deceive the entire world. No doubt he will mock the miracles of Christ, as of old Jannes and Jambres duplicated the miracles of Moses. His marvelous deeds will reach their climax in his own resurrection from the dead.

8. "Who is a liar but he that denieth that Jesus is the Christ? He is antichrist, that denieth the Father and the Son" (1 John 2:22). For our comments on the significance of this name "the Antichrist" we refer our readers to the fourth chapter. There it will be seen that we understand this official title to have a double significance, corresponding to the two main divisions in his career. First, he will pose as the true Christ; later he will stand forth as the avowed opponent of Christ. The above verse presents him as the Arch-apostate. He will, eventually, repudiate the distinguishing truth of *Judaism,* namely, that "Jesus is the Christ"; as he will also set himself against that which is vital in *Christianity*—the revelation of "the Father and the Son".

9. A brief word upon 1 John 4:3 and we must conclude.

"And every spirit that confesseth not that Jesus Christ is come in the flesh is not of God: and this is that spirit of Antichrist, whereof ye have heard that it should come; and even now already is it in the world". It is to the last clause we would here direct attention. The spirit of Antichrist, that which is preparing the way for his appearing, is even now already "in the world". This statement is parallel with 2 Thess. 2:7, "For the mystery of iniquity *doth already work:* only He who now letteth (hindereth) will let, until He be taken out of the way". The Mystery of Iniquity, which concerns the incarnation of Satan, is the direct antithesis of "the Mystery of Godliness" (1 Tim. 3:16) which has to do with the Divine incarnation. Just as there was a long preparation by God preceding the advent of His Son, so the Devil is now paving the way for the advent of the Son of Perdition. The Mystery of Iniquity "doth *already* work"; so in 1 John 4:3 of the spirit of Antichrist we read, "Even now *already* is it in the world"! How far advanced the preparations of Satan now are for the bringing forth of his Masterpiece is becoming increasingly evident to those who are granted wisdom to discern the signs of the times.

10

ANTICHRIST IN THE APOCALYPSE

THE scope of the Apocalypse is indicated by its place in the Sacred Canon. Coming as it does right at the close of the Scriptures, we should naturally expect to find it outlining the last chapters of the world's history. Such is indeed the case. The Revelation is mainly devoted to a description of the judgments which God will yet send upon the earth. It furnishes by far the most complete description of the conditions which are to obtain during the Tribulation period. It treats at greatest length with the character and career of the Antichrist, who will be the "Rod" in the hands of an angry God to chastise recreant Israel and apostate Christendom. All of this is, of course, preparatory to the establishment of Messiah's kingdom, which will exist during the last of earth's dispensations.

It is impossible to understand the Apocalypse without a thorough acquaintance with the books that precede it. The more familiar we are with the first sixty-five books of the Bible, the better prepared are we for the study of its sixty-sixth. There is little that is really new in the Revelation. Its varied contents are largely an amplification of what is to be found in the preceding scriptures. Each of its figures and symbols are explained if not on its own pages, then somewhere within the compass of the written Word. For Scripture is ever self-interpreting. Most of our difficulties with the Revelation grow out of our ignorance and lack of acquaintance with the earlier books. Daniel and Zechariah especially should be examined minutely, for they shed much light upon the visions and prophecies of the Patmos seer.

The Apocalypse not only reveals much concerning the person and work of the Man of Sin, but it describes his doom, as it also announces the complete overthrow of the Trinity of Evil. This, no doubt, accounts for much of the prejudice which obtains against the study and reading of this book. It is indeed remarkable that this is the only book in the Bible connected with which there is a distinct promise given to those who read and hear read its prophecy (1:3). And yet how very rarely *it is* read from the pulpits of those churches which are reputed as orthodox! Surely the great Enemy is responsible for this. It seems that Satan fears and hates above every book in the Bible this one which tells of his being ultimately cast into the Lake of Fire. But "we are not ignorant of his devices" (2 Cor. 2:11). Then let him not keep us from the prayerful and careful perusal of this prophecy which tells of those things "which must shortly come to pass".

1. We turn first to the sixth chapter of the Revelation, where a fourfold view is presented of the Son of Perdition. Just as at the beginning of the New Testament the Holy Spirit has given us a fourfold delineation of Christ in the Gospels, so at the commencement of His description of the judgments of God on the earth He has furnished us with a fourfold picture of Christ's great opponent. We believe that the contents of the first four of the "seals" describe four aspects of the Antichrist's character, and also outline four stages in his career. First, he is seen aping the Christ of God as the Righteous One. The *"white* horse" on which he is seated, speaking of righteousness. Just as we are told in 2 Cor. 11:14 that "Satan himself is transformed into an angel of light", and "therefore it is no great thing

if his ministers also be transformed as the ministers of *righteousness"*, so the Antichrist will pose as the friend of law and order. Second, he is seen mimicking the Christ of God as the mighty Warrior. Just as the Lord Jesus at His return will make a footstool of His enemies and trample in fury all who defy Him (Isa. 63:3), so the Man of Sin shall slay all who dare to oppose him. Third, he is seen imitating Christ as the Bread of Life, for the third seal views him as the Food-controller. Fourth, he is seen with his mask off, depicted as one whose name is Death and Hades, that is, as the Destroyer of men's bodies and souls.

Let us see how the *identity* of this Rider of the various colored horses is established. In 6:2 we are told, "And I saw, and behold a white horse: and he that sat on him had a bow; and a crown was given unto him: and he went forth conquering, and to conquer". Notice first, that he is here viewed as seated upon a "white horse". This is in imitation of the Christ of God, who, at the time of His second advent to the earth, will also appear seated upon "a white horse" (Rev. 19:11). Second, it is said that "a crown was given unto him". This at once serves to connect him with the first Beast—the Antichrist—of Rev. 13, for of him it is written, "And they worshipped the Dragon which *gave power* unto the Beast" (v. 4). Again; in 6:4 we are told, "And there went out another horse that was red: and power was given to him that sat thereon to take peace from the earth, and that they should kill one another: and there was given unto him a great sword." Notice first, the last clause—"There was given unto him a great sword". This stamps him plainly as the pseudo christ, for of the true Christ it is written, "Out of His mouth goeth a sharp sword" (19:15). Second, it is said "power was given to him to take peace *from the earth*."

So, too, of the first Beast of Rev. 13 we read, "And power was given him over *all* kindreds, and tongues, and *all* nations" (v. 7). In the third seal he is viewed as the Food-controller, weighing out the necessities of life at famine prices. This, no doubt, corresponds with what we read of in 13:17. Finally, in the fourth seal he is named "Death and Hell". This double title removes all doubt as to who is in view. When God remonstrates with Israel for having made the seven-years' treaty, He does so in the following language: "And your covenant with Death shall be disannulled, and your agreement with Hell shall not stand" (Isa. 28:18). Thus the Riders of the four horses of Rev. 6 are not four different persons, but one person presented in a fourfold way, as the Lord Jesus is in the four Gospels.

Before we pass from Rev. 6 a few words should be added by way of amplification of our remarks above, namely, that in the first part of Rev. 6 we have outlined *four stages* in the Antichrist's career. The preparation of the Man Christ Jesus for His public ministry—the long years spent quietly at Nazareth—are passed over by the four Evangelists. So here in Rev. 6 the early days of the Man of Sin—in his "little horn" character—are not noticed. Under the first seal he is viewed as seated on a white horse, having a bow. The color of the horse and the fact that no arrow is seen attached to the bow, suggests bloodless victories, for he goes forth "conquering and to conquer". This first seal at once conducts us to the time when the Prince of Darkness poses as the Christ of God and presents himself to the Jews for their acceptance. He does not come out in his true satanic character, rather does he simulate the Prince of Peace. The first seal is parallel with Dan. 11:21, 23, where we learn that he will gain the kingdom by flatteries and political diplomacy. But not for long will he fill this pacific role. War is in his heart (Psa. 55:21), and nothing short of universal dominion will satisfy his proud ambitions. As God has plainly warned, at the very time when men shall be saying, Peace and safety, "then sudden destruction cometh upon them, as travail upon a woman with child; and they shall not escape" (1 Thess. 5:3).

It is to this the second seal brings us. Here the Antichrist is seen no longer upon a white horse, but upon a *red* horse. And in perfect accord with this, it is added, "And power was given to him that sat thereon to take peace from the earth . . . . and there was given to him a great sword" (v. 4). Little wonder that he is called "the Destroyer of the Gentiles" (Jer. 4:7). At the time of his overthrow it will be exclaimed, "Is this the man that made the earth to tremble, that did shake kingdoms; that made the world as a wilderness, and destroyed the cities thereof?" (Isa. 14:17, 18). Jer. 25:29 throws light upon this "great sword" which is given to him—"For, lo, I begin to bring evil on the city which is called by my name, and should ye be utterly unpunished? Ye shall not be unpunished: for I will call for *a sword* upon *all* the inhabitants of the earth, saith the Lord of hosts" (read verses 15 to 33).

In the third seal he is portrayed as the Harbinger of famine conditions. This is intimated by the change of the color of the horse: for "black" in connection with famine see Jer. 14:1, 2 and Lam. 5:10. The symbolic significance of the "black" horse is intensified by the figure of the "pair of balances in his hand" (*compare* Hosea 12:7, Amos 8:4-6). What follows describes the wheat being doled out at famine prices. But it is added, "See thou hurt not the oil and the wine". This intimates that the famine is by no means universal: yea, it suggests that side by side with abject suffering there is abundance and luxury. We therefore regard this third seal as denoting the Antichrist's persecution of the godly Jews which, from other scriptures we learn, will be the fiercest during the last three and one half years of his career. Rev. 13:17 makes it known that they who will not be suffered to buy or sell are the ones who refuse to receive his mark. These, of course, are the faithful remnant of the Jews. But they who *do* render allegiance to the Beast will not want—"oil and wine" shall be their portion.

The fourth seal, plainly conducts us to the end of Antichrist's course. The fact that he is named Death and that we are told Hades (that which receives the soul) followed with him, makes known the awful doom which shall overtake this Son of Perdition and all his blinded followers—see Rev. 19:20, 21.

2. The next allusion to the Antichrist is found in Rev. 9:11 where he is given a threefold appellation, namely, King over the locusts, The Angel of the Abyss, and the Destroyer. A few remarks upon the context are required if we are to expound, even briefly, the significance of these three titles. The majority of pre-millennial commentators are agreed upon the identity of the personage named in Rev. 9:11, though there is considerable difference of opinion among them concerning the meaning of the context. We can here only offer a few remarks on the preceding verses according to our present light and submit the reasons for our conclusions.

The immediate context takes us back to the opening verse of Rev. 9 where a "star" is seen falling from heaven unto the earth, unto whom is given the key of the Bottomless Pit. This we believe refers to Lucifer, or "Day-Star" (see Isa. 14:12 margin). The reference, we think, is not to his original fall, but to what is described in Rev. 12:9. The fact that the key of the Abyss is given to *him* is in keeping with the fact that during the Tribulation period God allows him free rein and suffers him to do his worst. The R. V. correctly renders verses one and two as follows— "And there was given to him the key of *the Pit of* the Abyss. And he opened *the Pit of* the Abyss", etc., or, as it may literally be rendered, *"the well of* the Bottomless Pit."* This expression occurs nowhere else in Scripture. The "well of the Bottomless Pit" is to be distinguished from the Bottomless Pit itself, mentioned in 9: 11; 11:7; 17:8; 20:3. What the distinction is we shall presently suggest.

Out of *the well of* the Bottomless Pit issued a smoke, so great that the sun and the air were darkened (v. 2), and out of the smoke came "locusts upon the earth". We regard these "locusts" as identical with the creatures referred to in the prophecy of Joel (2:1-11). By noticing what is said of them in Joel 2 and Rev. 9 it is at once apparent that they are no ordinary locusts. Joel says of them, "A great people and a strong; there hath not been ever the like, neither shall be any more after it" (2:2). It is said, "When they fall upon the sword they shall not be wounded" (2:8). The fact that they issue from the Pit also denotes that they are supernatural beings. In the description furnished in Rev. 9 they seem to be a kind of *infernal cherubim,* for "the horse" (v. 7), the "man" (v. 7), the "lion" (v. 8), and "the scorpion" (v. 19) are combined in them. Their number is given as two hundred thousand thousand. Who, then, are these infernal beings? No commentator that we are acquainted with has attempted an answer. It is therefore with diffidence that we suggest, without being dogmatic, that they are, most likely, *fallen angels* now imprisoned in Tartarus. We give three reasons which, in our judgment, point to this conclusion.

First, we know from 2 Pet. 2:4 that the angels which sinned were "cast *down* to Tartarus", and in Rev. 9:2, 3 we are told there *"arose* a smoke out of the Pit . . . and there came out of the smoke locusts upon the earth". Now, as pointed out, these infernal "locusts" issue from *"the well of* the Pit", an expression occurring nowhere else in Scripture, and only the "locusts" are said to come from *there.* So also the term "Tartarus" is found nowhere but in 2 Pet. 2:4. It seems likely, then, that *"the well of* the Pit" may be only another name for "Tartarus" (with which *only* fallen angels are connected), just as "the Lake of Fire" is only another name for "Gehenna". Who else could these locusts be *but* the fallen angels? To say we do not know may savor of humility, but shall the writer be deemed presumptuous because he has sought to furnish an answer by comparing scripture with scripture?

In the second place, it is surely significant that the "king" of these "locusts" is termed in Rev. 9:11 "the *angel* of the Bottomless Pit"! A title which is nowhere else given to him. Just as Christ, the "Angel of the Covenant" (Mal. 3:1—cf Isa. 63:9, etc.) is, again and again, termed an "angel" in the Apocalypse (see 8:3, 10:1, 20:1, etc.), so the Antichrist is here denominated "the Angel of the Bottomless Pit". And just as we learn from Matt. 25:31 that "the Son of Man shall come in His glory, and *all* the *holy angels* with Him" (cf Matt. 24:31), so when the Son of Perdition is manifested, *all* the unholy angels will be *with him!*

In the third place, let the language of 2 Pet. 2:4 be carefully examined: "For if God spared not the angels that sinned, but cast them down to Tartarus, and delivered them into chains of darkness, to be reserved unto judgment". It is to the last clause we wish to direct attention. Let it be compared with the 9th verse of the same chapter—"The Lord knoweth how to deliver the godly out of temptations, and to reserve the unjust unto the day of judgment *to be punished*". Wicked human beings are said to be reserved "unto *the Day of* Judgment to be *punished*". But this is not what is said of the angels that sinned, though, of course, eternal punishment awaits them as we learn from Matt. 25:41. 2 Pet. 2:4 simply says they are "reserved unto judgment", and we believe this means that God is holding them in Tartarus until His time comes for Him to use them as one of His instruments of *judgment* upon an ungodly world. The *time* when God will thus use them is stated in Jude 6—it will be in "the judgment of the great day" (compare Rev. 6:17 for "the great day"). Confirmatory of this, observe that in Joel 2:11 the Lord calls the supernatural locusts *"His* army", then employed to inflict sore punishments on apostate Israel.* If our interpretation of 2 Pet. 2:4 be correct, namely, that it makes no reference to the future punishment of the fallen angels, this explains why the Lord in Matt. 25: 41 when referring to future punishment was careful to mention *them* specifically.

Returning now to Rev. 9:11 the Antichrist is here termed the "King over" the locusts. Let the reader pay careful attention to what is predicated of these infernal beings in Joel 2 and here in Rev. 9, and let him remember they number no less than two hundred millions, and then

---

* Psa. 78:49 speaks of God using "evil angels" (those mentioned in Rev. 12:7) in His judgments on Egypt.

see if it does not throw new light on Rev. 13:4, where concerning the Antichrist the question is asked, "Who is able to make *war* with *him?*"! ! How utterly futile to engage in conflict one who commands an "army" of two hundred millions, none of whom are subject to death! In the second place, he is here termed "the Angel of the Bottomless Pit", a title peculiarly appropriate as the leader of the fallen angels; and, as well, a title which denotes the superhuman nature of the Son of Perdition. In the third place, we are here told that his name "in the Hebrew tongue is Abaddon, but in the Greek tongue hath his name Apollyon". This title serves to establish beyond a shadow of doubt the identity of this "King" of the infernal "locusts", this "Angel of the Bottomless Pit". The Hebrew and the Greek names signify the same thing in English—the Destroyer. It is "the Destroyer of the Gentiles" of Jer. 4:7, translated "Spoiler" in Isa. 16:4 and Jer. 6:24. Suitable name is this for the one who is the great opponent of the *Saviour*. "Destroyer" is close akin to "Death" in Rev. 6:8. The reason why his name is given here in both Hebrew and Greek is because he will be connected with and be the destroyer of *both* Jews and Gentiles! But why give the Hebrew name first? Because the order in judgment, as in grace, is "the Jew first"—see Rom. 2:9 and 1:16 for each, respectively.

3. "And when they shall have finished their testimony, the Beast that ascendeth out of the Bottomless Pit shall make war against them, and shall overcome them, and kill them" (Rev. 11:7). This is the first time in the Revelation that the Antichrist is seen in his character of "the Beast". The last scripture which we have examined serves at once to identify him. He is termed "the Angel of the Bottomless Pit", because in a peculiar sense the Abyss is

his home. There he has been during all the centuries of this Christian era. In Acts 1:23 (cf Chapter 3, Section 3) the Pit is called "his *own* place". Here the Beast is shown ascending out of the Bottomless Pit. What, then, is the Abyss? It appears to be the special abode of infernal creatures. As we have seen, out of its "well" issue the fallen angels. From it comes the Beast. And in it Satan himself is incarcerated for the thousand years (Rev. 20:3). The "Abyss" is quite distinct from "Hades" in which the souls of lost *human* beings are now being tormented; as it must also be distinguished from "Gehenna" or "the Lake of Fire" in which *all* the lost shall suffer for ever and ever.

4. We come now to Rev. 13. A lengthy paper might readily be devoted to its exposition, but as we have had occasion to refer to its contents so frequently in earlier chapters, we shall here be as brief as possible. The contents of this chapter center around two "Beasts". As to which of them represent the Antichrist there is a difference of opinion. The majority of those who have written upon the subject regard the first Beast as the Man of Sin, and with them we are in hearty accord. We shall devote our next chapter to a setting forth of some of the many proofs that the first Beast *is* the Antichrist. Here we shall take the point for granted.

"And I stood upon the sand of the sea, and saw a beast rise up out of the sea, having seven heads and ten horns, and upon his horns ten crowns, and upon his heads the name of blasphemy" (v. 1). There is here, as frequently in Scripture, a *double* reference. Two objects quite distinct though intimately connected are in view. We believe that this "Beast" which arises from "the sea" points to the Roman Empire revived and in its final form, that is, resuscitated and confederated under the form of ten kingdoms. In Dan. 7:3 we read, "And four great beasts came up from the sea, diverse one from another". These "four great beasts" are interpreted in the verses which follow as four kingdoms. In v. 7 we are told this fourth Beast (the Roman Empire) "had ten horns". So the Beast of Rev. 13:1 also has "ten horns". Each of the successive Beasts or kingdoms of Dan. 7 retained the territory of the previous one, though enlarging on it. In the symbolic description there furnished the first Beast is likened unto "a lion" (v. 4); the second to "a bear" (v. 5); the third to "a leopard" (v. 6). So also in Rev. 13 the Beast there is "like unto a leopard", has feet like "a bear", and has the mouth of "a lion" (v. 2). Thus we learn that the Roman Empire in its final form will include within its borders the territory controlled by the earlier Empires and will also perpetuate the dominant characteristics of the ancient Babylonians, Medo-Persians, and Grecians.

But it is very clear from what follows in Rev. 13 that there is something more than the Empire here in view. In vv. 3-8 it is a *person* that is before us. We are satisfied that this same person is also described, symbolically, in the opening verses. As is frequently the case in the prophetic scriptures, the king and his kingdom are here inseparably united. Rev. 13:1, 2 portrays both the Empire and its last Emperor. One of the proofs for this is found in Dan. 9:26, 27, where (as we have shown in Chapter 9) the Antichrist is denominated "the prince" of that people who destroyed Jerusalem in A. D. 70. We shall therefore interpret here according to this principle.

"And I saw . . . . a Beast rise up out of the sea". In Scripture, the troubled "sea" is frequently a figure of restless humanity away from God. The Antichrist will come upon the scene at a time of unprecedented social disturbance and governmental upheaval. He will appear at a crisis in the history of the world. From other prophetic scriptures we gather that, following the removal of the Church from this earth and some time before Daniel's seventieth week begins, there will be a complete overthrow of law and order, both civil and political. All Divine restraint being removed, lawlessness will prevail. We have no doubt that Satan will designedly bring this about. It will create a situation beyond the diplomatic skill of earth's statesmen. This will provide the desired opportunity for the coming Superman, who will be a diplomatic genius. Just as many leaders today are satisfied that a League of Nations would be the best device for preserving peace, so in the day to come the Man of Sin will satisfy the world that this is the only solution to the baffling problems then confronting the Powers of earth. Thus will the Antichrist resurrect the old Roman Empire at a time of universal confusion and tumult. He will himself be the acknowledged head or Emperor, the last of the Cæsars. Hence the *double* significance of this figure—"a Beast rising out of *the sea*". Out of a state of anarchy will come forth this mighty Despot, who will speedily arrogate to himself *all* authority, both Divine and human; and in the end it will be seen that he embodies a lawlessness even worse and more fatal than that out of which he sprang. A *Beast* indeed will he soon appear to be. Pregnant with meaning is this title. Having rejected God's "Lamb"; a "Beast" shall be the world's ruler. *This* will be God's reply to the satanic teaching of "Evolution" now so popular almost everywhere. The leaders of modern thought insist on the *beastial* origin of man, and so a Beast shall yet lead the majority of his generation to Perdition!

"Having seven heads and ten horns". It is most significant that identically the same features are attributed to the Dragon in 12:3. He, too, is there said to have "seven heads and ten horns." This clearly implies his satanic origin: he will be a human replica of the Devil himself. As wrote the late G. H. Pember (from whom we have borrowed a number of valuable points), the Beast will be "the effulgence of the Antigod's glory, and the very image of his substance". We take it that the "seven heads" are symbolic of full intelligence, and the "ten horns" speak of imperial dominion.

"And the Beast which I saw was like unto a leopard, and his feet were as the feet of a bear, and his mouth as the mouth of a lion" (v. 2). Like the "Beast rising up out of the sea" of the previous verse, we believe the terms of this second verse have a *double* significance. First, as intimated above, they denote that the Empire will include the territory and preserve the dominant features of the earlier Empires. Second, they supply a figurative description of the Emperor himself. The Antichrist will combine in his personality the characteristics of the leopard (beauty and subtlety), of the bear (strength and cruelty), and of the lion (boldness and ferocity).

"And the Dragon gave him his power, and his seat, and great authority" (v. 2). This is the Devil's travesty of what God the Father will yet do to His Son:—"I saw in the night visions, and, behold, one like the Son of Man came with the clouds of heaven, and came to the Ancient of Days, and they brought Him near before Him. And there was *given Him* dominion, and glory, and a kingdom, that all people, nations, and languages, should serve Him" (Dan. 7:13, 14).

"And I saw one of his heads as it were wounded to

death; and his deadly wound was healed: and all the world wondered after the Beast" (v. 3). It is clear from a number of scriptures that during the early part of the second half of Daniel's seventieth "week" the Antichrist will be slain by the sword—cf Isa. 14:18, 19; 37:7; Ezek. 21:25 R. V.; Zech. 11:17: see our comments on these in the closing portion of Chapter 6. It is equally clear that this "wound of death" will be "healed" (Rev. 13:4) and that the Beast shall again "live" (Rev. 13:14).* Satan will be permitted to bring his son from the dead. This is no wild speculation of ours but a view which has been propounded by quite a number of devout students. In his "Coming Prince", Sir Robert Anderson said, "The language of Rev. 13:3, 12 suggests that there will be some impious travesty of the resurrection of our Lord". It is useless to reason about it: we simply believe the record of Scripture upon it. The raising of the Beast from the dead will remove whatever doubt men may have entertained concerning his supernatural character. *"All the world wondered after him"* is the statement which immediately follows the reference to the healing of his wound of death.

"And they worshipped the Dragon which gave power unto the Beast: and they worshipped the Beast, saying, Who is like unto the Beast? Who is able to make war with him?" (v. 4). This cry of the world, "Who is like unto the Beast?" is a travesty of the song of Moses. When celebrating Jehovah's overthrow of their enemies at the Red Sea, Israel sang, "Who is like unto Thee, O Lord, among the Gods! Who is like Thee, glorious in holiness, fearful in praises, doing wonders!" (Ex. 15:11). The additional exclamation, "Who is able to make war with

---

* "It is remarkable that just three times (the number of *resurrection*) the healing of the Antichrist's "wound of death" is referred to here in Rev. 13—see vv. 3, 12, 14!

him?" is evoked by the vast army of infernal creatures at his command, and by his own triumph over death in battle.

"And there was given unto him a mouth speaking great things and blasphemies" (v. 5). *This* is the one great distinguishing mark of the Antichrist—cf Psa. 52:1-4; Isa. 14:13, 14; Dan. 7:11, 20; 11:36; 2 Thess. 2:4, etc. But not for long will he be suffered to continue his God-defying course. Another "forty two months" and his career shall be ended. This number—here designedly used by the Holy Spirit, rather than three and one half years or twelve hundred and sixty days—is a very significant one. Its factors are 6 and 7, which stand for man and completeness. It is man in his fallen condition, here the Man of Sin, *fully* manifested. Forty-two stands for *intensified apostasy*. Thus Num. 33 gives the various stopping places of unbelieving Israel in the wilderness as forty-two in number. Judges 12:6 tells us that the number of the apostate Ephraimites which fell before the Gileadites were 42-thousand. See also 2 Kings 2:4 and 10:14.

"And it was given unto him to make war with the saints, and to overcome them: and there was given to him authority over every tribe and people and tongue and nation. And all they that dwell on the earth shall worship him, every one whose name hath not been written from the foundation of the world in the book of life of the Lamb that hath been slain" (vv. 7, 8, R. V.). The "saints" here mentioned are the godly Jewish remnant who will refuse to worship the Beast. Those "overcome" are they who disobeyed the command of Christ recorded in Matt. 24:16; those who obey will be preserved by God—see Rev. 12:6. Note how election is seen here: only they whose names were "written from the foundation of the world in the book of life" will be preserved from the unpardonable sin of worshipping the Antichrist—cf Matt. 24:22, 24.

"And I beheld another Beast coming up out of the earth; and he had two horns like a lamb, and he spake as a dragon" (v. 11). This brings before us the second Beast, called in 19:20 the False Prophet. He is the third person in the Trinity of Evil. As there is to be an Antichrist who will both counterfeit and oppose the Christ of God, so there will be an Anti-spirit who will simulate and oppose the Spirit of God. Just as the great work of the Holy Spirit is to glorify Christ, so the one aim of the Anti-spirit will be to magnify the false christ (see 13:12). Just as the coming of the Holy Spirit at Pentecost was visibly attended by "cloven tongues like as of fire" (Acts 2:3), so we read of the Anti-spirit that "he doeth great wonders, so that he maketh *fire* come down from heaven on the earth in the sight of men" (v. 13). And just as it is the Holy Spirit who now *quickens* dead sinners into newness of life, so of the Anti-spirit we are told, "He had power to give *life* unto the image of the Beast" (v. 15).

5. "And the third angel followed them, saying with a loud voice, If any man worship the Beast and his image, and receive his mark in his forehead, or in his hand, the same shall drink of the wine of the wrath of God, which is poured out without mixture into the cup of His indignation, and he shall be tormented with fire and brimstone in the presence of the holy angels, and in the presence of the Lamb" (Rev. 14:9, 10). This looks back to what we read of in the closing verses of the preceding chapter: "And he causeth all, both small and great, rich and poor, free and bond, to receive a mark in their right hand, or in their foreheads: and that no man might buy or sell, save he that

had the mark, or the name of the Beast, or the number of
his name" (13:16, 17). This "mark" will be the *official
sign* of allegiance to the Emperor stamped either upon the
hand or forehead of his loyal subjects. It will be the satanic travesty of the "seal" which the angel will stamp on
"the foreheads of God's servants" (7:3). This "mark"
on the persons of the subjects of the Beast will be, we believe, *the name of the Devil,* (cf Rev. 13:4), as the seal on
the foreheads of God's servants is defined in 14:1 as "having their Father's name written on their foreheads".
Here in Rev. 14:9-11 we have one of the most solemn
warnings in all the Bible. An angel from heaven will
announce the terrible punishment which shall be visited
upon those who honor the Beast. It is set over against the
threats of the Beast and the False Prophet, who will ter-
rify men by the sentence of physical death for all who
defy them. But here God, by His angel, declares that all
who heed the Beast and his coadjutor will share their
awful doom. This no doubt will strengthen the faith and
patience of the saints, and enable them to "endure unto
the end".

6. "And another angel came out from the altar, which
had power over fire; and cried with a loud cry, to him that
had the sharp sickle, saying, Thrust in thy sharp sickle,
and gather the clusters of the Vine of the earth; for her
grapes are fully ripe. And the angel thrust in his sickle
into the earth, and gathered the Vine of the earth, and
cast it into the great winepress of the wrath of God" (14:
19, 20). The "Vine of the earth" refers, we believe, to
the Man of Sin at the head of apostate Israel. This appellation points one more contrast. In John 15 we find the
Lord Jesus saying, "I am the true Vine, ye are the
branches". The true Vine, then, consists of the Christ of

God and His people in fellowship with Him. Over against this is "the Vine of the earth", which is the Antichrist and those allied to him, particularly, renegade Israel. In Deut. 32 there is a reference to the "Vine of the earth"—"For their rock is not as our Rock, even our enemies themselves being judges. For their Vine is of the vine of Sodom, and of the fields of Gomorrah: their grapes are grapes of gall, their clusters are bitter" (vv. 31, 32). That this is speaking of apostate Israel is clear from v. 28—"For they are a nation void of counsel, neither is there any understanding in them". That the passage is speaking of apostate Israel in the days of the Antichrist appears from v. 35—"To me belongeth vengeance, and recompense; their foot shall slide in due time: for *the day of their calamity is at hand, and the things which shall come upon them make haste*" (v. 35).

7. In Rev. 15:2 there is a brief allusion to the Beast, in connection with the godly Remnant: "And I saw as it were a sea of glass mingled with fire: and them that had gotten the victory over the Beast, and over his image, and over his mark, and over the number of his name, stand on the sea of glass, having the harps of God", etc. The reference is to those who had been slain by the Antichrist because they had refused to render him any honor or worship. The same company is seen again in 20:4.

8. Rev. 16 describes the "vial" judgments which are executed just before the end of the Tribulation. The Beast is noticed several times in the chapter. In v. 2 we read, "And the first went, and poured out his vial upon the earth; and there fell a noisome and grievous sore upon the men which had the mark of the Beast, and upon them which worshipped his image" (v. 2). This is a foretaste of the grievous torments awaiting the worshippers of the

Beast. Again in v. 10 we read, "And the fifth angel poured out his vial upon the seat of the Beast; and his kingdom was full of darkness; and they gnawed their tongues for pain". Here the Beast himself receives intimation of the doom awaiting him. In vv. 13 and 14 we are told, "And I saw three unclean spirits like frogs come out of the mouth of the Dragon, and out of the mouth of the Beast, and out of the mouth of the False Prophet. For they are the spirits of demons, working miracles, which go forth unto the kings of the earth and of the whole world, to gather them to the battle of that great day of God Almighty". Here we behold, in symbolic guise, each of the persons in the Evil Trinity. The figure of the "frog" is very suggestive. Frogs are creatures which love the darkness rather than the light: they wallow in the mire and filth: their croaking is heard in the dusk of twilight and by night. Thus they are an apt symbol of the persons in the Trinity of Evil. Their very form suggests inflation by pride. The reference here in Rev. 16:13, 14 indicates the superhuman character of the False Prophet as well as of the Beast and the Dragon.

9. Rev. 17 calls for a lengthy exposition, so we must defer to a later chapter the consideration of its details. The central figures in it are "the great whore" and the "Beast". While freely granting that, historically, the great whore has received its fulfillment in the Roman Catholic system, and while allowing that it will yet represent the whole of apostate Christendom, nevertheless, we believe that the ultimate reference is to apostate Israel. Here in Rev. 17 the "woman" is first seen sitting upon the scarlet colored Beast —the Antichrist in his imperial glory (v. 3); but later we see him suffering his ten kings to destroy her (v. 16). This accords perfectly with the dual relation of Antichrist to Is-

rael: first posing as their Benefactor (here seen in v. 3 *supporting* her), later standing forth as her great Enemy. The eighth verse (see our comments on it in Chapter 3, Section III, 6) is one of the scriptures which show that Antichrist is a re-incarnation of Judas.

10. Rev. 19:19, 20 describes the end of Antichrist's career. We need not enlarge now upon these verses for we have already commented on them in Chapter 7. The final reference to the Antichrist is in Rev. 20:10 where we read of the Devil being cast into the Lake of Fire where the Beast and the False Prophet are, to be, with them, tormented for ever and ever.

11

ANTICHRIST IN REVELATION 13

IN the thirteenth chapter of Revelation *two* "Beasts'"
are there described. The first is the final Head of
the last great Empire before the establishment of
the millennial kingdom of our Lord. The second Beast is
denominated, in other passages, "the False Prophet".
There is a difference of opinion as to which of these
"Beasts'" represents the Antichrist. In the Appendix to
our book "The Redeemer's Return", where this subject is
discussed and from which we shall here freely transcribe,
we have stated that opinion is about equally divided. But
during the last five years we have made a much wider investigation, and as the result we have found that the great
majority of those who have written on the subject regard
the *first* Beast as the Antichrist, and that only a comparative few—nearly all of whom belong to a particular school
—favor the alternative view. However, the writings of the
few have had a wide circulation and have exerted a considerable influence on students of prophecy, and therefore
these papers on the Antichrist would lack completeness,
and probably some of our readers would be disappointed,
if we said nothing on the subject. It is in no spirit of con-
troversy that we now present our own reasons for believing
it is the first Beast of Rev. 13 who is the Antichrist.

The book of Revelation makes known the fact that there
is a Trinity of Evil. Each of these three evil persons
comes into view in Rev. 13. First, there is "the Beast"
(v. 2). Second, there is "the Dragon" (v. 2). Third,
there is "another Beast" (v. 11). The fact that of this
third Beast it is said "He spake as a dragon" (v. 11) at

once intimates his satanic nature and character, for the speech corresponds to the heart. The demonaical nature of each of these evil persons comes out clearly in Rev. 16: 13, 14, where we read, "And I saw *three* unclean spirits like frogs come out of the mouth of the Dragon, and out of the mouth of the Beast, and out of the mouth of the False Prophet. For they are the spirits of demons, working miracles". Finally, in Rev. 19:19, 20 we are told, "And the Beast was taken, and with him the False Prophet. . . . these both were cast alive into a lake of fire burning with brimstone", and then in 20:10 we read, "And the Devil that deceived them was cast into the lake of fire and brimstone, where the Beast and the False Prophet are, and shall be tormented day and night for ever and ever."

The above scriptures clearly establish the fact that there is a Trinity of Evil. Now it surely needs no argument to prove that these three evil persons are opposed to and are the antithesis of the three Persons in the Godhead. The Devil stands opposed to God the Father—"Ye are of your *father,* the Devil", John 8:40, etc. The Antichrist stands opposed to God the Son—his very name shows this. The remaining evil person stands opposed to God the Spirit. If this be the case, then our present task is greatly simplified: it is merely a matter of noting what is separately predicated of the two Beasts in Rev. 13 so as to ascertain which of them stands opposed to Christ and which to the Holy Spirit.

Now there are only two arguments of any plausibility which have been advanced to support the view that it is the second Beast of Rev. 13 which is the Antichrist, but so far as we are aware *no one has endeavored to show that the first Beast represents the third Person in the Trinity of Evil!* Yet he *must* be so if the second is the Antichrist!

This is unmistakeably clear from Rev. 16:13, 14 and 19: 19, 20. The first argument used is drawn from the language of 13:11, where of the second Beast it is said, "He had two horns *like a lamb,* and he spake as a dragon". This, we are told, indicates that it is the Antichrist who is here in view, aping the Lamb of God. Personally, we are amazed that such an assertion should have been made in soberness. It is difficult to imagine anything more wide of the mark, seeing that not only is it not said this beast with the two horns was "like *the* lamb" but in this same book "the Lamb" is pictured with *"seven* horns" (see 5: 6). But if this second Beast, the False Prophet, be the opponent of God the Spirit, then the *two* horns have a pertinent significance, for two is the number of *witness,* and just as Christ declared the Spirit of God should "testify (lit., bear witness) of Me" (John 15:26), so the third person in the Trinity of Evil bears witness to the first Beast—see 13:12, 14, 16. In the second place, it is said that the first Beast of Rev. 13 is presented as the *political* Head, while it is the second who is viewed as the *religious* Head. But if this is not a bad mistake, it certainly needs to be modified. It is the first Beast, not the second, who is *worshipped* (v. 12) ! Having thus noticed briefly the two leading objections which have been brought against the position we are about to define and defend, we shall now present some of the many arguments on the other side.

In the first place, to regard the Antichrist as *limited* to the *religious* realm and *divorced* from the *political,* seems to us, to leave out entirely an essential and fundamental element of his character and career. The Antichrist will claim to be the true Christ, the Christ of God. Hence, it would seem that he will present himself to the Jews as their long-expected Messiah—the One foretold by the Old

Testament prophets—and that before apostate Christendom, given over by God to believe the Lie, he will pose as the *returned* Christ. Therefore, must we not predicate, as an *inevitable corollary,* that the pseudo christ, will usher in a false millennium, and rule over a mock messianic kingdom? That this conclusion is fully borne out by Scripture we shall show in a moment.

Why was it (from the human side) that, when our Lord tabernacled among men, the Jews rejected Him as their Messiah? Was it not because He failed to fulfill their expectations that He would take the government upon His shoulder and wield the royal sceptre as soon as He presented Himself to them? Was it not because they looked for Him to restore the Kingdom to Israel there and then? Is it not therefore reasonable to suppose that when the Antichrist presents *himself* to them, that *he will* wield great *temporal* power, and rule over a vast earthly empire? It would certainly seem so. Happily we are not left to logical deductions and conclusions. We have a "thus saith the Lord" to rest upon. In Dan. 11:36—a scripture upon which all are agreed concerning its application—the Antichrist is expressly termed *"The King* (which) shall do according to his will". Here then is unequivocal proof that Antichrist *will exercise* political or governmental power. He will be a king—"the king"—and if a king he must be at the head of a kingdom.

In the second place, if the Antichrist is to be *a perfect counterfeit* of the true Christ, if he is to ape the *millennial* Christ as set forth in Old Testament prophecy—for, of course, he will not mimick the "suffering" Christ of the first advent—then it necessarily follows that he will *fill the role of king,* yea, that he will reign as a King of kings, as Satan's parody of the Son of man seated upon "the throne of His glory". That the Antichrist will *also* be at the head of the religious world, that he will demand and receive Divine honors, is equally true. Just as in the Millennium the Lord Jesus will *"be a Priest upon His Throne"* (Zech. 6:13), so the Antichrist will *combine* in his person the headships of both the political and the religious realms—see our notes on Ezek. 21:25, 26 in Chapter 9. And just as the Son of Man will be the Head of the fifth world-empire (Dan. 2:44) so, the Man of Sin will be the Head of the revived fourth world-empire (Dan. 2:40).

In the third place, to make the Antichrist and "the False Prophet" one and the same person is to involve us in a difficulty for which there seems to be no solution. In Rev. 19:20 we read, "And the Beast was taken, and with him the False Prophet that wrought miracles before him. . . . These both were cast alive into a lake of fire burning with brimstone". Now, if the "False Prophet" be the Antichrist, then who is "the Beast" that is cast with him into the Lake of Fire? The Beast here cannot be the Roman Empire (the people in it), for no member of the human race (as such) is cast into the Lake of Fire until *after* the Millennium (see Rev. 20). That "the Beast" is a separate entity, another individual than "the False Prophet" is also clear from Rev. 20:10—"And the Devil that deceived them was cast into the lake of fire and brimstone, where the Beast and the False Prophet are". In this last quoted scripture, each of the three persons in the Trinity of Evil is specifically mentioned, and if "the Beast" is not the Antichrist, the Son of Perdition, the second person in the Trinity of Evil, who is he?

In the fourth place, what is predicated of the *first* "Beast" in Rev. 13 comports much better with what is elsewhere revealed concerning the Antichrist, than what is here said of the second "Beast". In proof of our assertion we submit the following:

Points of resemblance between the first Beast of Rev. 13 and the Man of Sin of 2 Thess. 2:—

1. The first Beast receives his power, seat, and great authority from the Dragon, Rev. 13:2. Cf. 2 Thess. 2:9— "Him, whose coming is after the working *of Satan* with all power and signs and lying wonders".

2. "All the world" wonders after the first Beast, Rev. 13:2. Cf. 2 Thess. 2:11, 12—"And for this cause God shall send them strong delusion, that they should believe the Lie; that they *all* might be damned", etc.

3. The first Beast is *"worshipped"*, Rev. 13:4. Cf 2 Thess. 2:4—"He *as God* sitteth in the temple of God".

4. The first Beast has a mouth "speaking great things", Rev. 13:5. Cf 2 Thess. 2:4—"Who . . . . *exalteth himself* above all that is called God". Note also that in Rev. 13: 5 it is said of the *first* Beast, he "has a mouth speaking great things and *blasphemies"*. Is not this one of the chief characteristic marks of the Antichrist?

5. The first Beast makes war on the saints, Rev. 13:7. Cf 2 Thess. 2:4—"Who *opposeth* . . . . all that is called God", that is, he will seek to exterminate and obliterate everything on earth which bears God's name.

From these points of analogy it is evident that the first Beast of Rev. 13 and the Man of Sin of 2 Thess. 2 are one and the same person.

In the fifth place, that the *second* "Beast" is *not* "the Man of Sin" appears from the fact that the second Beast causeth the earth to worship the *first* Beast (Rev. 13:12), whereas the Man of Sin *"exalteth himself"* (2 Thess. 2: 4), and compare Dan. 11:36: "And he *exalteth himself"*.

As already intimated, there are several things which show plainly that the second Beast is the *third* person in the Trinity of Evil, that is, the one who is the satanic parody of the Holy Spirit. The point now before us supplies further confirmation. There is nothing in Rev. 13, nor elsewhere, to show that this second Beast is worshipped, rather does he direct worship away from himself, to the first Beast. Therefore, he cannot be the pseudo christ, for the Lord Jesus *did,* again and again, receive worship (see particularly Matthew's Gospel), and will be worshipped on His return. But this second Beast, who directs worship *away from himself,* accurately imitates the Holy Spirit in this respect, for nowhere in the New Testament is the third Person of the Holy Trinity presented as a distinct Object of worship; instead, He is to "glorify" Christ (John 16: 14) by drawing out our hearts unto that blessed One who loved us and gave Himself for us.

Again; it has been generally recognized by prophetic students that our Lord referred to the Antichrist when He said, "I am come in My Father's name, and ye receive Me not: if another shall come *in his own name,* him ye will receive" (John 5:43). If the one here mentioned as coming "in his own name" *is* the Antichrist, then it is certain that the *second* Beast of Rev. 13 cannot be the Antichrist, for he *does not* come "in his own name". On the contrary, the second Beast comes in the name of the first Beast as is clear from Rev. 13:12-15. Just as the Holy Spirit—the *third* Person in the Holy Trinity—speaks "not of Himself" (John 16:13), but is here to glorify Christ, so the second Beast—the *third* person in the Evil Trinity—seeks to glorify the first Beast, the Antichrist.

If it should be objected that the second Beast is represented as *working miracles* (Rev. 13:13, 14) and, that as the Man of Sin is also said to come "after the working of Satan with all power and signs and lying wonders" (2 Thess. 2:9), therefore, the second Beast must be the Antichrist, the answer is, This by no means follows. The power to work miracles *is common to each person* in the Trinity of Evil. Just as God the Father, God the Son, and God the Holy Spirit, each perform miracles, so does the Dragon, the Beast, and the False Prophet (see Rev. 16:13, 14 for proof). Three things are said in connection with the second Beast which correspond closely with the work of the Holy Spirit. First, "he maketh *fire* come down from heaven" (Rev. 13:13), cf Acts 2:1-4. Second, "he had power to *give life* unto the image of the Beast" (Rev. 13:15), cf John 3:6—"born of the Spirit". Third, "he causeth all, both small and great, rich and poor, free and bond, to *receive a mark* in their right hand, or in their foreheads" (Rev. 13:16), cf Eph. 4:30—"Grieve not the Holy Spirit of God, *whereby ye are sealed* unto the day of redemption".

Finally; the second Beast is clearly *subordinate* to the first Beast. But would the Jews receive as their Messiah and King one who was himself the vassal of a Roman? Was not this the very reason why the Jews of old *rejected* the Lord Jesus, i. e., because *He was* subject to Caesar, and because He refused to deliver the Jews *from* the Romans!

In the sixth place, as we have seen, in Dan. 11:36 the Antichrist is termed "the King", and if a king he must possess a kingdom, and can there be any doubt as to the identity of this kingdom? Will not Antichrist's kingdom be the very one which Satan offered in vain to Christ? namely, "all the kingdoms of the world, and the glory of them" (Matt. 4:8). That the kingdom of the Antichrist will be much wider than Palestine appears from Dan. 11:

40-42—"And at the time of the end shall the king of the South push at him (the Antichrist) : and the king of the North (the Antichrist, as King of Babylon) shall come against him (the King of the South) like a whirlwind, with chariots, and with horsemen, and with many ships: and he (the Antichrist) shall enter into the countries, and shall overflow and pass over. He (the Antichrist) shall enter also into the glorious land, and many countries shall be overthrown: but these shall escape out of his (the Antichrist's) hand, even Edom and Moab, and the chief of the children of Ammon. He (the Antichrist) shall stretch forth his hand upon the countries: and the land of Egypt shall not escape". From this scripture it is also clear that the Antichrist will be at the head of a great army and therefore must be a *political* ruler as well as a religious chief.

In the seventh place, it is generally agreed among those students of prophecy who belong to the Futurist school, that the rider upon the four horses in Rev. 6 is the Antichrist. If this be the case, then we have further proof that the Antichrist and *the Head* of the revived Roman Empire is one and the same person. This may be seen by comparing three scriptures. In Rev. 6:8, of the rider on "the pale horse", we read, "His name that sat on him was *Death* and *Hell* followed with him". In Isa. 28:18, those who will be in Jerusalem during the Tribulation period are addressed by Jehovah as follows: "And your covenant with *Death* shall be disannulled, and your agreement with *Hell* shall not stand". What "covenant" can this be, except the one mentioned in Dan. 9:27, where we read of the Roman Prince (the Head of the revived Roman Empire) confirming the covenant with the many for seven years? Now reverse the order of these three passages, and what do

we learn?   In Dan. 9:27 we learn that the Head of the
Roman Empire makes a "covenant" with the Jews.   In
Isa. 28:18 this "covenant" is said to have been made with
"Death and Hell". While in Rev. 6:8 the rider on the pale
horse (whom it is generally admitted is the Antichrist) is
named "Death and Hell".   Hence, from whatever angle
we approach the subject it is seen that the Antichrist is the
Head of the fourth world-kingdom.

12

TYPES OF THE ANTICHRIST

"I N the volume of the book it is written of Me" (Heb. 10:7), said the Lord Jesus. Christ is the key to the Scriptures—"Search the Scriptures . . . . they are they which testify of Me", are His words; and the "Scriptures" to which He had reference were not the four Gospels, for they were not then written, but the writings of Moses and the prophets. The Old Testament Scriptures, then, are something more than a compilation of historical narratives, something more than the record of a system of social and religious legislation, or a code of ethics. The Old Testament Scriptures are, fundamentally, a stage on which is shown forth, in vivid symbolry, stupendous events then future. The events recorded in the Old Testament were actual occurrences, yet were they also typical prefigurations. Throughout the Old Testament dispensations God caused to be shadowed forth things which must yet come to pass. This is in full accord with a basic law in the economy of God. Nothing is brought to maturity at once. As it is in the natural world, so it is in the spiritual: there is first the blade, then the ear, and then the full corn in the ear. So there is first the shadow, and then the substance; the type, and then the antitype.

"Whatsoever things were written aforetime were written for our learning" (Rom. 15:4). Israel's tabernacle was *"a figure* for the time then present" (Heb. 9:8, 9), as well as the example and *"shadow of heavenly things"* (Heb. 8:5). Concerning the history of Abraham, his wives and his children, the apostle was inspired to write "which things are *an allegory"* (Gal. 4:24). These and other passages which might be quoted witness plainly to the typical meaning of portions of the Old Testament. But there are some brethren who will own the typical significance of *these* things, who refuse to acknowledge that anything else in the Old Testament has a typical meaning save those which are expressly interpreted or mentioned in the New. But surely this is a mistake. Ought we not to regard those Old Testament types which *are* expounded in the New Testament as *samples* of others which are not explained? Are there no more prophecies in the Old Testament than those which in the New Testament are expressly said to be "fulfilled"? Assuredly there are. Then why not admit the same in connection with the types? Nothing is said in the New Testament that the history of Joseph has a profound and wonderful typical significance, yet who with anointed eyes can fail to see in the experiences of Jacob's favorite son a remarkable foreshadowing of the person and work of Christ!

There will probably be few who read this chapter that will dispute what we have said above. No doubt the majority of our readers have already been instructed in much of the typology of the Old Testament. Many of God's servants have written at length upon the Passover, the brazen serpent, the Tabernacle, etc., as well as upon the many ways in which such men as Abel, Noah, Isaac, Moses, David, etc. prefigured the Saviour. But strange to say, very little seems to have been written upon those who adumbrated the Antichrist. So far as we are aware practically nothing has been given out concerning the many Bible characters of ill fame, who foreshadowed that coming one, that occupies such a prominent place in the prophetic scriptures. A wide field is here opened for study, and we take pleasure in now submitting to the careful perusal of the reader the results of our own imperfect researches, hoping that it may lead others to make a more complete examination of the subject for themselves.

It was well said by one of the Continental Puritans that "When we read the Scriptures, we are to judge beforehand, that then only do we understand them, when we discover in them a wisdom unsearchable and worthy of God" (Witsius). Such is the inexhaustible fulness of the written Word of God that not only are its words significant of things, but even the things, which are first signified by the words, also represent other things, which they were appointed to prefigure long before they happened. Besides the plain and literal sense of Scripture, there is also a mystical sense, hidden beneath the surface and which can only be discovered as we, in dependance on the Holy Spirit, diligently compare scripture with scripture. In pursuing the latter we need not only to proceed with due caution, but in "fear and trembling", lest we devise mysteries out of our own imagination, and thus pervert to one use what belongs to another. The principle which will safeguard us is to thoroughly acquaint ourselves with the antitypes. Let nothing be regarded as a type unless we are sure there is an exact correspondence with the antitype. This will preserve us from erroneously supposing that any person who is clearly a type of either Christ or the Antichrist *is so* in *every* detail of his life. Thus Moses was plainly a type of Christ as our Mediator, and in many other respects too, but in his failures and in other details of his personal history he was not a type of Christ. So, too, with those who foreshadowed the Antichrist: not everything recorded of them prefigured the character or deeds of the Man of Sin. Should it still be inquired, How are we to ascertain *in which* respects the actions of Old Testament characters were, and were not, typical? the answer, as given above, is, By comparing the antitype. This will save us from the wild allegorizing of Origen and others of the "Fathers". We shall now look at ten Bible characters, each of which strikingly typified the Antichrist.

1. *Cain.* It is indeed solemn to discover that the very first man born into this world prefigured the Man of Sin. He did so in at least seven respects. First, we may observe that in 1 John 3:12 we are told "Cain was of that Wicked one", i. e. the Devil. Of none other is this particular expression used. The Antichrist will also, in a special sense, be "of that Wicked one", for the Devil is said to be his "father" (John 8:44). Second, Cain was a religious hypocrite. This is seen in the fact that at first he posed as a worshipper of God, but the emptiness of his pretensions were quickly evidenced; for, when the Lord refused his offering, Cain was "very wroth" (Gen. 4:5). As such he clearly prefigured that one who will first claim to be the Christ, only to stand forth later as His denier (1 John 2:22). Third, by his primogeniture Cain occupied the position of *ruler*. Said the Lord to him, "Unto thee shall be his desire, and thou shalt *rule over* him", that is, over Abel (Gen. 4:7). Such, too, will be the position filled by the Antichrist—he shall be a Ruler over men. Fourth, in murdering his brother Abel, Cain foreshadowed the wicked martyrdom of the Tribulation saints by the Son of Perdition. Fifth, Cain was a *liar*. After the murder of Abel, when the Lord asked Cain, "Where is Abel thy brother?", he answered, "I know not" (Gen. 4:9). In like manner deceit and falsehood will characterize him who is appropriately named "the Lie" (2 Thess. 2:11). Sixth, God's judgment descended upon Cain. So far as we know from the Scripture record, no human eye witnessed the dastard-

ly murder of Abel, and doubtless Cain deemed himself secure from any penal consequences. But if so, he reckoned without God. The Lord announced to him, "Thy brother's blood crieth unto Me from the ground", and then He declared, "And now art thou cursed from the earth" (Gen. 4:10). So, too, in his reckless conceit, the Antichrist will imagine that he can defy God and slay His people with impugnity. But his blasphemous delusions will be quickly dispelled. Seventh, Cain was made to exclaim, "My punishment is greater than I can bear" (Gen. 4:13). Such indeed will be the awful portion meted out to the Antichrist—he shall be "cast alive into the lake of fire burning with brimstone" (Rev. 19:20).

2. *Lamech.* And Lamech said unto his wives: Adah and Zillah, hear my voice; Ye wives of Lamech, hearken unto my speech: For I have slain a man for wounding me, and a young man for bruising me. If Cain shall be avenged sevenfold, Truly Lamech seventy and seven fold" (Gen. 4:23, 24, R. V.). The record of this man's life is exceedingly brief, but from the little that is recorded about him we may discover at least seven parallelisms between him and the Antichrist. First, the meaning of his name. Lamech signifies "powerful". This was an appropriate name for one who foreshadowed the Man of Sin who, as the Head of the United States of the World, will be powerful governmentally. He will also be mighty in his person, for we are told that the Dragon shall give power unto him (Rev. 13:4). Second, in the fact that Lamech was a descendant of Cain (Gen. 4:17-19), not Seth, we see that he sprang from the *evil* line. Third, he was the *seventh* from fallen Adam, as though to intimate that the cycle of depravity was *completed in him.* So the Antichrist will be not only the culmination of satanic craft and power, but

as well, the climax of human wickedness—the Man of Sin. Fourth, the first thing predicted of Lamech is his "lawlessness". "Lamech took unto him *two* wives" (Gen. 4:19). As such he violated the marriage-law and disobeyed the command of God (Gen. 2:24). Clearly, then, he foreshadowed the "Lawless One" (2 Thess. 2:8, R. V.). Fifth, like Cain before him, Lamech was a murderer. His confession is, "I have *slain* a man for wounding me, and a young man for bruising me" (Gen. 4:23). In this, too, he foreshadowed the Man of blood and of violence. Sixth, he was *filled with pride*. This comes out in two details. First, he says to his wives, "Hear *my* voice; Ye wives of Lamech, hearken unto *my* speech" (Gen. 4:23). Second, in his arrogant self-importance—"If Cain shall be avenged sevenfold, *truly* LAMECH seventy and seven fold" (Gen. 4:24). This appears to mean that Lamech had slain a man for wounding him, and mad with passion, he jeered ironically at God's dealings with Cain. Seventh, in the fact that the very next thing recorded after the brief notice of Lamech is the *birth of Seth* (the one from whom, according to the flesh, Christ descended) who *set aside* the line of Cain—for on his birth Eve exclaimed, "God hath appointed me another seed instead of Abel whom Cain slew" (Gen. 4:25)—thus we have a beautiful foreshadowing of the millennial reign of the Lord Jesus following the *overthrow* of the Antichrist.

3. *Nimrod*. This personal type of the Antichrist is deeply interesting and remarkably full in its details. His exploits are recorded in Gen. 10 and 11, and it is most significant that his person and history are there introduced at the point immediately preceding God's call of Abraham from among the Gentiles and His bringing him into the promised land. Thus will history repeat itself. Just be-

fore God again gathers Abraham's descendants from out of the lands of the Gentiles (many, perhaps the majority of whom, will be found dwelling in Chaldea, in Assyria, the "north country"—see Isa. 11:11; Jer. 3:18, etc.) there will arise one who will fill out the picture here typically outlined by Nimrod.

Let us examine the details of this type. First, the meaning of his name is most suggestive. Nimrod signifies "The Rebel". A fit designation was this for a man that foreshadowed the Lawless One, who shall *oppose* and exalt himself above all that is called God (2 Thess. 2:4), and who shall "stand up against the Prince of princes" (Dan. 8:25). Second, we are told that he was a son of Cush— "And Cush begat Nimrod" (Gen. 10:8), and Cush was a son of Ham, who was curst by Noah. Nimrod, then, was not a descendant of Shem, from whom Christ sprang, nor of Japheth; but he came from Ham. It is remarkable that these men who typified the Antichrist came from the *evil* line. Third, we are told that Nimrod "began to be a mighty one in the earth" (Gen. 10:8). Four times over is this term "mighty" connected with this one who prefigured him "whose coming is after the working of Satan, *with all power* and signs and lying wonders" (2 Thess. 2: 9). But observe that it is first said, "He *began* to be mighty", which seems to suggest the idea that he *struggled for the pre-eminence* and obtained it by mere force of will. How this corresponds with the fact that the Man of Sin first appears as "the *little* horn" and by force of conquest attains to the position of King of kings needs only to be pointed out. It is also significant that the Hebrew word for "mighty" in Gen. 10:9 is "gibbor" which is translated several times "Chief" and "Chieftain". Fourth, it is also added, "Nimrod the mighty hunter *before the Lord*", which means that he pushed his designs in brazen defiance of his Maker. The words "mighty hunter before the Lord" are found twice in Gen. 10:9. This repetition in so short a narrative is highly significant. If we compare the expression with a similar one in Gen. 6:11,—"The earth also (in the days of Noah) was corrupt *before God*"—the impression conveyed is, that this "Rebel" pursued his impious designs in open defiance of the Almighty. The contents of Gen. 11 abundantly confirm this interpretation. In like manner, of the Antichrist it is written, "And the King shall do according to *his* will, and he shall exalt himself and magnify himself above every god (ruler), and shall speak marvelous things against the God of gods" (Dan. 11:36). Fifth, Nimrod was a "Man of Blood". In 1 Chron. 1:10—"And Cush begat Nimrod; he began to be *mighty* upon the earth". The Chaldea paraphrase of this verse says, "Cush begat Nimrod who began to prevail in wickedness for he slew innocent blood and rebelled against Jehovah". This, coupled with the expression "a mighty Hunter before the Lord", suggests that he relentlessly sought out and slew God's people. As such, he accurately portrayed the *bloody* and *deceitful* Man (Psa. 5:6), the *violent* Man (Psa. 140:1). Sixth, Nimrod was a King— "the beginning of his *kingdom* was Babel" (Gen. 10:10). Thus he was King of Babylon, which is also one of the many titles of the Antichrist (Isa. 14:4). In the verses which follow in Gen. 10 we read, "He went out into Assyria and builded Ninevah, and the city Rehoboth, and Calah", etc. (Gen. 10:11). From these statements it is evident that Nimrod's ambition was to establish a *world-empire*. Seventh, mark his inordinate desire for *fame*. His consuming desire was to make for himself *a name*. Here again the antitype marvellously corresponds with the type, for the Man of Sin is expressly denominated "King over all the children of pride" (Job 41:34).

What is recorded in Gen. 10 about Nimrod supplies the key to the first half of Gen. 11 which tells of the building of the Tower of Babel. Gen. 10:10 informs us that the beginning of Nimrod's kingdom was *Babel*. In the language of that day Babel meant "the gate of *God*", but afterwards, because of the judgment which the Lord there inflicted, it came to mean "Confusion". That at the time Nimrod founded Babel this word signified "the gate (the figure of official position) *of God*", intimates that he not only organized an imperial government over which he presided as king, but that he also instituted a new and idolatrous system of worship. If the type be perfect, and we are fully assured it is so, then, as the Lawless One will yet do, Nimrod demanded and received *Divine honors*. In all probability, it was at this point that idolatry was introduced.

Nimrod is not directly mentioned in Gen. 11, but from the statements made about him in chap. 10 there cannot be any doubt that *he* was the "Chief" and "King" who organized and headed the movement and rebellion there described: "And they said, Go to, let us build us a city and a tower, whose top may reach unto heaven; and let us make us a name, lest we be scattered abroad upon the face of the whole earth" (11:4). Here we behold a most blatant defiance of God, a deliberate refusal to obey His commands given through Noah—"Be fruitful, and multiply, and replenish *the earth*" (9:1). But they said, "Let us make us a name *lest we be* scattered upon the face of the whole earth". As we have seen, Nimrod's ambition was to establish a *world-empire*. To accomplish this two things, at least, were necessary. First, a *center,* a great headquarters; and second, a *motive* for the inspiration and encouragement of his followers. The former was furnished in the city of Babylon: the latter was to be supplied in the "let us make us a name". It was inordinate desire for fame. The idea of the "Tower" (considered in the light of its setting) seems that of *strength,* a stronghold, rather than eminence.

To sum up. In Nimrod and his schemes we behold Satan's initial attempt to raise up an universal ruler of men. In his inordinate desire for fame, in the mighty power that he wielded, in his ruthless and brutal methods, in his blatant defiance of the Creator, in his founding of the kingdom of Babel, in his assuming to himself Divine honcrs, in the fact that the Holy Spirit has placed the record of these things *just before* the inspired account of God's bringing Abraham into Canaan—pointing forward to the re-gathering of Israel in Palestine, immediately after the overthrow of the Lawless One—and finally, in the Divine destruction of his kingdom—described in the words, "Let Us *go down* and there confound their language" (Gen. 11:7), which so marvellously pictures the *descent* of Christ from heaven to vanquish His impious rival—we cannot fail to see that we have a wonderfully complete typical picture of the person, the work, and the destruction of the Antichrist.

4. *Chedorlaomer.* The history of this man is recorded in Gen. 14 which is a chapter of deep interest to the student of typology. The chapter opens with the words "And it came to pass in the days" of. "This is an expression which occurs six times (in the Hebrew) and always marks a time of trouble ending in blessing—cf Ruth 1:11; Isa. 7:1; Jer. 1:3; Esther 1:1; 2 Sam. 21:1" (Companion Bible). Such is plainly the case here. The first half of Gen. 14 depicts Tribulation conditions, and this is followed by

a scene foreshadowing millennial glory. The *time* when Chedorlaomer lived is the first point in the type. His history is recorded just before the first mention of Melchizedek, the priest-king, who came forth and blessed Abraham —an unmistakeable foreshadowment of Christ in millennial glory, blessing Israel. Second, the name of this man is highly significant. Gesenius, in his lexicon, says of the meaning of his name, "If it be a Phoenicio—Shemetic word 'a handful of sheaves' . . . . perhaps its true etymology should be sought in the *ancient* Persian". The latter is doubtless correct, for "Elam", of which Chedorlaomer was king (Gen. 14:1), is the ancient name for Persia. Col. Rawlinson searched for his name on the tablets of ancient Assyria, and there he found that his official title was, "Ravager of the west"! Thus was he a true type of the coming one who shall wade through a sea of blood to his coveted position as Emperor of the world. Third, it is indeed remarkable to find that just as Rev. 13:1 shows us that the empire of which the Antichrist will be the Head (see our notes on this verse in Chapter 11) includes within it the territory and perpetuates the characteristics of the earlier empires (Babylon, Persia, Greece and Rome), so in Gen. 14 Chedorlaomer is seen connected with *the same dominions:* "And it came to pass in the days of Amraphel king of Shinar, Arioch king of Ellasar, Chedorlaomer king of Elam, and Tidal king of nations". Now "Shinar" is one of the names of *Babylon* (see Dan. 1:2) ; "Elam" is the ancient name of *Persia;* "Ellasar" is translated "Hellas" in the Sept., which is the ancient name of *Greece;* while "Tidal king of the nations" evidently stands for *Rome,* the last of the world empires. Fourth, but what is even more striking, is the fact that in Gen. 14:5 Chedorlaomer is seen *at the head of* the kings mentioned in v. 1. They act as his vassals, and thus bow to the superiority of this one who was evidently a King of kings. Fifth, Chedorlaomer was a Warrior of renown. He was the Attila, the Napoleon of his day. He defeated in battle the kings of Sodom and Gomorrah and brought them into subjection and servitude (see 14:2-4). Later, they rebelled, and gathering his forces together he went forth, vanquished, and slew them (14:9, 10). Thus did he foreshadow the "Destroyer of the Gentiles" (Jer. 4:7). Sixth, in Gen. 14:12 we read, "And they took Lot, Abraham's brother's son, who dwelt in Sodom, and his goods, and departed". This prefigured the persecution of Israel by Antichrist and his subordinates in a coming day. Finally, we learn how that Abraham and his servants pursued Chedorlaomer and his forces, and that "Chedorlaomer and the kings that were with him" were slain "in the kings dale" (14:17), which strikingly adumbrated the future overthrow of Antichrist and the kings who shall be with him, in the dale of Megiddo (see Rev. 19:19).

5. *Pharaoh*. We have in mind the Pharaoh of the book of Exodus. His history and character are described at much greater length than the other personal types of the Antichrist which have been before us, and therefore more parallelisms are to be found here. We shall aim to be suggestive rather than exhaustive. First, Pharaoh was king of Egypt which, in Scripture, is the lasting symbol of the world. In like manner, the one whom he so strikingly prefigured will be Head of the world-kingdom. Second, the Pharaoh of Exodus came from Assyria (Isa. 52:4); so also will the Antichrist first rise in that land. Third, Ex. 1 presents him to our view as the merciless persecutor of the Hebrews, embittering their lives by hard bondage. Fourth, he is next seen as the one who sought to cut off

Israel from being a nation, giving orders that all the male children should be slain in infancy. Fifth, he was the blatant defier of God. When Moses and Aaron appeared before him and said, "Thus saith the Lord God of Israel, Let My people go, that they may hold a feast unto Me in the wilderness", his arrogant reply was, "Who is the Lord, that I should obey His voice to let Israel go?" (Ex. 5:1, 2). Sixth, God's *two witnesses* performed miracles before Pharaoh (Ex. 7:10); so, too, will God's two witnesses in the Tribulation period work miracles before the Beast (Rev. 11:6, 7). Seventh, Pharaoh had magical resources at his disposal (Ex. 7:11), as the Antichrist will have at his (2 Thess. 2:9). Eighth, Pharaoh made fair promises to the Hebrews, only to break them (Ex. 8:8, 15). In this, too, he foreshadowed the Antichrist in his perfidy and treachery toward Israel. Ninth, he met with a drastic end at the hands of God (Psa. 136:15). Tenth, he was overthrown at the time that Israel started out for the promised land: so Antichrist will be cast into the Lake of Fire just before Israel enters into everlasting possession of their promised inheritance. In all of these ten respects (and in others which the student may search out for himself) Pharaoh was a striking and accurate type of the Antichrist.

6. *Abimelech*. First, Abimelech signifies "father of the king". Gideon, deliverer of Israel, was his father. But his mother was a concubine, and this name was given to him, no doubt, for the purpose of hiding the shame of his birth. Looking from the type to the antitype—*"Father of the King"*—calls attention to the satanic origin of the Antichrist. Second, Abimelech slew seventy of his own brethren (Judges 9:5), and was therefore a bloody persecutor of Israel. Third, Judges 9:6, 22 tell us that he

was "king over Israel".' Fourth, it is significant to note that he occupied the throne at the time of Israel's apostasy (see Judges 8:33, 34). Fifth, it is also most suggestive that we are told he commenced his career at the stone (Judges 9:6), or pillar, which Joshua erected in Ebal (facing Gerizim), the mount where all the *curses* of a broken law were announced—Deut. 11:29; 27:4, 12, 13; Josh. 8:30. Sixth, he was a mighty warrior, a violent man (see Judges 9:40-50, and cf Psa. 140:1 for the Antichrist as such). Seventh, he was slain by the *sword* (Judges 9: 54 and see Zech. 11:7; Rev. 13:3 for the antitype).

7. *Saul.* In at least ten respects Saul foreshadowed the Antichrist. Almost the first thing told us about Saul is that he was "from his shoulders and upward higher than any of the people" (1 Sam. 9:2, which is repeated in 10: 23). As such he fitly prefigured the coming Super-man, who in intelligence, governmental power, and satanic might, will so tower above all his contemporaries that men shall exclaim, "Who is like unto the Beast?" (Rev. 13:4). Second, Saul was king of Israel (1 Sam. 10:24), so also will the Antichrist be. Third, Saul was a priest-king, blatantly performing the office of the Levite (see 1 Sam. 13:9, and cf Ezek. 21:25, 26 R.V.). Fourth, the *time* of his reign was immediately before that of David, as that of the Antichrist will immediately precede that of David's Son and Lord. Fifth, he was a mighty Warrior (see 1 Sam. 11:11; 13:1-4; 15:4; 7:8). Sixth, he was a rebel against God (1 Sam. 15:11). Seventh, he hated David (1 Sam. 18:7, 8, 11; 26:2, etc.). Eighth, he slew the servants of God (1 Sam. 22:17, 18). Ninth, he had intercourse with the powers of evil (1 Sam. 29). Tenth, he died by the *sword* (1 Sam. 31:4).

8. *Goliath.* First, his name means "Soothsayer" which

at once connects him with the powers of evil. Second, he was a giant, and thus, like Saul, prefigured the Super-man. Third, he was the enemy of Israel. Fourth, his consuming egotism was displayed in his blatant chal-lenge, "I defy the armies of Israel" (1 Sam. 17:10). Fifth, the mysterious number 666 (the number of the Antichrist) is connected with Goliath. Note the three sixes. (a) He was *"six* cubits high" (1 Sam. 17:4). (b) *Six* pieces of armor are enumerated—helmet, coat of mail, greaves, target, staff, and shield (1 Sam. 17:5-7). (c) His spear's head weighed *"six* hundred shekels of iron (1 Sam. 17:7). Sixth, he was slain by the *sword* (see 1 Sam. 17:51). Seventh, he was slain by David—type of Christ. In each of these respects he foreshadowed the Antichrist.

9. *Absalom.* First, the meaning of his name is very significant. "Absalom" means "father of peace". A care-ful reading of his history reveals the fact that, again and again, he posed as a man of peace, while war was in his heart. So the Antichrist will pose as the promised Prince of peace, and for a time it will appear that he has actually ushered in the Millennium. But ere long his violent and bloody character will be revealed. Second, Absalom was the son of David, and therefore a Jew. Third, but Absa-lom was a son of David by Maacah, the daughter of the Gentile king of Jeshur (2 Sam. 3:3). So, too, will the Antichrist also be connected with the Gentiles. Fourth, Absalom was a man of imposing personality (2 Sam. 14: 25). So the Antichrist will be a veritable king among men. Fifth, Absalom was a man of blood (2 Sam. 13, etc.). Sixth, Absalom sought to obtain the kingdom by flatteries (2 Sam. 15:2-6); cf Dan. 11:21, 23. Seventh, he cloaked his rebellion by a pretense of religion (read 2 Sam. 15:7, 8). Eighth, he was the immediate cause of

the faithful followers of David being driven from Jerusalem into the wilderness (2 Sam. 15:14-16). Ninth, he reared up a "pillar" unto himself (2 Sam. 18:18), which clearly foreshadowed the "image" which the Antichrist will cause to be set up unto himself. Tenth, he met with a violent end (2 Sam. 18:14).

There are quite a number of others who foreshadowed the Antichrist in one or more of the outstanding features of his character and career. For instance, there is Balak who, accompanied by Baalam the prophet sought to curse and destroy Israel—a striking foreshadowing of the Beast with his ally the False Prophet. There is Adoni-zedek, mentioned in Joshua 10, and who headed a federation of ten kings; it is remarkable that his name signifies "lord of righteousness" which is what the Antichrist will claim to be as he comes forth on "the *white* horse" (Rev. 6). Then there is Adoni-kam, with whom is associated the mystical number 666—see Ezra 2:13; and how profoundly significant that his name signifies "the Lord hath risen". We believe that this mystic number in connection with the Antichrist will apply to him only after his resurrection— 666 is *three* sixes, and three is the number of *resurrection,* and six the number of man! Sennacherib (2 Kings 18) prefigured the Antichrist in a number of ways: as the king of Assyria, the blatant defier of God, smitten by the sword, etc. Haman, four times denominated "the Jews' enemy" (Esther 3:10 etc.), and termed "the adversary" (Esther 7:6), was another typical character. Nebuchadnezzar, king of kings, who demanded universal worship, who set up an image to himself, and decreed that all should worship it under pain of death, etc., manifestly pointed forward to the Man of Sin, and so we might continue. Almost every prominent feature of the Antichrist's person and career was foreshadowed by some Old Testament character. The subject is intensely interesting, and we trust that many of our readers will be encouraged to pursue it further for themselves. In closing this chapter we shall look at one New Testament type of the Antichrist.

10. *Herod.* At the beginning of the New Testament there meets us a typical foreshadowing of the Antichrist. We refer to what is recorded in Matt. 2. The description there furnished of Herod obviously contains a prophetic adumbration of his great prototype. Notice, first, that three times over he is denominated *"the king"* (vv. 1, 3, 9), as such he prefigured the last great king, before the appearing of the King of kings. Second, observe his *hypocrisy.* When the "wise men", who had followed the star which heralded the Saviour's birth, were summoned into Herod's presence, we are told that he said unto them, "Go and search diligently for the young child; and when ye have found Him, bring me word again, *that I may come and worship Him also*" (v. 8). That nothing could have been further from his mind is plain from his subsequent acts. But, nevertheless, he first posed as a devout worshipper. Such is the role that the Antichrist will first fill in Palestine. Third, next he *threw off* his religious mask and displayed his wicked heart: "Then Herod, when he saw that he was mocked of the wise men, was exceeding wroth, and sent forth, and slew all the children that were in Bethlehem", etc. (v. 16). Similarly will the Antichrist act in Jerusalem. Three and one half years before his end comes he will discard his religious pretensions and stand forth in his true character. Fourth, in this edict of slaying the young children in Bethlehem and the coasts thereof, he was aiming, of course, at Christ Himself. Thus did he accurately foreshadow that one who will yet fulfill

the terms of Gen. 3:15, where we read of a *double* "enmity"—between Satan and the woman (Israel), and between her Seed (Christ) and the Serpent's "seed" (the Antichrist). In the fifth place, we may also discover in Herod's destruction of the children, a forecast of the fiendish assaults which the Antichrist will make upon *the Jews,* when he seeks to cut them off from being a nation. In the sixth place, we may note how *the consequence* of Herod's cruelty will reappear in the future—"In Ramah was there a voice heard, lamentation, and weeping, and great mourning, Rachel weeping for her children, and would not be comforted, because they are not" (Matt. 2:18). This is a quotation from Jer. 31:15. But like most, if not all, prophecies, this will receive another and final fulfillment at the close of the Tribulation period. Our authority for this is found in the words which immediately follow in Jer. 31: "Thus saith the Lord, Refrain thy voice from weeping, and thine eyes from tears: for thy work shall be rewarded, saith the Lord; and they shall come again from the land of The Enemy. And there is hope in *thine end,* saith the Lord, that thy children shall come again to their own border". Thus it is clear that "bitter weeping and lamentation" will again be heard in Ramah just before Christ returns and restores Israel. Seventh, the accuracy of the typical picture supplied by Matt. 2 may be discovered in *the failure* of Herod to destroy the Christchild. Just as God foiled Herod, so will He yet bring to nought the wicked designs of the Antichrist; and just as we read of Christ coming and dwelling at Nazareth after the *death* of Herod, so Christ shall again dwell in that land after the death of the false King. Surely, this remarkable typical picture of the Antichrist should cause us to search more diligently for other esoteric allusions to him in the New Testament.

13

BABYLON AND THE ANTICHRIST

WE arrive now at a branch of our subject upon which the Lord's people are in evident need of instruction: they have less light here than on most prophetic themes. And perhaps we should not be surprised at this. The very name Babylon means *confusion,* and widely prevails the confusion concerning it. Yet here and there God has raised up individuals who have borne faithful testimony to the teaching of His Word concerning the past and future of Babylon, and to their witness the writer acknowledges his indebtedness. In view of the ignorance which generally obtains we shall proceed the more cautiously. We here propose to examine carefully the principal scriptures in the Old Testament bearing upon our present theme.

"Babylon was a mighty city of old; its beginnings were in Shinar in the days shortly after the flood; it played an important part in the history of Israel and of Judea; it was the head of the kingdoms of the earth in the days of Nebuchadnezzar; after its capture by the Medes and Persians it fell from its high estate, but for some centuries after Christ it was still a city of importance, and the head of a district. In the New Testament it is first mentioned by Peter (1 Pet. 5:13), and here in the book that tells of the events that occur in the *Day of the Lord* we read of it as a city again dominating the world, and that at a time when Israelites are again prominent in the story of the earth. Here, too, Babylon reappears in its ancient dual aspect, political and social, the first city of earth and also the leader of the worship and religion of the world powers.

The site of old Babylon is known at the present day; it covers a wide extent of ground, and parts of it are inhabited, as for instance Hillah, where there are some five or six thousand people. When the long-talked-of Euphrates Valley Railway becomes a reality, Babylon will be one of the most important places on the line" (Col. VanSomeron—"The Great Unfolding"). This quotation supplies a brief but fairly comprehensive outline of our subject.

The earliest mention of Babel in Scripture is in connection with the name of him who first after the deluge attained to greatness in the earth—greatness apart from God. Nimrod was the grandson of Ham, who called down upon him the curse of his father, Noah. "The sons of Ham were Cush . . . . and Cush begat Nimrod: he began to be a mighty one in the earth. He was a mighty hunter before the Lord, and the beginning of his kingdom was *Babel, in the land of Shinar*" (Gen. 10:7-10). Let the reader turn back to the previous chapter for our comments on Nimrod as a type of the Antichrist. "Thus mightiness in the earth and commencement of kingly rule are first mentioned in connection with one, the seat of whose power was Babylon and the land of Shinar. Nimrod—Nebuchadnezzar—Antichrist, are, as we shall see, the three great names connected with that region and with that city" (B. W. Newton: "Babylon; Its Revival and Final Destruction"—1859).

The first mention of anything in Scripture always calls for the most particular attention, inasmuch as the initial occurrence of any term or expression in the Word of God invariably defines its meaning and forecasts its subsequent significance and scope. The passage just quoted from Gen. 10 is inseparably connected with and is in fact the key to what is found in Gen. 11. There we learn that the land of Shinar is mentioned as the place where men first united in confederate action against God. God had commanded that men should spread abroad—Gen. 9:1. But they, in blatant defiance, preferred to centralize. They determined to make for themselves a name, saying, "Go to, Let us build us *a city* and a tower, whose top may reach unto heaven; and let us make us a name, lest we be scattered abroad upon the face of the whole earth" (Gen. 11: 4). And this, we are told, was "In the *land of Shinar*" (11:2). But the Lord interfered, came down, confounded their speech, and scattered them—"And they left off to build the city. Therefore is the name of it called *Babel;* because the Lord did there confound the language of all the earth", etc. (Gen. 11:8, 9). Thus we see that at the beginning, the land of Shinar and the city of Babylon were the scene of confederate evil, and of judgment from the hand of God.

Shinar, then, was the land around Babel. Now, though the building of the city of Babylon was checked during the days of Nimrod, yet his kingdom was not overthrown. In Gen. 14:1 we read of "Amraphal king of Shinar". It would appear from several scriptures that "the land of Chaldea"—the capital of which was the city of Babylon— is but another name for "the land of Shinar". In Dan. 5: 30 Belshazzar is termed "the king of the Chaldeans", while in 7:1 he is called "the king of Babylon"—cf Isa. 47:1; Jer. 50:8; 51:54; Ezek. 12:13. In addition to these passages, Dan. 1:2, 3 seems to positively establish this conclusion, for there we are expressly told that the Babylon of Nebuchadnezzar's day was situated in "the land of *Shinar*"! This serves to confirm the fact that Chaldea or Babylonia was the most ancient of the early empires. It was from "Ur" *of Chaldea* (Gen. 11:28) that Abram was called; and it was "the *Chaldeans*" who plundered Job (Job 1:17); and in Josh. 7:21 we read of the "goodly *Babylonish* garment" which tempted Achan, among the spoils of Jericho. In striking accord with this is the statement found in Jer. 5:15, where the Holy Spirit terms the Babylonians an *"ancient"* as well as a "mighty" nation. After the days of Joshua, Babylon was not directly referred to again till the days of Esar-Haddan, of whom it is said, "And the king of Assyria brought men from Babylon, and from Cuthah, and from Ava, and from Hamath, and from Sepharvaim, and placed them in the cities of Samaria instead of the children of Israel: and they possessed Samaria, and dwelt in the cities thereof" (2 Kings 17:24, and cf Ezra 4:2). Closely connected with the land of Shinar is *Assyria*. For a time the supremacy alternated between Assyria and Babylonia, until in the days of Nabapolasser, the father of Nebuchadnezzar, Ninevah was conquered and Assyria became subject to Babylon.

But though Shinar and its capital are referred to in Gen. 10 and 11, and though there are occasional allusions to them in the centuries that followed, it was not until Israel's apostasy had been fully manifested that we find Babylon coming into the place of prominence and dominion. "Until Jerusalem had been sufficiently tried, to see whether she would prove herself worthy of being God's city, Babylon was kept in abeyance. The founder of Babylon's greatness was that great king who was raised up to scourge Jerusalem, and who commenced the 'Times of the Gentiles', by receiving from God that endowment of power which was taken from Israel, and remains vested in the Gentiles, till Jerusalem shall be forgiven and cease to be trodden down. It was Nebuchadnezzar who 'walked in the palace of the kingdom of Babylon. The king spoke and said, Is not this great Babylon which I have built for the house of the kingdom by the might of my power and for the honor of my majesty?' (Dan. 4). The *greatness* of Babylon dates only from Nebuchadnezzar" (B.W.N.).

The fifth chapter of Daniel tells how Belshazzar, the successor of Nebuchadnezzar, was slain by Darius, who took over the kingdom. Neither the city nor the kingdom was then destroyed, and so far from it being made desolate and without inhabitant, it remained for long centuries a city of note. Two hundred years after its capture by Darius, Alexander the Great, after his conquest over the Persians, selected Babylon as the intended capital of his vast dominion, and, in fact, died there. In the first century of the Christian era Babylon still stood, for Peter refers to a church there! (See 1 Pet. 5:13). Several of the church "Fathers" refer to Babylon, and at the beginning of the sixth century A.D. the famous Babylonian Talmud was issued by the Academies of Babylonia. Mr. Newton tells us that "Ibn Hankel in A.D. 917 speaks of Babylon as a small village. Even in the tenth century, therefore, it had not wholly disappeared". Slow and almost undiscernible was its decline and decay. Even in this day there is still a small town, Hillah, standing on the original site of ancient Babylon. What, then, of the future?

That there will yet be another Babylon, a Babylon eclipsing the power and glory of that of Nebuchadnezzar's day, has long been the firm conviction of the writer. Nor are we by any means alone in this conviction. A long list of honored names might be given of those who have arrived, independently, at the conclusion that the Scriptures plainly teach that Babylon is going to be re-built. But there is no need to buttress our conviction by an appeal to human authority. Better that the faith of the reader rest on the Word of God, than in the wisdom of the best of men. Before we set forth some of the many scripture *proofs* on which our conviction rests, let us ask, Would it not be passing strange if Babylon had no place in the End-time? Scripture tells us that Jerusalem, which has been so long trodden down by the Gentiles, is to be restored by human agency, and have a re-built temple (Matt. 24:15). Egypt and Assyria have yet an honored future before them, as is clear from Isa. 19:23, 24. Moab, Edom, and Seir are to figure in the coming day, as is intimated in Num. 24:17, 18. Greece awaits her final judgment from God (Zech. 9:13). And so we might go on. Why, then, should *Babylon* be exempted from the general renovation of the East?

But we are not left to logical deductions, the Word of God expressly affirms that Babylon *will* play a prominent part at the Time of the End. The empire over which the Antichrist will reign is described in the identical symbols which were applied to the four world-kingdoms of Dan. 7. In Dan. 7:3 Daniel beheld "four great beasts" come up from *the sea,* and in Dan. 7:17 we are told "these great beasts, which are four, are four kings (or kingdoms) which shall arise out of the earth". These four beasts or kingdoms were the Babylonian, the Medo-Persian, the Grecian, and the Roman. Dan. 7:4 says "The first was like a *lion*". 7:5 says "The second was like a *bear*". 7:6 says the third was "like a *leopard*". 7:7 says the fourth was "dreadful and terrible". Now, in Rev. 13:1, 2, where we have a symbolical description of the empire which the Antichrist shall head, we are told that John saw "a Beast rise up out of *the sea*", and then it is added, "the Beast . . . was like unto a *leopard,* and his feet were as the feet of a *bear,* and his mouth as the mouth of a *lion*". Of the fourth beast of Dan. 7 we read, "It had *ten horns*" (7:7) ; so in Rev. 13:1 the Beast there has *"ten horns"*. Who, then, can doubt that Rev. 13:1, 2 is given for the express purpose of teaching us that the four great world-kingdoms of the past—not merely the fourth but *all* of the four—are to be revived and restored at the Time of the End? But as this point is disputed by some, we tarry to advance further proof.

It is to be noted that the Beast (kingdom) of Rev. 13:1 is said to have "seven heads". This has puzzled many of the commentators, but once it is seen that the Beast of Rev. 13:1, 2 is a symbolic description, first of a *composite* kingdom, made up of and perpetuating the features of the four world-empires of old; and second, a symbolic description of the one who shall head it, all difficulty disappears. That we have here in Rev. 13: 1, 2 a *composite* kingdom is clear from the "seven heads". Now note that in Dan. 7 the first, second and fourth kingdoms are not said to have more than one head, but the third has *"four* heads" (Dan. 7: 6). Thus the beasts of Dan. 7 have, three of them one head each, and the third four heads, or *seven* in all; which tallies perfectly with Rev. 13:1. But even this does not exhaust the proofs that the *four kingdoms* of Dan. 7 are to be restored, and play their final parts immediately before the Millennium.

If the reader will turn to Dan. 2, which is parallel with Dan. 7—the "image" in its *four parts* (the head, the breast and arms, the belly and thighs, the legs and feet) corresponding with the *four beasts*—it will be found that when we come to v. 45, which speaks of Christ (under the figure of "the Stone cut out of the mount without hands") returning to earth to destroy the forces of evil, and then set up His kingdom, we discover that the Stone "brake in pieces the iron (Rome), the brass (Greece), the clay (apostate Israel), the silver (Medo-Persia), and the gold (Babylon). What we desire the reader to note particularly is that the Stone strikes not only the iron, but the brass, clay, silver, and gold; in fact, v. 35 tells us, expressly, they shall be "broken to pieces *together*"! If, then, they are destroyed "together", they *must* all be on the scene at the time of Christ's return to earth to inaugurate His millennial reign, and if so, each of them must have been *revived* and *restored!!* As our present inquiry concerns not the renovation of Persia, Greece and Rome, but only that of Babylon, we shall confine ourselves to the scriptures which speak of the last mentioned.

1. Isa. 13 and 14 contain a remarkable prophecy bearing directly on the theme before us. It is termed in the opening verse, "The burden of Babylon". It tells of the terrible judgment which God shall send on this city. It speaks of the total and final destruction of it. It declares that "Babylon, the glory of kingdoms, the beauty of the Chaldees' excellency, shall be as when God overthrew Sodom and Gomorrah". It shall never be inhabited, neither shall it be dwelt in from generation to generation (vv. 19, 20). Now the one point pertinent to our present inquiry is, Whether Isa. 13 describes the doom which befell the Babylon of Belshazzar's day, or the judgment which shall overtake the Babylon of the coming day. Upon this point there is, for those who desire to be subject to God's Word, no room for uncertainty. The sixth verse expressly declares that this "burden of Babylon" is to receive its fulfillment in "the Day of the Lord". This, we need hardly add, is the name for that Day which follows the present Day of Salvation (2 Cor. 6:2). If the reader will consult a concordance he will find that "the Day of the Lord" nev-

er refers to a period now past, but always has reference to one which is yet future! If any doubt remains as to whether or not Isa.13 is speaking of a *future* Day, the contents of v. 10 should forever remove it. There we are told that "the stars of heaven and the constellation thereof shall not give their light: the sun shall be darkened in his going forth, and the moon shall not cause her light to shine". All students of prophecy will see at a glance that these cosmic phenomena are what are to be witnessed during the Tribulation period—cf Matt. 24:29. There is not a hint anywhere either in Scripture or (so far as we are aware) in secular history, that such disturbances among the heavenly bodies occurred at the captivity of Babylon by Darius. And it is at *that* time, in "the Day of the Lord" when the sun is darkened and the moon shines not, that Babylon is overthrown (v. 19). This one scripture is quite sufficient to establish the futurity of Babylon and its coming overthrow*.

2. The 14th of Isaiah reads right on from 13, completing the "burden of Babylon" there begun. It supplies further proof that there is to be another Babylon. The chapter opens with a declaration of Israel's coming restoration. It declares "the Lord will have mercy on Jacob, and will yet choose Israel, and set them in their own land" (v. 1). It goes on to say, "It shall come to pass *in the day that* the Lord shall give thee rest from thy sorrow, and from thy fear, and from the hard bondage wherein thou wast made to serve, That thou shalt take up this taunting speech against the king of *Babylon,* and say, How hath the oppressor ceased! the golden city ceased!" (vv. 3, 4). Should the quibble be raised that these verses are speaking

---

* There is no room for a quibble about the meaning of "Babylon", for v. 19 expressly terms it "The beauty of the *Chaldees'* excellency".

of the restoration of Israel to Palestine following the captivity of Nebuchadnezzar's time, it is easily silenced. The verses that follow those just quoted make it unmistakeably clear that this prophecy *yet awaits* its fulfillment. Thus we read in vv. 7, 8, "The whole earth is at rest, and is quiet: they break forth into singing. Yea, the fir trees rejoice at thee, and the cedars of Lebanon, saying, Since thou art laid down, no feller is come up against us". The whole earth never has been "at rest" since the days of Cain (except it were during the brief period when the Word tabernacled among men). But it will be during the Millennium! Notice, too, that following the overthrow of "the golden city", Israel exclaims, "Since thou art laid down, (laid low) *no* feller (no *cutter off*) is come up against us"! This establishes, unequivocally, the time of which this prophecy treats. Long after the days of Belshazzar, the Romans came up against Israel and cut them off. But none shall do this again when the *last* king of Babylon is destroyed!

Above, we have quoted to the end of the 8th verse of Isa. 14. In the 9th verse the prophet suddenly turns from Babylon to its last king. Verses 9 to 20 contain a striking portrait of the lofty arrogance and fearful doom of the Man of Sin. Then, in verse 21, the "burden" returns again to the *subjects* of the Antichrist: "Prepare slaughter for his children for the iniquity of their fathers; that they do not rise, nor possess the land, nor fill the face of the world with cities. For I will rise up against them, saith the Lord of hosts, and cut off from Babylon the name, and remnant, and son, and nephew, saith the Lord. I will also make it a possession for the bittern, and pools of water: and I will sweep it with the besom of destruction, saith the Lord of hosts" (vv. 21-23). Finally, the prophet

concludes with a parting word concerning the Antichrist:
"The Lord of hosts hath sworn, saying, Surely as I have
thought, so shall it come to pass; and as I have purposed,
so shall it stand: That I will break the Assyrian in my
land, and upon my mountains tread him under foot: then
shall his yoke depart from off them, and his burden depart from off their shoulders. This is the purpose that
is purposed upon the whole earth: and this is the hand
that is stretched upon all the nations. For the Lord of
hosts hath purposed, and who shall disannul it? And His
hand is stretched out, and who shall turn it back?" (vv.
24-27). Well has it been said, "These are remarkable
and significant words, and certainly we cannot say they
have been fulfilled. Will any one affirm that God's purpose which He hath purposed upon the whole earth was
accomplished when Babylon was overthrown by the Medes
and Persians? Did the hand that was stretched out over
all the nations, *then* fulfill its ultimate designs? Was the
Assyrian then trodden under foot in THE LAND, AND
ON THE MOUNTAINS OF ISRAEL, and, that at a time
when the yoke of bondage is finally broken from off the
neck of Israel? If this were so we should no longer see
Jerusalem trodden down now. 'The times of the Gentiles'
would have ended. Israel would be gathered, and Jerusalem be 'a praise in the earth'. The concluding words of
this prophecy, therefore, might alone convince us that it
yet remains to be fulfilled" (B. W. N.).

3. We appeal next to the 50th chapter of Jeremiah. The
opening verses contain a prophecy which certainly has not
received its complete fulfillment in the past. It declares,
"The words that the Lord spake against Babylon and
against the land of the Chaldeans by Jeremiah the prophet. Declare ye among the nations, and publish, and set

up a standard; publish, and conceal not: say, Babylon is taken, Bel is confounded, Merodach is broken in pieces; her idols are confounded, her images are broken in pieces. For out of the north there cometh up a nation against her, which shall make her land desolate, and none shall dwell therein: they shall remove, they shall depart, both man and beast. In those days, *and in that time,* saith the Lord, the children of Israel shall come, they and the children of Judah *together,* going and weeping: they shall go, and seek the Lord their God. They shall ask the way to Zion with their faces thitherward, saying, Come, and let us join ourselves to the Lord in a perpetual covenant which shall not be forgotten" (vv. 1-5). Mark carefully three things in these verses. First, it is announced that the *land* of Babylon shall be made so desolate that neither man nor beast shall dwell therein. Second, the time for this is defined as being when Israel and Judah *together* (and since the days of Rehoboam they have never been united) shall "seek the Lord". Third, it is when Israel and Judah shall join themselves to the Lord in "a perpetual covenant"! Still more explicit is the time-mark in v. 20: *"In those days, and in that time,* saith the Lord, the iniquity of Israel shall be sought for, and there shall be *none;* and the sins of Judah, and they shall not be found".

4. The whole of Jer. 51 should be carefully studied in this connection. Much in it we reserve for consideration in the two chapters which will follow this. Here we simply call attention to vv. 47-49: "Therefore, behold, the days come, that I will do judgment upon the graven images of Babylon: and her whole land shall be confounded, and all her slain shall fall in the midst of her. Then the heaven and the earth, and all that is therein, shall sing for Babylon: for the Spoiler shall come upon her from the north,

saith the Lord. As Babylon hath caused the slain of Israel to fall, so at Babylon shall fall the slain of all the earth". Surely little comment is needed here. When did the slain "of all the earth" (i. e. of all nations) fall in the midst of Babylon? And when did heaven and earth and all that is therein rejoice at her overthrow? "When Babylon passed into the hands of the Medes there was little occasion for such joy. It made little difference to the earth whether Babylon was reigned over by Chaldeans, or by Persians, or Greeks, or Romans, There was little cause for thanksgiving in *such* transfer of authority from one proud hand to another. But if there be a fall of Babylon that is to be immediately succeeded by the kingdom of Him, of whom it is said, 'All nations shall call Him blessed' . . . . then there is indeed sufficient reason why heaven and earth, and all that is therein should sing" (B. W. N.).

5. "Be in pain, and labour to bring forth, O daughter of Zion, like a woman in travail: for now shalt thou go forth out of the city, and thou shalt dwell in the field, and thou shalt go even to *Babylon;* there shalt thou be delivered; *there* the Lord shall redeem thee from the hand of thine enemies" (Micah 4:10). In the light of such scriptures as Micah 5:3, Matt. 24:8 ("sorrows" literally means "birth-pangs"), etc., there can be no room for doubt as to the time to which this prophecy refers. It is at the close of the Great Tribulation. And at that time a remnant of Israel will be found in *Babylon* and they shall be delivered by the Lord.

6. Both the prophecies of Isaiah and Jeremiah as well as the Apocalypse speak of the *immediateness* of the blow which is to destroy Babylon. "Come down, and sit in the dust, O virgin daughter of Babylon, sit on the ground:

there is no throne, O daughter of the Chaldeans: for thou shalt no more be called tender and delicate . . . . therefore hear now this, thou that art given to pleasures, that dwellest carelessly, that sayest in thine heart I am, and none else besides me; I shall not sit as a widow, neither shall I know the loss of children: But these two things shall come to thee *in a moment, in one day,* the loss of children, and widowhood: they shall come upon thee in thy perfection for the multitude of thy sorceries, and for the great abundance of thine enchantments" (Isa. 47:1, 8, 9). "Babylon is *suddenly* fallen and destroyed: howl for her" (Jer. 51:8). "Alas, alas, that great city Babylon, that mighty city! for *in one hour* is thy judgment come" (Rev. 18: 10). There has been nothing in the past history of Babylon which in any-wise corresponds with these prophecies.

7. Isaiah, Jeremiah, and the Revelation each declare that Babylon shall be *burned* with fire. "And Babylon, the glory of kingdoms, the beauty of the Chaldees' excellency shall be *as* when God overthrew *Sodom and Gomorrah*" (Isa. 13:19). "The mighty men of Babylon have forborne to fight, they have remained in their holes: their might hath failed; they became as women: they have *burned* her dwelling places; her bars are broken. . . . Thus saith the Lord of hosts; the broad walls of Babylon shall be utterly broken, and her high gates shall be *burned with fire*" (Jer. 51:30, 58). "And cried when they saw the smoke of her *burning,* saying, What city is like unto this great city!" (Rev. 18:18). We know of nothing in either Scripture or secular history which shows that Babylon was "burned" *in the past.*

"But it will be said, perhaps, How can this be? Has not Babylon already been smitten? Has it not already been swept with the besom of destruction? Our answer is—Not

at the time and with the concomitant circumstances speci-
fied in the passages just quoted. It is true indeed that the
Euphratean countries have been smitten—sorely smitten
under the hand of God. God is wont in His goodness to
give premonitory blows—He is accustomed to warn before
He finally destroys. Egypt, Jerusalem, and many other
places, have all experienced premonitory desolations, and
so has Babylon. Its present ruin (which came on it slow-
ly, and if I may so speak, gently), is a memorial of what
God's righteous vengeance can do, and a warning of what
it will more terribly do, if human pride in contempt of all
His admonitions, shall again attempt to rear its goodly
palaces when He has written desolation. But if it be the
habit of God thus graciously to warn, it is equally the
habit of man to say, 'The bricks are fallen down, but we
will build with hewn stone; the sycamores are cut down,
but we will change them into cedars'. Unbidden, the
hand of man revived what God had smitten (that is what
happened in Chicago and San Francisco! A.W.P.). Without therefore undervaluing the lesson given by past visi-
tations of God's judgments—without hiding, but rather
seeking to proclaim the reality and extent of the ruin, His
holy hand has wrought, we have also to testify, that the
hand of man uncommissioned from above will, sooner or
later, reconstruct the fabric of its greatness—its last evil
greatness, on the very plains which teem with the me-
morials of a ruin entailed by former and yet unrepented of
transgressions. Egypt, Damascus, Palestine, and in a
measure, Jerusalem, are already being revived. And if
these and neighboring countries which have been visited
by inflictions similar to those which have fallen on Babylon, are yet to revive and flourish with an evil prosperity

at the time of the end, why should *Babylon* be made an exception?" (B.W.N.).

That the Antichrist will be intimately connected with the land of Chaldea is clear from a number of scriptures, notably, those which speak of him as "the Assyrian" and "the king of Babylon". But as this is a disputed point we are obliged to pause and make proof of it. Let us turn, then, first to Isa. 10 and 11 which form one continuous prophecy. We can not now attempt even an outline of this long and interesting prediction, but must merely single out one or two statements from it which bear on the point now before us.

In the fifth verse of Isa. 10, the Lord addresses the Antichrist as follows: "O Assyrian, the rod of mine anger, and the staff in their hand is mine indignation". This intimates, as pointed out in a previous chapter, that the Son of Perdition is but a tool in the hands of the Almighty, His instrument for threshing Israel. His consuming egotism and haughtiness come out plainly in the verses that follow (7-11). But when God has accomplished His purpose by him, He "will punish the fruit of the stout heart of the king of Assyria, and the glory of his high looks" (v. 12). How this serves to identify him with the "little horn" of Dan. 7:20, the Man of Sin of 2 Thess. 2:4!—cf further his proud boastings recorded in Isa. 10:13, 14. In v. 23 is another statement which helps us to fix with certainty the period of which the prophet is speaking, and the central actors there in view: "For a consummation, and that determined, shall the Lord, the Lord of hosts, make in the midst of all the earth" (R.V.). The words "consummation" and "that determined" occur again in Dan. 9:27—"He (Antichrist) shall make it (the temple) desolate, even until *the consummation, and that determined*

shall be poured upon the Desolator". The "King of Assyria" and "the Desolator" are thus shown to be the same.
In Isa. 10, vv. 24 and 25 we read, "Therefore thus saith
the Lord God of hosts, O My people that dwellest in Zion,
be not afraid of the Assyrian: he shall smite thee with a
rod, and shall lift up his staff against thee, after the manner of Egypt. For yet a very little while, and *the indignation shall cease,* and Mine anger in their destruction."
Clearly this is parallel with Dan. 11:36: "And the King
shall do according to his will; and he shall exalt himself,
and magnify himself above every god, and shall speak
marvellous things against the God of gods, and shall prosper till *the indignation be accomplished."* In the 11th
chapter of Isaiah there is a statement even clearer, a proof
conclusive and decisive: "And He shall smite the earth
with the rod of His mouth and with the breath of His lips
shall He slay the wicked" (11:4). These very words are
applied to the Man of Sin in 2 Thess. 2:8.

In Isa. 14 we have a scripture which very clearly connects the Antichrist with Babylon. The opening verses
(which really form a parenthesis) tell of the coming restoration of Israel to Jehovah's favor, and then in v. 4 they
are bidden to take up "a taunting speech (marginal rendering) against the King of Babylon". The taunting
speech begins thus: "How hath the Oppressor ceased! the
golden city ceased! the Lord hath broken the staff of the
Wicked" (vv. 4, 5). As to *who* is in view here there is
surely no room for doubt. He is Israel's Oppressor in the
End-time; he is the Wicked One. In the verses which follow there are many marks by which he may be positively
identified. In v. 6 this "King of Babylon" is said to be
"He who smote the people (i. e. Israel) in wrath with a
continual stroke". In v. 12 he is called "Lucifer (Day-

star), Son of the morning", a title which marks him out as none other than the Son of Perdition. Whatever backward reference to the fall of Satan there may be in this verse and the ones that follow, it is clear that they describe the blasphemous arrogance of the Antichrist. In v. 13 we read, "For thou hast said in thine heart, I will ascend into heaven, I will exalt my throne above the stars of God: I will sit also upon the mount of the congregation, in the sides of the north". Then, in vv. 15 and 16 we are told, "Yet thou shalt be brought down to hell, to the sides of the Pit. They that see thee shall narrowly look upon thee, and consider thee, saying, Is this the *man* that made the earth to tremble, that did shake kingdoms?" Clearly it is the Man of Sin that is here in view.

In Isa. 30 we have another scripture which links Antichrist with Babylonia. Beginning at v. 27 we read: "Behold, the name of the Lord cometh from far, burning with His anger, and the burning thereof is heavy: his lips are full of indignation, and his tongue as a devouring fire: And his breath, as an over-flowing stream, shall reach to the midst of the neck, to sift the nations with the sieve of vanity: and there shall be a bridle in the jaws of the people, causing them to err. Ye shall have a song, as in the night when a holy solemnity is kept; and gladness of heart, as when one goeth with a pipe to come into the mountain of the Lord, to the mighty One of Israel". Clearly it is the very end of the Tribulation period which is here in view. The reference is to the return of the Lord to earth in great power and glory, when He shall overthrow those who are gathered together against Him, and put an end to the awful career of the Antichrist. Continuing, we find this passage in Isa. 30 closes as follows: "For through the voice of the Lord shall *the Assyrian* be beaten down, which smote with a rod. And in every place where the grounded staff shall pass, which the Lord shall lay upon him, it shall be with tabrets and harps: and in battles of shaking will he fight with it. For Tophet is ordained of old; yea, for the King it is prepared; He hath made it deep and large: the pile thereof is fire and much wood; the breath of the Lord, like a stream of brimstone, doth kindle it"—cf "the breath of the Lord" here with Isa. 11:4. For further references to Antichrist and Assyria see Isa. 7:17-20; 8:7, etc.

The next two chapters will be devoted to a consideration of Babylon in the New Testament, when Rev. 17 and 18 will come before us. May the Lord in His grace give us the wisdom we so sorely need, and preserve the writer and reader from all error.

14

BABYLON AND THE ANTICHRIST
(Continued)

IN the last chapter we confined ourself to the Old Testament, in this and the one that follows we shall treat mainly of Babylon in Rev. 17 and 18, though, of necessity, we shall examine these in the light of Old Testament passages. In the previous chapter, we briefly reviewed the Old Testament evidence which proves there is to be a re-built Babylon, over which the Antichrist shall reign during the Time of the End. Now as both the Old and New Testaments have one and the same Divine Author, it cannot be that the latter should conflict with the former. "If the Old and New Testaments treat of the circumstances which are immediately to precede the Advent of the Lord in glory, the substantive facts of that period must be alike referred to in both. If the Old Testament declares that Babylon and 'the Land of Shinar' is to be the focus of influential wickedness at the time of the end, it is impossible that the Revelation, when professedly treating of the same period, should be silent respecting such wickedness, or respecting the place of its concentration. If the Old Testament speaks of an individual of surpassing power who will connect himself with this wickedness, and be the king of Babylon, and glorify himself as God, it is not to be supposed that the Revelation should treat of the same period and be silent respecting such an event. If, therefore, in the Old Testament, the sphere be fixed—the locality named—the individual defined—it is impossible that the Revelation, when *detailing the events of the same period,* should alter the localities, or change the individuals. There cannot be two sovereign individ-

uals, nor two sovereign cities in the same sphere at the
same time. If the mention of the 'Land of Shinar', and of
'Assyria', and of 'the king of Babylon', be intended in the
Old Testament to render our thoughts fixed and definite,
why should similar terms, applied in the Revelation to a
period avowedly the same, be less definite?" (B.W.New-
ton).

Of Rev. 17 and 18 it has been well said, "There is, perhaps, no section of the Apocalypse more fraught with difficulty than the predictions concerning Babylon. Enig-
matical and inconsistent with each other as, at first sight,
they seem to be, we need to give careful attention to every
particular, and much patient investigation of other scriptures, if we would penetrate their meaning and possess
ourselves of their secret" (Mr. G. H. Pember, M.A.). In
prosecuting our present study we cannot do better than
borrow again from the language of Mr. Pember, "Nor is
the present necessarily brief and imperfect essay written
in any spirit of dogmatic certainty that it solves the mystery; but only as the conclusion, so far as light has been
already vouchsafed, to one who, having received mercy of
the Lord, has been led to much consideration of this and
kindred subjects".

An exposition of the Revelation or any part thereof
should be the last place for dogmatism. Both at the beginning and close of the book the Holy Spirit expressly
states that the Apocalypse is a "prophecy" (1:3; 22:19),
and prophecy is, admittedly, the most difficult branch of
Scripture study. It is true that during the last century
God has been pleased to give His people not a little light
upon the predictive portions of His Word, nor is the Apocalypse to be excepted. Yet, the more any one reads the
literature on the subject, the more should he become con-

vinced that dogmatism here is altogether unseemly. During the last fifteen years the writer has made it a point to read the Revelation through carefully at least three times a year, and during this period he has also gone through over thirty commentaries on the last book of the Bible. A perusal of the varied and conflicting interpretations advanced have taught him two things: First, the wisdom of being cautious in adopting any of the prevailing views; second, the need of patient and direct waiting on God for further light. To these may be added a third, namely, the possibility, yea, the probability, that many of the prophecies of the Revelation are to receive a double, and in some cases, a treble, fulfillment.

"All Scripture is given by inspiration of God, and is *profitable"*. This applies equally to the Prophets as to the Epistles, and it was just as true five hundred years ago as it is today. That being so, the right understanding of the *final* fulfillment of the prophecies in the Revelation cannot be the only value that book possesses. There must also be that in it which had a pertinent and timely message for the people of God of this dispensation in *each* generation. There must be that in it which strengthened the faith of those saints who read it during the "Dark Ages", and that which enabled them to detect and keep clear from that which was opposed to God and His Christ. In other words, its prophecies must have received a gradual and partial fulfillment all through the centuries of the Christian era, though their final fulfillment be yet future. Such is the case with Rev. 17 and 18. Ever since John received the Revelation there has always existed a system which, in its *moral features,* has corresponded to the Babylon of the 17th chapter. There exists such a system today; there will exist such a system after the Church is raptured to

heaven. And there will also come into existence another and final system which will 'exhaust the scope of this prophecy.

The position which the Apocalypse occupies in the Sacred Canon is surely indicative of the character of its contents. The fact that it is placed at the close, at once suggests that it treats of that which concerns the *end* of things. Moreover, it is taken for granted that the student of this sixty-sixth book of the Bible is already acquainted with the previous sixty-five books. Scripture is self-interpreting, and we may rest assured that whatever appears vague or difficult in the last book of Scripture is due to our ignorance of the meaning of the books preceding, and particularly of the Prophets. In the Apocalypse the various streams of prediction, which may be traced through the Old Testament Scriptures, are seen emptying themselves in the sea of historical accomplishment. Or, to change the figure, here we are given to behold the last act of the great Dispensational Drama, the earlier acts of which were depicted in the writings of the seers of Israel. And yet, as previously intimated, these final scenes have already had a preliminary rehearsal during the course of the Christian centuries.

It will thus be seen that we are far from sharing the views of those who *limit* the prophecies of the Revelation to a *single* fulfillment. We believe there is much of truth in both the Historical and Futurist interpretations. We are in entire accord with the following words from the pen of our esteemed brother, Mr. F. C. Jennings: "How many of the controversies that have ruled, alas, amongst the Lord's people, have been due to a narrow way of limiting the thoughts of God, and seeking to confine or bend them by our own apprehension of them. How often two, or more, apparently opposing systems of interpretation may really both be correct; the breadth, the length, and height, and depth, of the mind of God, including and going beyond both of them". Let us now come more directly to our present theme.

The first time that Babylon is mentioned in the Apocalypse is in 14:8: "And there followed another angel, saying, Babylon is fallen, is fallen, that great city, because she made all nations drink of the wine of the wrath of her fornication". Now what is there here to discountenance the natural conclusion that "Babylon" means *Babylon?* Two or three generations ago, students of prophecy received incalculable help from the simple discovery that when the Holy Spirit spoke of Judea and Jerusalem in the Old Testament Scriptures He meant Judea and Jerusalem, and not England and London; and that when He mentioned Zion He did not refer to the Church. But strange to say, few, if any of these brethren, have applied the same rule to the Apocalypse. Here they are guilty of doing the very thing for which they condemned their forebears in connection with the Old Testament—they have "spiritualised". They have concluded, or rather, they have accepted the conclusions of the Reformers, that Babylon meant Papal Rome, ultimately being refined to signify apostate Christendom. But what is there in Rev. 14:8 which gives any hint that "Babylon" there refers to the Papal system? No; we believe that this scripture means what it says, and that we need not the annals of secular history to help us to understand it. What then? If to regard "Jerusalem" as meaning *Jerusalem* be a test of intelligence in Old Testament prophecy, shall we be counted a heretic if we understand "Babylon" to mean *Babylon,* and not Rome or apostate Christendom?

The next reference to Babylon is in Rev. 16:18, 19: "And there were voices, and thunders, and lightnings; and there was a great earthquake, such as was not since men were upon the earth, so mighty an earthquake, and so great. And the great city was divided into three parts, and the cities of the nations fell: and great Babylon came in remembrance before God, to give unto her the cup of the wine of the fierceness of His wrath". The remarks just made above apply with equal force to this passage too. Surely it is a literal city which is in view, and which is divided into three parts by a literal earthquake. If it does not mean this then the simple reader might as well turn from the Apocalypse in dismay. More than a hint of the literalness of this great city Babylon is found in the context, where we read of the river *Euphrates* (v. 12). This is sufficient for the writer: whether or not it is for the reader, we must leave with him.

We come now to Rev. 17, and as soon as we read its contents we are at once struck with the noticeable difference there is between it and the other passages which have just been before us. Here the language is no longer to be understood literally, but symbolically; here the terms are not plain and simple, but occult and mysterious. But God, in His grace, has provided help right to hand. He *tells us* that here is "mystery" (v. 5). And what is more, He *explains* most (if not all) of the symbols for us—see vv. 9, 12, 15, 18. With these helps furnished it ought not to be difficult to grasp the general outline.

The central figures in Rev. 17 are "the great whore", the "scarlet-colored Beast", and the "ten horns". The Beast is evidently the first Beast of Rev. 13. The "ten horns" are stated to be "ten kings" (v. 12). Who, then, is figured by "the great Whore"? There are a number of statements

made concerning "the great Whore"—"the woman"—
"the Mother of harlots"—which are of great help toward
supplying an answer to this question. First, it is said that
she "sitteth upon many waters" (v. 1), and in v. 15 these
are said to signify "peoples, and multitudes, and nations,
and tongues". Second, it is said, "The kings of the earth
have committed fornication" with her (v. 2). Third, she
is supported by "a scarlet-colored Beast" (v. 3), and from
what is said of this Beast in v. 8 it is clear that he is the
Antichrist, here viewed at the head of the last world-empire. Fourth, the woman "was arrayed in purple and
scarlet color and decked with gold and precious stones" (v.
4). Fifth, "Upon her forehead was a name written—Mystery: Babylon the great", etc. (v. 5). Sixth, the woman
was "drunken with the blood of the saints and with the
blood of the martyrs" (v. 6). Seventh, in the last verse it
is said, "And the woman which thou sawest is that great
city, which reigneth over the kings of the earth". These
seven points give an analysed summary of what is here
told us about this "woman".

Now the interpretation which has been most widely accepted is, that the "Whore" of Rev. 17 pictures the Roman
Catholic system. Appeal is made to the fact that though
she poses as a virgin, yet has she been guilty of the most
awful spiritual fornication. Unlike the blessed One, who,
in His condescension and humiliation, had "not where to
lay His head", Romanism has coveted silver and gold, and
has displayed herself in meretricious luxury. She has had
illicit intercourse with the kings of the earth, and she has
made herself drunken with the blood of saints. Other
parallelisms between the woman of Rev. 17 and the Roman Catholic system may be pointed out. What, then,
shall we say to these things?

The points of correspondence between Rev. 17 and the history of Romanism are too many and too marked to be set down as mere co-incidences. Undoubtedly the Papacy has supplied *a* fulfillment of the symbolic prophecy found in Rev. 17. And therein has lain its practical value for God's people all through the dark ages. It presented to them a warning too plain to be disregarded. It was the means of keeping the garments of the Waldenses (and many others) unspotted by her filth. It confirmed the faith of Luther and his contemporaries, that they were acting according to the revealed will of God, when they separated themselves from that which was so manifestly opposed to His truth. But, nevertheless, there are other features in this prophecy which *do not* apply to Romanism, and which compel us to look elsewhere for the *complete* and *final* fulfillment. We single out but two of these.

In Rev. 17:5 Babylon is termed *"the Mother* of harlots and abominations of the earth". Is this an accurate description of Romanism? Were there no "harlot" systems before her? Is the Papacy the *mother* of the "abominations of the earth"? Let scripture be allowed to interpret scripture. In 1 Kings 11:5-7 we read of "Ashtoreth the goddess of the Zidonians, and after Milcom the *abomination* of the Ammonites . . . . then did Solomon build an high place for Chemosh, the *abomination* of Moab, in the hill that was before Jerusalem, and for Molech, the *abomination* of the children of Ammon"! The Papacy had not come into existence when John wrote the Revelation, so that *she* cannot be held responsible for all the "abominations" which preceded her. Again; in Rev. 17:2 we read of "the great Whore" that "the kings *of the earth* have committed fornication" with her. Is that applicable in its fulness to Rome? Have the kings of Asia and the kings of Africa committed fornication with the Papacy? It is true that the Italian pontiffs have ruled over a wide territory, yet it is also true that there are many lands which have remained untouched by their religious influence.

It is evident from these two points alone that we have to go back to something which long antedates the rise of the Papacy, and to something which has exerted a far wider influence than has any of the popes. What, then, is this something? and where shall we look for it? The answer is not hard to find: the word "Babylon" supplies us with the needed key. Babylon takes us back not merely to the days of Nebuchadnezzar, but to the time of *Nimrod*. It was in the days of the son of Cush that "Babylon" began. And from the Plain of Shinar has flown that dark stream whose tributaries have reached to *every* part of the earth. It was then, and there, that idolatry began. In his work on "The Two Babylons"* Dr. Hislop has proven conclusively that all the idolatrous systems of the nations had their origin in what was founded by that mighty Rebel, the beginning of whose kingdom was Babel (Gen. 10:10). But into this we cannot now enter at length. We refer the reader back to our comments on Nimrod in chapter 13. Babylon was founded in rebellion against God. The very name Nimrod gave to his city, proves him to have been an idolator—the *first* mentioned in Scripture—for Bab-El signified "the gate of God"; thus he, like his anti-type, determined to exalt himself above all that is called God (2 Thess. 2:4). This, then, was the source and origin of all idolatry. Pagan Rome, afterwards Papal Rome, was only one of the polluted streams from this corrupt source—one of the filthy "daughters" of this unclean Mother of Harlots. But to return to Rev. 17.

---

* A book of intense interest for the antiquarian, but dull and wearisome for the average reader.

In v. 5 we read, "And upon her forehead was a name written—mystery: Babylon the great, the Mother of harlots and abominations of the earth". We believe that the English translators have misled many by printing (on their own authority) the word "mystery" in large capital letters, thus making it appear that this was a part of "the woman's" name. This we are assured is a mistake. That the "mystery" is connected with the "Woman" herself and not with her "name" is clear from v. 7, where the angel says unto John, "I will tell thee *the mystery of the Woman,* and of the Beast which carrieth her".

The word "mystery" is used in the New Testament in two ways. First, as a *secret,* unfathomable by man but explained by God: see Matt. 13:11; Rom. 16:25, 26; Eph. 3:3, 6, etc. Second, the word "mystery" signifies a *sign* or *symbol.* Such is its meaning in Eph. 5:32, where we are told that a man who is joined to his wife so that the two become "one flesh" is a "great mystery, (that is, a "great sign" or "symbol") of Christ and the Church". So, again, in Rev. 1:20 we read of "the mystery (sign or symbol) of the seven stars", etc.

As we have seen, the term "mystery" has *two* significations in its New Testament usage, and we believe it has a *double* meaning in Rev. 17:5, where it is connected with the "Woman". It signifies both a *symbol* and a *secret,* that is, something not previously revealed. It should also be noted that, in keeping with this, the name given to the Woman is a *dual* one—"Babylon the great", *and* "the Mother of harlots and abominations of the earth". Who, then, is symbolized by the Woman with this dual name? V. 18 tells us, "And the Woman which thou sawest is that great city, which reigneth over the kings of the earth". Now to get the force of this it is essential that we should bear in mind that, in the Apocalypse, the words "is" and "are" almost always (in the symbolical sections) signify *"represent"*. Thus, in 1:20 "the seven stars *are* the seven churches" means "the seven stars *represent* the seven churches"; and "the seven candlesticks *are* the seven churches", signifies, "the seven candlesticks *represent* the seven churches". So in 17:9 "the seven heads *are* (represent) seven mountains"; 17:12 "the ten horns *are* (represent) ten kings"; 17:15 "the waters . . . . *are* (represent) peoples", etc. So in 17:18 "the woman which thou sawest *is* that great city" must mean "the woman *represents* that great city". What, then, is signified by the "great city"?

In keeping with what we have just said above, namely, that the term "mystery" in Rev. 17:5 has a two-fold significance, and that the woman has a dual name, so we believe "that Great City" has a *double* force and application. First, it signifies a *literal* city, which shall yet be built in "the Land of Shinar", on the banks of the "Euphrates". Proof of this was furnished in our last chapter so that we need not pause here to submit the evidence. *Six* times (significant number!) is "Babylon" referred to in the Apocalypse, and nowhere is there a hint that the name is not to be understood literally. In the second place, the "great city" (unnamed) signifies an *idolatrous system*— "mother of harlots" a system of idolatry which originated in the Babylon of Nimrod's day, and a system which is to culminate and terminate in another Babylon in a day soon to come. This we think is clear and on the surface. What, then, is the *secret* here disclosed, which had hitherto been so closely guarded?

In seeking the answer to our last question it is important to note that there is another "Woman" in the Revelation, between whom and this one in chapter 17 there are some striking comparisons and some vivid contrasts. Let us note a few of them. First, in Rev. 12:1 we read of "a Woman clothed with the sun, and the moon under her feet, and upon her head a crown of twelve stars", which symbolically signifies that she occupies a position of *authority* and *rule* (cf Gen. 37:9); so also the Woman of chapter 17 is pictured as "ruling over the kings of the earth" (v. 18). Second, this Woman of Rev. 12 is a mother, for she gives birth to the Man-child who shall rule all nations (v. 5); so the Woman of chapter 17 is "the *Mother* of harlots". Third, in 12:3 we read of a great red Dragon "having seven heads and ten horns", and he *persecutes* the Woman (v. 14); but in striking contrast, the Woman of chapter 17 is seen *supported by* a scarlet-colored Beast "having seven heads and ten horns" (v. 3). Fourth, in Rev. 19:7 the Woman of chapter 12 is termed the Lamb's Wife (v. 7); whereas the Woman of chapter 17 is the Devil's Whore. Fifth, the Wife of Rev. 19 is "arrayed in fine linen, clean and white" (v. 8); but the Whore of chapter 19 is arrayed in purple and scarlet, and has in her hand a golden cup "full of abominations and filthiness of her fornication" (v. 4). Sixth, the Lamb's Wife is also inseparably connected with a great city, even the holy Jerusalem (21:10); so the Whore of Rev. 17 is connected with a great city, even Babylon. Seventh, the chaste Woman shall dwell with the Lamb forever; the Whore shall suffer endless torment in the Lake of Fire.

Once we learn who is symbolized by the chaste Woman, we are in the position to identify the corrupt Woman, who is compared and contrasted with her. As to whom is signified by the former, there is surely little room for doubt— it is the faithful portion of Israel. *She* is the one who gave birth to the Man-child—i. e. Judah, in contrast from the unfaithful ten tribes, who because of idolatry were, at the time of the Incarnation, in captivity. So in Rev. 19 and 21 there are a number of things which show clearly (to any unprejudiced mind) that the Bride, the Lamb's Wife, is redeemed Israel, and not the Church. For example, in Rev. 19:6, 7, when praise bursts forth because the marriage of the Lamb is come, a great multitude cry, *"Alleluia:* for the Lord God omnipotent reigneth. Let us be glad and rejoice, and give honor to Him: *for* the marriage of the Lamb is come". "Alleluia (which occurs nowhere in the New Testament but in this chapter) is a peculiarly *Hebrew* expression, meaning "Praise the Lord". In the second place, the word for "marriage" (gamos) or "wedding-feast" is the same as is used in Matt. 22:2, 3, 8, 11, 12, where, surely, it is *Israel* that is in view. In the third place, note that we are told "His wife hath *made herself ready"* (v. 7). Contrast this with Eph. 5:26, where we learn that *Christ* will make the Church ready—see Matt. 23:39 for *Israel* making herself "ready". In the fourth place, in 19:8 we read, "And to her was granted that *she should be* arrayed in fine linen, clean and white, for the fine linen is the righteousness of saints". The Church will have been arrayed years before the time contemplated here. In the fifth place, note it is said that "the marriage of the Lamb is come" (v. 7), just as He is on the point of leaving heaven for earth (v. 11); but the Church will have been with Him in the Father's House for at least seven years (probably forty years, or more) when that hour strikes. In the sixth place, in Rev. 21:9, 10 the Lamb's Wife is inseparably connected with that great city, the holy *Jerusalem,* and in the description which follows we are told that on the twelve gates of the city were written "the names of the twelve tribes of the children *of Israel"*

(v. 12) ! Surely that is conclusive evidence that it is not the Church which is in view. In the seventh place, in Rev. 21:14 we are told that in the twelve foundations of the City's wall were "the names of the twelve apostles of the Lamb" (cf Matt. 19:28!). Is it thinkable that the name of the apostle *Paul* would have been omitted if the Church was there symbolically portrayed?*

If, then, the Chaste Woman of Rev. 12, 19, 21, symbolizes *faithful* Israel, must not the Corrupt Woman (who is compared and contrasted with the former) represent *faithless* Israel? But if so, *why* connect her so intimately with Babylon, the "great city"? It will help us here to remember that the Chaste Woman of the Apocalypse is also indissolubly united to a city. In Rev. 21:9 we read that one of the seven angels said to John, "Come hither, *I will show thee the Bride,* the Lamb's Wife". And immediately following we read, "And he carried me away in the spirit to a great and high mountain, *and showed me that great city,* the holy Jerusalem, descending out of heaven from God". Thus, though separate, the two are intimately connected. The Bride *will dwell* in the holy Jerusalem. So here in Rev. 17, though distinct, the Whore is intimately related to the City, Babylon. One of the many proofs that the Harlot of Rev. 17 is apostate Israel is found in Isa. 1, where we read, "How is the faithful city become an *harlot*"! (v. 21). In the verses which follow it will be seen that the Lord of hosts is addressing Israel, and describing conditions which will prevail in the End-time. After indicting Israel for her sins, the Lord declares, "I

---

* "He that *hath* the Bride" (John 3:29), spoken by John the Baptist—the "friend of the Bridegroom"—demonstrates that "the Bride" was in view during our Lord's ministry unto the lost sheep of the house of Israel. The believing Remnant who "received" Him, form the nucleus and were representative of redeemed Israel, millennial Israel, the Bride of the Lamb.

will ease Me of Mine adversaries, and avenge Me of Mine enemies". Clearly, this has reference to the Tribulation period. Then the Lord continues, "And I will turn Mine hand upon thee, and purely purge away thy dross", etc., and then He adds, "Afterwards thou shalt be called, The city of righteousness, the *faithful* city". How clear it is then that God calls Israel "an *Harlot*" for her unfaithfulness. For further proofs see Jer. 2:20; 3:6, 8; Ezek. 16: 15; 20:30; 43:8, 9; Hosea 2:5, etc.

We would next call attention to some of the scriptures which prove that there will be Israelites dwelling in Babylon and the land of Assyria at the End-time. In Jer. 50: 4-7 we read, "In those days, and in that time, saith the Lord, the children of Israel shall come, they and the children of Judah together, going and weeping: they shall go, and seek the Lord their God. They shall ask the way to Zion with their faces thitherward, saying, Come, and let us join ourselves to the Lord in a perpetual covenant that shall not be forgotten", etc. Clearly these verses treat of the closing days of the time of "Jacob's trouble". Immediately following we read, "Remove out of the midst of *Babylon,* and go forth out of the land of the *Chaldeans*" (v. 8). Then, in the next verse, a reason is given, showing the urgency of this call for the faithful Jews in Babylon to come out: "For lo, I will raise and cause to come up against Babylon an assembly of great nations from the north country: and they shall set themselves in array against her; from thence she shall be taken" (v. 9). Again, in Jer. 51:44, the Lord says, "And I will punish Bel in *Babylon,* and I will bring forth out of his mouth that which he hath swallowed up: and the nations shall not flow together any more unto him: yea, the wall of Babylon shall fall". And then follows the Call for the faithful Jews to separate themselves from the mass of their apostate brethren in Babylon—"My people, go ye out of the midst of her, and deliver ye every man his soul from the fierce anger of the Lord". Isa. 11:11; 27:13; Micah 4:10, all show that Israel will be intimately connected with Babylon in the End-time.

It was of incalculable help to students of the past when they discovered that *Israel* is the key which unlocks prophecy, and that the Nations are referred to only as they affect the fortunes of Jacob's descendants. There were other mighty peoples of old besides the Egyptians and the Chaldeans, but the Holy Spirit has passed them by, because their history had no bearing on that of the chosen Nation. The same reason explains why the empires of Babylon, Medo-Persia, Greece, and Rome, *do* occupy such a prominent notice in the book of Daniel—they were the enemies into whose hands God delivered His wayward people. These principles have received wide recognition by prophetic students, and therefore it is the more strange that so few have applied them in their study of the final prophetic book. *Israel* is the key to the Revelation, and the Nations are only mentioned therein as they immediately affect *Israel's* fortunes. The *ultimate* design of the Apocalypse is not to take notice of such men as Nero and Charlemagne and Napoleon, nor such systems as Mohammedanism and the Papacy. Nor would so much be said about Babylon unless this "great city" was yet to be the home of apostate Israel. After these preliminary considerations, which though lengthy were necessary, we are now prepared to examine a few of the details supplied by Rev. 17 and 18. Nor can we now do more than offer a bare outline, and even that will require a further chapter on Rev. 18.

"And there came one of the seven angels which had the

seven vials, and talked with me, saying unto me, Come hither; I will show unto thee the judgment of the great whore that sitteth upon many waters: with whom the kings of the earth have committed fornication, and the inhabitants of the earth have been made drunk with the wine of her fornication" (Rev. 17:1, 2). The "great whore", in the final accomplishment of this prophecy, describes apostate Israel in the End-time—i. e. Daniel's seventieth week. The figure of an unfaithful woman to represent apostate Israel is a common one in the Scriptures: see Jer. 2:20; 3:6, 8; Ezek. 16:15; 20:30; 43:8, 9; Hosea 2:5, etc. She is here termed "the *great* whore" for two reasons: first, because (as we shall show later) she will, at the end, worship Mammon as she never has in the past; second, because of her idolatrous alliance with the Beast. The apostle is here shown her "judgment". This is in contrast from what we have in Rev. 12, where we learn that the chaste "Woman" will be preserved. That apostate Israel will yet sit "upon many waters" ("peoples", etc., v. 15), and that the kings of the earth will commit fornication with her, we reserve for consideration in the next chapter.

"So he carried me away in the spirit into the wilderness: and I saw a woman sit upon a scarlet colored Beast, full of names of blasphemy, having seven heads and ten horns. And the woman was arrayed in purple and scarlet color, and decked with gold and precious stones, and pearls, having a golden cup in her hand full of abominations and filthiness of her fornication" (vv. 3 and 4). The Woman seated on the Beast does not signify that she will rule over him, but intimates that he will support her. The ultimate reference here is to the Devil's imitation of the Millennium, when the Jews (even now rapidly coming into prominence) shall no longer be the tail of the Nations, but the head. How the Devil will bring this about will appear when we examine Rev. 18. As the result of the Beast's *support* (v. 3), apostate Israel will be lifted to heights of worldly power and glory (v. 4).

"And upon her forehead was a name written, mystery: BABYLON THE GREAT, THE MOTHER OF HARLOTS AND ABOMINATIONS OF THE EARTH" (v. 5). In a re-built Babylon will culminate the various systems of idolatry which had their source in the first Babylon of Nimrod's day. It is in this city that the most influential Jews will congregate at the Time of the End. From there, Jewish financiers will control the governments of earth. That apostate Israel, in Babylon, should be clothed in "purple and scarlet" (emblems of royalty and earthly glory) *before* the Kingdom of Messiah is set up, was indeed a "mystery" (secret) disclosed by none of the Prophets, but now made known in *the Revelation.*

"And I saw the woman drunken with the blood of the saints, and with the blood of the martyrs of Jesus: and when I saw her, I wondered with a great wonder" (v. 6, R.V.). The final reference is, again, to apostate Israel in the End-time. The most relentless enemies of the godly Jews will be their own apostate brethren—cf our notes on Luke 18 in chapter 9. The second half of v. 6, correctly rendered in the R. V., "And when I saw her I wondered with a great wonder", ought to show us that it is not Romanism which is here in view. Why should John, who was himself then suffering from the hatred of Rome (Pagan) wonder at Rome (Papal) being clothed with governmental power and glory, and drunken with the blood of saints? But that the kings of the earth (her worst enemies for three thousand years) should commit fornication with

Israel, and that the apostate portion of the Nation should be drunken with the blood of their own brethren according to the flesh, was well calculated to fill him with amazement.

"And the angel said unto me, Wherefore didst thou marvel? I will tell thee the mystery of the woman, and of the Beast that carrieth her, which hath the seven heads and ten horns" (v. 7). It should be noted that in the interpretation which follows, far more is said about "the Beast" than about "the Woman". We believe the chief reason for this is because the 18th verse tells us the Woman represents "that great city, which reigneth over the kings of the earth", and the City receives fuller notice in the chapter that follows—Rev. 18.

"And here is the mind which hath wisdom. The seven heads are seven mountains, on which the woman sitteth. And there are seven kings: five are fallen, and one is, and the other is not yet come; and when he cometh, he must continue a short space. And the Beast that was, and is not, even he is the eighth, and is of the seven, and goeth into perdition" (vv. 9-11). Here is the mind which hath wisdom (v. 9): "This repetition of 13:18 identifies and connects these two chapters. The word rendered 'mind' in 17:9 and 'understanding' in 13:18 is the same. This 'wisdom' is, to understand that, though a 'Beast' is seen in the vision, it is not a wild beast that is meant, but one great final super-human personality; namely, a man energized by satanic power" (Dr. E. W. Bullinger).

The 9th verse should end with the word "wisdom": what follows belongs to v. 10. The R. V., which in this verse follows a number of reliable translations, renders thus: "The seven heads are seven mountains, on which the woman sitteth, *and they are* seven kings". This at once disposes of the popular interpretation which regards these "seven *mountains*" as referring to the seven *hills* on which the city of Rome is built. The Holy Spirit expressly tells us that the seven mountains are (*represent*) seven kings. Of these seven kings it is said, "five are fallen, and one is (i. e. the sixth existed when John wrote the Apocalypse), and the other (the seventh) is yet to come; he must continue a short space". And then in v. 11 we read, "And the Beast that was, and is not, is himself also an eighth, and is of the seven, and he goeth into perdition". Upon these verses we cannot do better than give extracts from Mr. Newton's "Thoughts on the Apocalypse":

"This passage is evidently intended to direct our thoughts to the various forms of executive government or kingship which have existed, or shall exist in the prophetic earth, until the hour when the sovereignty of the world shall become the sovereignty of the Lord and of His Christ. We might expect to find such a reference in a chapter which professedly treats of him who is to close the history of human government by the introduction of a new and marvellous form of power—a form new as to its mode of administration and development, yet not unconnected with the past, for it will be constructed upon principles drawn from the experience of preceding ages, and will have the foundations of its greatness laid by the primeval efforts of mankind. He will be the eighth; but he is *of* (ek) the seven.

"The native energy and intrepidity of him who is said to have been a mighty hunter before the Lord—an energy essential to men who were settling in a forlorn and unsubdued earth, surrounded by beasts of the forest and countless other difficulties and dangers, very naturally gave the first form to *kingship,* and hence its parentage may be said to spring. 'The beginning of his kingdom was Babel'. The supremacy of Nimrod was not derived from any previously existing system. He neither inherited his power from others, nor did he, like Nebuchadnezzar afterwards, receive it as a gift from God. He earned it for himself, by the force of his own individual character—but it was without God. Great progress was made in the kingdom which he founded in the land of Shinar, in civilization and refinement; for we early read of the goodly Babylonish garment, and of the skill and learning of the Chaldees; but their dominion was repressed and kept, as it were, in abeyance by the hand of God, until the trial of Israel, His people, had been fully made, that it might be seen whether they would prove themselves worthy of *supremacy* in the earth.

"The form of government in Israel was a theocracy; as was seen in the reigns of David and Solomon, who were types (*imperfect* types indeed) of Him that is to come. The monarch was independent of and uncontrolled by those whom he governed, but he was dependent upon God, who dwelt in the temple, ever near to be consulted, and whose law was given as the final standard of appeal. He stood between God and the people, not to be their functionary and slave—not to be the expression of *their* judgments, and the reflection of *their* will; but as set *over* them by God, his office was to mould *them* and to fashion *them* by principles which he himself had received from above. But the possession of power like this, held in companionship with God, required a holiness that was not found in man in the flesh, and therefore it was soon forfeited. Divine sanction, however, has many times since been coveted, and the name of 'the Lord's anointed' assumed. The last great king of the Gentiles, indeed, will do more than this, for he will take the place of Divinity itself, and sit upon the mount of the congregation on the sides of the north, saying he is like the Most High. But all this is unauthorized assumption.

"The third form is developed when the Gentile dynasty was formally constituted by God in the person of Nebuchadnezzar. He, like the monarchs of Israel, had absolute sovereignty granted to him—but God was not with him in it. He and his successors received it as delegated power, to be exercised according to their own pleasure, though in final responsibility to God. It is not necessary here to pursue the painful history of the Gentiles. It is sufficient to say, as regards the history of power, that the Gentile monarchs from the beginning, not knowing God so as to lean upon Him, and too weak to stand alone; exposed to the jealousy and hatred of those whom they governed—a jealousy not unfrequently earned by their own evil, found it necessary to lean upon something inferior to themselves: and thus the character of power has been deteriorated from age to age, until at last the monarchy of these latter days has consented not only to own the people as the basis and source of its power, but has also submitted to be directed in the exercise of that power by given rules prescribed by its subjects.

"The native monarchy of Nimrod, the theocracy of Israel, the despotic authority of Nebuchadnezzar, the aristocratic monarchy of Persia, and the military monarchy of Alexander and his successors, had all passed away when John beheld this vision. All these methods had been tried —none had been found to answer even the purposes of man; and now another had arisen, the half military, half popular monarchy of the Caesars,—the iron empire of Rome. 'Five have fallen, and one is, and the other is not yet come; and when he cometh he must continue a little space'.

"That other (though it cannot yet be said to have *come* so as to fulfill this verse)* has nevertheless appeared and is found in the constitutional monarchy of this present hour. This is the seventh, (we are rather inclined to believe that the "seventh" is *commercialism,* that is, the moneyed-interests in control—A.W.P.) and, with one brief exception, the last form that is to be exhibited before the end shall come, and it is under this form that the system of Babylon is matured. It is obvious that a monarchy, guided not by the people numerically, but by certain classes of the people, and those classes determined by the possession of property, must be the form adapted for the accumulation of wealth, and the growth of commercial power; for it gives (which pure democracy has ever failed to do), the best security for property without unduly fettering the liberty of individual enterprise".

For lack of space we are obliged to pass over the intervening verses now, and in closing this chapter we offer a brief word on v. 18. "And the woman which thou sawest is that great city, which reigneth over the kings of the earth". This verse tells us that the Whore represents a City. This city is named in 14:8; 16:19; 17:5; 18:2; 10, 21; and it is surely significant that it is thus named in the Apocalypse *six* times—the number of *man;* whereas the new Jerusalem is referred to *three* times (3:12; 21:2, 10) the *Divine* number. Babylon, must therefore be understood *literally,* otherwise we should have the anomaly of a figure representing a figure. But from the very fact that we are here told the Woman represents the City, we learn

---

* It will not have come in the sense of this verse, until it pervades the Roman world. When *all* the ten kingdoms have been constitutionalized, it may be said to have come.

that she is not literal, but *figurative*.   In the next chapter we shall further review Rev. 17 and offer some comments on Rev. 18.

15

BABYLON AND THE ANTICHRIST
(Continued)

IN our last chapter we sought to show that in Rev. 17 "the great Whore", and "Babylon the great", though intimately connected, are yet distinct; the former being the representative of the latter. While allowing, yea insisting upon it, that many features of the symbolic prophecy contained in Rev. 17 have had a striking fulfillment already, still *that* in which *all* its varied terms are to find their complete realization is yet future. We also reminded our readers that *Israel* supplies the solution to most of the problems of prophecy, and this is becoming more and more evident as the last prophetic book in the Bible is receiving wider and closer study. Fifty years ago the majority of the commentators "spiritualised" the first half of Rev. 7 and made the "twelve tribes of Israel", there mentioned, to refer to the Church. But this has long since been discredited. So, the popular interpretation of Rev. 12 which made the "woman" there a figure of the Church has also been abandoned by many. An increasing number of Bible students are recognizing the fact that "the Lamb's Wife," "the Bride" of Rev. 19 and 21 also contemplates Israel rather than the Church. That the Church is the Bride (a statement nowhere affirmed in Scripture) has been sedulously proclaimed by the Papacy for over a thousand years, and the tradition has been echoed throughout Protestantism. But, as we have said, there is a steadily increasing number who seriously question this, yea, who are bold to repudiate it, and declare in its stead that the new Israel, saved Israel, will be "the Bride". As this truth becomes more clearly discerned, we believe it will also be apparent that the great Whore is not the apostate church but *apostate Israel*.

The future of Israel is a wide subject, for numerous are the scriptures which treat of it. It is, moreover, a subject of profound interest, the more so because what is now prophetic is so soon to become historic. The Zionist movement of the last twenty-five years is something more than the impracticable ideal of a few visionaries; it is steadily preparing the way for the re-establishment of the Jews in Palestine. It is true that the Zionists have been frowned upon by many in Jewry, and that, for a very good reason. God's time is not yet fully ripe, and He has permitted the mercenary spirit of many of Jacob's descendants to hold it, temporarily, in check. The millions of Jews now comfortably settled and prospering in this land, and in the capitals of the leading European countries, are satisfied with their present lot. The love of money outweighs sentimental considerations. Zionism has made no appeal to their avarice. To leave the markets and marts of New York, London, Paris, and Berlin in order to become *farmers* in Palestine is not sufficiently alluring. Mammon is now the god of the vast majority of the descendants of those who, of old, worshipped the golden calf.

At present, it is (with few exceptions) only those who are oppressed in greater Russia, Hungary, etc. who are really anxious to be settled in Palestine. But soon there will be a change of attitude. Even now there are faint indications of it. As Palestine becomes more thickly populated, as the prospects of security from Turkish and Arabian depredations grow brighter, as the country is developed and the possibilities of commercial aggrandizement loom on the horizon, the better class of Jews will be quick to see and seize the *golden* opportunity. Few American

Jews are anxious to emigrate to Palestine when there is nothing more than a spade and a hoe at the end of the journey. But as hospitals, colleges, universities, banking-houses are opened, and all the commercial adjuncts of civilization find a place in the land of David, then rapidly increasing numbers of David's descendants will turn their faces thitherward. High finance is the magnet which will draw the covetous Hebrews.

Once Palestine becomes a thorough Jewish State it is not difficult to forecast the logical corollary. We quote from the excellent exposition on Zechariah by Mr. David Baron—his comments on the fifth chapter*. "Without any spirit of dogmatism, and without entering at this place into the question of the identity and significance of the Babylon in the Revelation—whether mystical or actual—we would express our conviction that there are scriptures which cannot, according to our judgment, be satisfactorily explained except on the supposition of a revival and yet future judgment of literal Babylon, which for a time will be the center and embodiment of all the elements of our godless 'civilization', and which especially will become the chief *entrepot* of commerce in the world.

"To this conviction we are led chiefly by the fact that there are prophecies in the Old Testament concerning the literal Babylon which have never in the past been exhaustively fulfilled, and that Scripture usually connects the final overthrow of Babylon with the yet future restoration and blessing of Israel.

"And it is very striking to the close observer of the signs of the times how things at the present day are rapidly developing on the very lines which are forecast in the prophetic scriptures. 'The fears and hopes of the world—po-

---

*Mr. Baron is probably the ablest and most widely known and esteemed Hebrew Christian. *Zechariah*, published by Kregel Publications.

litical, commercial, and religious', writes one in a monthly journal which lies before me, 'are at the present day being increasingly centered upon the home of the human race—Mesopotamia. . . . As the country from which the father of the Jewish nation emigrated to the land of promise, it is also occupying the thoughts and aspirations of the Jews'.

"Whatever may be the outcome of the negotiations which have been carried on recently with the Turkish Government by the Jewish Territorialists 'for the establishment of a Jewish autonomous State' in this very region, in which many Zionists and other Jews were ready to join, there is so much truth in the words of another writer that when once a considerable number of such a commercial people as the Jews are re-established in Palestine, *'the Euphrates would be to them as necessary as the Thames to London or the Rhine to Germany. It would be Israel's great channel of communication with the Indian seas, not to speak of the commerce which would flow towards the Tigris and Euphrates from the central and northern districts of Asia! It would be strange, therefore, if no city should arise on its banks of which it might be said that her merchants were the great men of the earth' ''*.

Zech. 5 is most intimately connected with Rev. 18, and a grasp of the former is of such importance in studying the latter that we must here give it a brief consideration. But first let us outline in the fewest possible words the contents of the first four chapters of Zechariah. After a brief introduction we learn, first, that God's eye is ever upon Israel (1:7-17). Second, that His eye is also upon her enemies and desolators (1:18-21). Third, assurance is given of her future blessing (2) and of her cleansing (3). Fourth, we learn of the blessings which shall follow her restoration (4). Fifth, we are taken back to behold the punishment of apostate Israel: the "flying roll" symbolizes the destruction of wicked Jews (5:1-4). Then follows the vision of "the Ephah" in 5:5-11—let the reader please turn to it.

We cannot do more than now call attention to the prominent features in this vision. First, the prophet sees an "ephah" (or "bath") which was the largest measure for dry goods among the Jews. It would, therefore, be the natural symbol for *Commerce*. Next, we note that twice over it is said that the ephah "goeth forth" (vv. 5, 6). As the whole of the preceding visions concern *Jerusalem and her people,* this can only mean that the center of *Jewish* commerce is to be transferred from Palestine elsewhere. Next, we are told that there was a "woman" concealed in the midst of the ephah (v. 7). We say "concealed", for in vv. 5 and 6 the "woman" is not seen—the leaden cover (cf v. 8) had to be "lifted" before she could be beholden. The writer is satisfied that this hidden "woman in the ephah" is "the Woman" which is fully *revealed* in *Revelation* 17 and 18. Next, we are told that "wickedness" (lawlessness) was cast into the ephah, before its cover was closed again. Then, in what follows, we are shown this ephah, with the "woman" and "wickedness" shut up therein, being rapidly conveyed from Palestine to *"the land of Shinar"* (v. 11). The purpose for this is stated to be, "to build it a house", i. e. a settled habitation. Finally, we are assured, "it shall be established, and set *there* (in the land of Shinar) upon her own base". This vision or prophecy contains the germ which is afterwards expanded and developed in such detail in Rev. 17 and 18, where it is shown that "the house" which is established for this system of commerce is "Babylon the great". Let it be remembered, that this vision is found in the midst of a series of prophecies which have to do with, first the faithful, and then the faithless in Israel, and we have another clear and independent proof that the Corrupt Woman of the Apocalypse is none other than apostate Israel!

In his helpful and illuminative work on the Babylon of the future, the late Mr. Newton devoted a separate chapter to Zech. 5. His remarks are so excellent that we cannot forbear from making an extract: "If human energy is to be permitted again to make the Euphratean regions the scene of its operation—if prosperity is to be allowed for a brief moment to re-visit the Land of Babylon, it might be expected that the Scriptures would somewhere allude, and that definitely, to such an event. And we find it to be so. The Scripture does speak of an event yet unaccomplished, of which the scene is to be the Land of Babylon. The passage to which I refer is at the close of the fifth chapter of Zechariah.

"That the event predicted in this remarkable passage remains still unaccomplished, is sufficiently evident from the fact of Zechariah's having prophesied *after* Babylon had received that blow under which it has gradually waned. Zechariah lived after Babylon had passed into the hands of the Persians, and since that time, it is admitted by all, that declension—not 'establishment'—has marked its history. From that hour to the present moment there has been no 'preparation of an house', no establishment of anything—much less of an Ephah in the Land of Shinar. But an Ephah is to be established *there,* and a house to be built for it *there,* and *there* it is to be set firmly upon its base.

"An Ephah is the emblem of commerce. It is the symbol of the merchants. In the passage before us the Ephah is described as 'going forth'; that is, its sovereign influence is to pervade the nations, and to imprint on them a character derived from itself, as the formative power of their institutions. In other words, *commerce is for a season to reign*. It will determine the arrangements, and fix the manners of Israel, and of the prophetic earth. The appearance of every nation that falls under its control is to be mercantile. 'He said, moreover, this is their appearance (or aspect) throughout all the earth' ".

The theme is of deep interest, and we are tempted to enter at length into details. But that is scarcely necessary. Every one who has a general knowledge of the past, and who is at all in touch with political conditions in the world today, knows full well the radical change which the last two or three centuries have witnessed. For a thousand years the Church (the professing church) controlled the governments of Europe. Following the Reformation, the aristocracy (the nobility) held the reins. During the first half of last century democratic principles obtained more widely. But in the last two or three generations the governmental machines of this country and of the leading European lands have been run by the Capitalists. Of late, Labor has sought to check this, but thus far with little success. In the light of Zech. 5 and Rev. 18 present-day conditions are profoundly significant. It is *commerce* which is more and more dominating the policies and destinies of what is known as the civilized world. "If we turn our eyes abroad upon the world, we shall find that the one great object before the nations of the earth today is this image of commerce, drawing them with all the seductive influence a siren woman might exercise upon the heart of men. The one great aim on the part of each is to win the favor of this mighty mistress. The world powers are engaged in a

Titanic struggle for commercial supremacy. To this end mills are built, factories founded, forests felled, lands sown, harvests reaped, and ships launched. Because of this struggle for mastery of the world's market the nations reach out and extend their borders" (Dr. Haldeman). The recent war was caused by commercial jealousies. The root trouble behind the "reparation" question, the "Strait's" problem, the cancellation or demanding repayment of United States loans to Europe, each go back to commercial considerations.

Sixty years ago it was asked, "Is not commerce the sovereign influence of the day? If we were asked to inscribe on the banners of the leading nations of the earth, an emblem characteristically expressive of their condition, could we fix on any device more appropriate than an ephah?" With how much greater pertinency may this be said today! And how this is preparing the way for and will shortly head up in what is portrayed in Rev. 18, it is not difficult to see. There we read, "Thy *merchants* were the *great* men of the earth" (v. 23). This was not true four hundred years ago: for then the ecclesiastics were "the great men of the earth". Nor was it true one hundred years ago, for then the nobility were "the great men of the earth". But today. Ah! Ask the man on the street to name half a dozen of the "great men" now alive, and whom would he select? And who are behind and yet one with the "merchants"? Is it not the financiers? And who are the leading ones among them? Who are the ones that are more and more controlling the great banking-systems of the world? And, as every well-informed person knows, the answer is, *Jews*. How profoundly significant, then, that the head on the image in Nebuchadnezzar's dream (which symbolized the *Babylonian* Empire) should be of *gold,* and that the final Babylon should be denominated "the *golden* city" (Isa. 14:4). And how all of this serves, again, to confirm our interpretation of Rev. 17, namely, that "the great Whore" with "the *golden* cup in her hand" (17:4) is apostate Israel, whose final home shall be that "great city", soon to be built on the banks of the Euphrates. Not yet is it fully evident that the wealth of the world is rapidly filling Hebrew coffers—only a glimpse of the "woman" in *"the midst of* the Ephah" was obtained before it became established in the Land of Shinar. But it cannot be long before this will become apparent. At the End-time it will fully appear that *"the woman . . . .* is (represents) that great city" (17:18). This explains the words of Rev. 17:5, where we learn that the words "Babylon the great" are written upon "her *forehead"*—it will be obvious then to all! Apostate Israel, then controlling the wealth of the world, will personify Babylon.

And what part will the Antichrist play in connection with this? What will be his relation to Babylon and apostate Israel? The Word of God is not silent on these questions, and to it we now turn for the Divine answer. As to Antichrist's relation to Babylon, Scripture is very explicit. He will be "the King of Babylon" (Isa. 14:4); the "King of Assyria" (Isa. 10:12). As to his relation to apostate Israel, that is a more intricate matter and will require more detailed consideration. We shall therefore devote a separate chapter (the next one) to this interesting branch of our subject. Here we shall deal briefly with what Rev. 17 and 18 say thereon.

Rev. 17 presents the relation of apostate Israel to the Antichrist in three aspects. First, she is *supported by* him. This is brought before us in 17:3, where we are shown the corrupt Woman seated upon the scarlet-colored Beast. This, we believe, is parallel with Dan. 9:27, which tells us that "the Prince that shall come" will make a Covenant with Israel. This covenant, league, or treaty, will insure her protection. It is significant that Dan. 9:27 tells us the "covenant" is made by the one who is then at the head of the revived Roman Empire, which corresponds with the fact that Rev. 17:3 depicts him as a "scarlet colored Beast . . . . having seven heads and *ten horns*". It is the Antichrist no longer in his "little horn" character, but as one that has now attained earthly glory and dominion. As such, he will, for a time, uphold the Jews and protect their interests.

Second, Rev. 17 depicts apostate Israel as *intriguing with* "the kings of the earth". In v. 2 we read that the kings of the earth shall commit fornication with her. Note how this, as an item of importance, is *repeated* in 18:3. This, we believe, is what serves to explain 17:16 which, in the corrected rendering of the R. V. reads, "And the ten horns which thou sawest *and the Beast,* these shall *hate* the Harlot, and shall make her desolate and naked, and shall eat her flesh, and shall burn her utterly with fire". What it is which causes the Beast to turn against the Harlot and hate and destroy her is her *unfaithfulness* to him. Not content with enjoying the protection the Beast gives her, apostate Israel will aspire to a position of rivalry with the one over the ten horns. That she succeeds in this we learn from the last verse of the chapter—"And the woman which thou sawest is (represents) that great city, which *reigneth over* the kings of the earth". As to how apostate Israel will yet "reign over" the kings of the earth we hope to show in the next chapter.

Third, Rev. 17 makes it known that apostate Israel will

ultimately be *hated by* the Beast and his "ten horns" (v. 16). The 12th verse tells us that the ten horns are "ten kings". This has presented a real difficulty to many. In 17:16 it says that the ten horns (kings) and the Beast *hate* the Whore, and make her desolate and naked, and shall eat her flesh (that is, appropriate to themselves her substance, her riches), and burn her with fire; whereas in 18:9 we read, "The kings of the earth who have committed fornication and lived deliciously with her, shall *bewail* her, and lament for her, when they shall see the smoke of her burning". Yet the solution of this difficulty is very simple. The difficulty is created by confusing "the kings of the earth" with the "ten horns", whose kingdoms are within the limits of the old Roman Empire (see Dan. 7:7). The "kings of the earth" is a much wider expression, and includes such kingdoms as North and South America, China and Japan, Germany and Russia, etc., all in fact, outside the bounds of the old Roman Empire. It is the intriguing of apostate Israel with "the kings of the earth" which brings down upon her the hatred of the Beast and *his* "ten kings".

In closing this chapter we wish to call attention to some of the many and striking verbal correspondencies between Rev. 17 and 18 and the Old Testament Prophets:—

1. In Rev. 17:1 we are told the great Whore "sitteth upon many waters".

In Jer. 51:13 Babylon (see previous verse) is addressed as follows: "O thou that dwellest upon many waters".

2. In Rev. 17:2 it is said that, "The inhabitants of the earth have been made drunk with the wine of her fornication".

In Jer. 51:7 we read, "Babylon hath been a golden cup

in the Lord's hand, that made all the earth drunken: the nations have drunken of her wine".

3. In Rev. 17:4 the great Whore has "a golden cup in her hand".

In Jer. 51:7 Babylon is termed "a golden cup in the Lord's hand".

4. In Rev. 17:15 we are told, "The waters which thou sawest, where the Whore sitteth, are peoples, and multitudes, and nations, and tongues".

In Jer. 51:13 we read, "O thou that dwellest upon many waters, abundant in treasures".

5. Rev. 17:16 tells us that Babylon shall be burned with fire—cf 18:8.

So in Jer. 51:58 we read, "The broad walls of Babylon shall be utterly broken, and her high gates shall be burned with fire".

6. In Rev. 17:18 we are told that the woman who represents the great city "reigneth over the kings of the earth".

In Isa. 47:5 Babylon is denominated "the lady of kingdoms".

7. Rev. 18:2 tells us that after her fall, Babylon becomes "the habitation of demons, and the hold of every foul spirit, and a cage of every unclean and hateful bird".

Isa. 13:21 says, "But wild beasts of the desert shall lie there; and their houses shall be full of doleful creatures; and owls shall dwell there, and satyrs shall dance there".

8. Rev. 18:4 records God's call to the faithful Jews— "Come out of her My people".

In Jer. 51:45 God also says, "My people, go ye out of the midst of her".

9. In Rev. 18:5 it is said, "Her sins have reached unto heaven".

In Jer. 51:9 it reads, "For her judgment reacheth unto heaven".

10. In Rev. 18:6 we read, "Reward her as she rewarded you".

In Jer. 50:15 it says, "Take vengeance upon her; as she hath done, do unto her".

11. In Rev. 18:7 we find Babylon saying in her heart, "I sit a queen, and am no widow, and shall see no sorrow".

In Isa. 47:8 we also read that Babylon says in her heart, "I am, and none else beside me; I shall not sit as a widow, neither shall I know the loss of children".

12. In Rev. 18:8 we read, "Therefore shall her plagues come in one day".

Isa. 47:9 declares, "But these two things shall come to thee in a moment, in one day.

13. In Rev. 18:21 we read, "And a mighty angel took up a stone like a great millstone, and cast it into the sea, saying, Thus with violence shall that great city Babylon be thrown down, and be found no more at all".

So in Jer. 51:63, 64 we are told, "And it shall be, when thou hast made an end of reading this book, that thou shalt bind a stone to it, and cast it into the midst of the Euphrates: And thou shalt say, Thus shall Babylon sink, and shall not rise from the evil that I will bring upon her".

14. In Rev. 18:23 we read, "And the light of the candle shall shine no more at all in thee, and the voice of the bridegroom and of the bride shall be heard no more at all in thee".

In Isa. 24:8, 10 it is said of Babylon, "The mirth of tabrets ceaseth, the noise of them that rejoice endeth, the joy of the heart ceaseth . . . . the City of Confusion is broken down: every house is shut up, that no man may come in . . . . all joy is darkened, the mirth of the land is gone".

15. In Rev. 18:24 we read, "And in her was found the blood of prophets, and of saints, and of all that were slain upon the earth".

In Jer. 51:49 we read, "As Babylon hath caused the slain of Israel to fall, so at Babylon shall fall the slain of all the earth".

These parallelisms are so plain they need no comments from us. If the reader still insists that the Babylon of Rev. 17 and 18 is the ultimate development of the Papacy as it envelopes apostate Christendom, it is useless to discuss the subject any farther. But we believe that the great majority of our readers—who have no traditions to uphold· —will be satisfied that the Babylon of the Apocalypse is the Babylon of Old Testament prophecy, namely, a literal, re-built city in "the land of Nimrod" (Micah 5:6), a city which shall be the production of covetousness ("which is *idolatry*"—Col. 3:5), and a city which shall yet be the home of apostate Israel.

16

ISRAEL AND THE ANTICHRIST

IT is a ground for thanksgiving that during the last three or four generations the people of God have given considerable attention to the prophecies of Scripture which treat of the future of Israel. The old method of "spiritualizing" these predictions, and making them apply to the Church of the present dispensation, has been discarded by the great majority of pre-millennarians. With a steadily increasing number of Bible students it is now a settled question that Israel, as a nation, shall be saved (Rom. 11:26), and that the promises of God to the fathers will be literally fulfilled under the Messianic reign of the Lord Jesus (Rom. 9:4). Jerusalem, which for so many centuries has been a by-word in the earth, will then be known as "the city of the great King" (Matt. 5:35). His throne shall be established there, and it shall be the gathering-point for all nations (Zech. 8:23; 14:16-21). Then shall the despised descendants of Jacob be "the head" of the nations, and no longer the tail (Deut. 28:13); then shall the people of Jehovah's ancient choice be the center of His earthly government; then shall the Fig Tree, so long barren, "blossom and bud, and fill the face of the world with fruit" (Isa. 27:6). All of this is common knowledge among those who are in any-wise acquainted with dispensational truth.

But the same Word of Prophecy which announces the glorious future awaiting the children of Israel, also contains another chapter in the history of this peculiar people; a chapter yet unfulfilled, setting forth a period in their history darker and sadder than any of their past experiences. Both the Old and New Testaments plainly tell of a season of suffering for the Jews which will be far more acute than even their afflictions of old. Dan. 12:1 says, "And there shall be a time of trouble, such as never was since there was a nation even to that same time". And in Matt. 24:21, 22 we read, "For there shall be great tribulation, such as was not since the beginning of the world to this time, no, nor ever shall be. And except those days should be shortened, there should no flesh be saved".

The reasons or causes of this future suffering of Israel are as follows. First, God has not fully visited upon Israel's children the sins of their fathers. "When Solomon and her kings had by transgression lost their blessings, and the glory of the reign of Solomon had faded away, the supremacy, which was taken from them, was given to certain Gentile nations, who were successively to arise and bear rule in the earth, during the whole period of Israel's rejection. The first of these was the Chaldean Empire under Nebuchadnezzar. The period termed by our Lord the 'Times of the Gentiles', commences with the capture of Jerusalem by Nebuchadnezzar. It is a period coincident from its beginning to its close, with the treading down of Jerusalem. 'Jerusalem shall be trodden down of the Gentiles till the Times of the Gentiles be fulfilled'. Nebuchadnezzar therefore, and the Gentile empires which have succeeded him, have only received their pre-eminence in consequence of Jerusalem's sin; and the reason why they were endowed with that pre-eminence was, that they might *chasten* Jerusalem; and when they shall have fulfilled that purpose, they shall themselves be set aside and be made, because of their own evil, 'like the chaff of the summer threshing-floors'. In this we have another evidence that the earthly dispensations of God revolve around the Jews as their center" (B. W. Newton).

A further reason or cause of the future sufferings of Israel lies in the rejection of their Messiah. First and foremost Christ was "a Minister *of the Circumcision,* for the truth of God, to confirm the promises made unto the fathers" (Rom. 15:8). He was sent "but unto the lost sheep of the house of Israel" (Matt. 15:24). And in marvellous grace He tabernacled among them. But He was not wanted. "He came unto His own, and His own received Him not" (John 1:11). Not only did they receive Him not, they "despised and rejected Him"; they "hated Him without a cause". So intense was their enmity against Him that with one voice they cried, "Away with Him, crucify Him". And not until His holy blood had been shed, and He had died the death of the accursed, was their awful malice against Him appeased. And for this they have yet to answer to God. Vengeance is His, and He will repay. Not yet has the murder of God's Son been fully avenged*. It could not be during this "Day of Salvation". But the Day of Salvation will soon be over, and it shall be followed by "the great Day of His Wrath" (Rev. 6:17; Joel 2:11). Then will God visit the earth with His sore judgments, and though the Nations shall by no means escape the righteous retribution due them for their part in the crucifixion of Christ, yet, the ones who will be punished the most severely will be they who took the lead in that crime of crimes.

The form which God's judgment will take upon the Jews is to be in full accord with the unchanging law of recompense—what they have sown, *that* shall they also

*What they suffered in A. D. 70 was, first, for the sins of their fathers, see Luke 11:50, 51; and second, for the murder of Christ, see Matt. 22:7.

reap. This was expressly affirmed by our Lord Jesus: "I am come in My Father's name, and ye receive Me not: if another shall come in his own name, him ye will receive" (John 5:43). Because they rejected God's Christ, Israel shall receive the Antichrist. The same thing is stated in 2 Thess. 2:7—"For this cause (i. e. "because they received not the love of the Truth, that they might be saved") *God* shall send them strong delusion that they should believe the Lie". The immediate reference here, we believe, is to the Jews, though the principle enumerated will also have its wider application to apostate Christendom. The chief reason why God suffers the Man of Sin to come on the scene and run his awful course, is in order to *inflict punishment upon guilty Israel*. This is clearly taught in Isa. 10:5, where of the Antichrist God says, "O Assyrian, the rod (the instrument of chastisement) of Mine anger, and the staff in their hand is Mine indignation. *I will send him* against an hypocritical nation, against *the people of My wrath* will I give him a charge, to take the spoil, and to take the prey, and to tread them down like the mire of the street", and cf. our brief comments on Jer. 6:26, 27 and 15:8 in chapter 9.

It must be borne in mind that the Jews are to return to Palestine and there re-assume a national standing whilst yet unconverted. There are a number of passages which establish this beyond question. For example, in Ezek. 22: 19-22 we are told, "Therefore thus saith the Lord God; because ye are all become dross, behold, therefore I will gather you into the midst of Jerusalem, as they gather silver, and brass, and iron, and lead, and tin, into the midst of the furnace, to blow the fire upon it, to melt it; so will I gather you in Mine anger and in My fury, and I will leave you there, and melt you. Yea, *I will gather*

you, and blow upon you in the fire of My wrath, and ye
shall be melted in the midst thereof". The first six verses
of Isa. 18 describe how the Lord will gather the Jews to
Jerusalem, there to be the prey of "fowls and beasts".
The closing chapters of Zechariah lead to the inevitable
conclusion that the Jews return to their land in unbelief,
for if their national conversion takes place in Jerusalem
(Zech. 12:10), they must have returned to it unconverted.

When the Antichrist is manifested, great companies of
the Jews will already be in Palestine, and in a flourishing
condition. What, then, will be his relations with them?
It is by no means easy to furnish a detailed answer to this
question, and at best we can reply but tentatively. Doubtless, there are many particulars respecting this and all
other related subjects, which will not be cleared up until
the prophecies concerning them have been fulfilled. We,
today, occupy much the same position with regard to the
predictions concerning the Antichrist, as the Old Testament saints did to the many passages which foretold the
coming of the Christ. Their difficulty was to arrange
those passages in the order they were to be fulfilled, and to
distinguish between those which spoke of Him in humiliation and those which foretold His coming glory. A similar perplexity confronts us. To ascertain the *sequence* of
the prophecies relating to the Antichrist is a real problem.
Even when we confine ourselves to those passages which
speak of him in his connections with Israel, we have to
distinguish between those which concern only the godly
remnant, and those which relate to the great apostate mass
of the Nation; and, too, we have to separate between those
prophecies which concern the time when Antichrist is posing as the true Christ, and those which portray him in the

final stage of his career, after he has thrown off his mask
of religious pretension.

It would appear that the first thing revealed in prophecy
concerning the Antichrist's dealings with Israel is the entering into a "covenant" with them. This is mentioned
in Dan. 9:27: "And he shall confirm the covenant
("make a firm covenant", R.V.) with many for one week"
i. e. seven years. The many here can be none other than
the mass of the Jewish people, for they are the principal
subjects of the prophecy. The one who makes this covenant is the "Prince that shall come" of the previous verse,
the Head of the restored Roman Empire. Thus the relations between this Prince, the Antichrist, and the mass of
the Jews shall, at the first, be relations of apparent friendship and public alliance. That this covenant is not forced
upon Israel, but rather is entered into voluntarily by
them, as *seeking Antichrist's patronage,* is clear from Isa.
28:18, where we find God, in indignation, addressing
them as follows—"And *your* covenant with Death shall be
disannulled, and *your* agreement with Hell shall not
stand; when the overflowing scourge shall pass through,
then ye shall be trodden down by it". And this, we believe, supplies the key to Dan. 2:43.

Nebuchadnezzar's vision of the great image and the interpretation given to Daniel, outlines the governmental
history of the earth *as it relates to Palestine,* further details
being supplied in the other visions found in the book of
Daniel. "The earthly dispensations of God revolve around
Jerusalem as their center. The method which it hath
pleased God to adopt in giving the prophetic history of
these nations, is in strict accord with this principle. As
soon as they arose into supremacy and supplanted Jerusalem, prophets were commissioned, especially Daniel, to de-

lineate their course. We might perhaps, have expected that their history would have been given minutely and consecutively from its beginning to its close. But instead of this, it is only given in its connection with Jerusalem; and as soon as Jerusalem was finally crushed by the Romans and ceased to retain a national position, all detailed history of the Gentile Empires is suspended. Many a personage most important in the world's history has since arisen. Charlemagne has lived, and Napoleon—many a monarch, and many a conqueror—battles have been fought, kingdoms raised and kingdoms subverted—yet Scripture passes silently over these things, however great in the annals of the Gentiles. Because Jerusalem has nationally ceased to be, 1800 years ago, the *detail* of Gentile history was suspended—it is suspended still, nor will it be resumed until Jerusalem re-assumes a national position. Then the history of the Gentiles is again minutely given, and the glory and dominion of their last great King described. He is found to be especially connected with *Jerusalem and the Land* . . . . The subject of the book of Daniel as a whole, is the indignation of God directed through the instrumentality of the Gentile Empires upon Jerusalem" (B. W. Newton "Aids to Prophetic Enquiry", first Series).

The method which the Holy Spirit has followed in the book of Daniel is to give us, first, a general outline of Gentile dominion over Jerusalem, and this is found in the vision of the Image in chapter 2; and second, to fill in this outline, which is given in the last six chapters of that book. It is with the former we are now more particularly concerned. Much of the prophetic vision of Dan. 2 has already become history. The golden head (Babylon), the silver breast and arms (Medo-Persia), the brazen belly and thighs (Greece), the iron legs (Rome), have already appeared before men. But the *feet* of the Image, "part of iron and part of clay", have to do with a time yet future. The break between the legs and feet corresponds with the break between the sixty-ninth and seventieth "weeks" of Dan. 9:24-27. The present dispensation comes in as a parenthesis during the time that Israel is outside the Land, dispersed among the Gentiles.

What, then, is represented by the "iron and the clay" toes of the feet of the Image? If we bear in mind that this portion of the Image exactly corresponds to the seventieth week, we have an important key to the interpretation. Dan. 9:26, 27 treats of the seventieth week—the "one week" yet remaining. These verses speak of the Prince (of the restored Roman Empire) making a seven years' Covenant with the Jews. Thus the prophecy concerning the seventieth week presents to us two prominent subjects —the Romans, at whose head is the Antichrist, and apostate Israel, with whom the Covenant is made. Returning now to Dan. 2 we find that when interpreting the king's dream about the Image, the prophet declares that the "iron" is the symbol for the "fourth kingdom" (v. 40), which was Rome, who succeeded Babylon, Persia, and Greece; the "feet" with their ten toes forecasting this Empire in its final form. Thus, we have Divine authority for saying that the "iron" in the feet of the Image represent the peoples who shall yet occupy the territory controlled by the old Roman Empire. In a word, the "iron" symbolizes *the Gentiles*—specifically those found in the lands which shall be ruled over by the "ten kings".

Who, then, is symbolized by "the clay"? Here we are obliged to part company with the commentators, who unanimously take the clay to be the figure of democracy.

So far as we are aware none of them has offered a single proof text in support of their interpretation, and as the Word is the only authority, to it we must look. Assured that Scripture is its own interpretor, we turn to the concordance to find out what the "clay" signifies elsewhere, when used symbolically. In Isa. 64, which records the Cry of the Remnant at the End-time, we find them saying, "But now, O Lord, Thou art our Father; *we are the clay,* and Thou our Potter; and we all are the work of Thy hand". Again, in Jer. 18 the same figure is employed. There the prophet is commanded to go down to the potter's house, where he beheld him manufacturing a vessel. The vessel was marred in the hands of the potter, so he "made it again another vessel". Clearly, this is a picture of Israel in the past and in the future. The interpretation is expressly fixed in v. 6: "O house of Israel, cannot I do with you as this potter? saith the Lord. Behold, *as the clay* is in the potter's hand, *so are ye* in Mine hand, *O house of Israel".* How clear it is then that "clay" is God's symbol for *Israel*.*

In its final form, then, the revived Roman Empire—the kingdom of Antichrist—will be partly Gentilish and partly Jewish. And is not this what we must expect? Will not that be the character of the kingdom of that One which the Antichrist will counterfeit? Such scriptures as Psa. 2:6-8; Isa. 11:10; 42:6; Rev. 11:15, etc., make plain the *dual* character of the kingdom over which our Lord

*That the Hebrew word for "clay" in these passages is a different one from that employed in Dan. 2 is exactly what a reflecting mind would naturally expect. Isa. 64 and Jer. 18 treat of the Israel that shall be restored, whereas Dan. 2 speaks of the *apostate* portion of Israel, irrevocably given up to judgment. In striking accord with this, we may add, that the word used in Isa. 64 and Jer. 18 refers to clay in its native and mouldable stage; but the word in Dan. 2 signifies *"burnt* clay", which denotes its *final* condition: here, as always, "burning" tells of Divine *judgment!*

will reign during the Millennium. That the Antichrist *will be* intimately related to both Jews and the Gentiles we have proven again and again in the previous chapters—Rev. 9:11 is quite sufficient to establish the point. Therefore, we should not be surprised to find that that part of the Image which specifically depicts the kingdom over which the Man of Sin shall reign, should be composed of both "iron" *and* "clay". It would be passing strange were it otherwise. It is indeed striking to note that the "clay" is mentioned in Dan. 2 just *nine* times—the number of judgment!

In Dan. 2:43 we read, "And whereas thou sawest iron mixed with miry clay, they shall mingle themselves with the seed of men: but they shall not cleave one to another, even as iron is not mixed with clay"—a verse that has sorely puzzled the expositors. We believe that the reference is to the coming intimacy between Jews and Gentiles. The apostate Jews (members of the Corrupt *Woman)* shall "mingle themselves with the seed of men"—the Gentiles. This is amplified in Rev. 17, where we read of the great Whore "with whom the kings of the earth have committed fornication, and the inhabitants of the earth have been made drunk with the wine of her fornication". "But they shall not cleave one to another" (Dan. 2:43) is explained in Rev. 17:16—"And the ten horns which thou sawest upon the Beast, these shall *hate* the Whore, and shall make her desolate and naked", etc.! There is a remarkable verse in Hab. 2 which confirms our remarks above, and connects the Antichrist himself with the "clay". The passage begins with the third verse, which, from its quotation in Heb. 10:37, 38 we know, treats of the period immediately preceding our Lord's return. In vv. 4 and 5 we have a description of the Antichrist, and then in v. 6 we

read, "Shall not all these take up a parable against him,
and a taunting proverb against him, and say, Woe to him
that increaseth that which is not his! how long? and to
him that ladeth himself with *thick clay*". The reference
is clearly to this "proud Man's" fellowship with apostate
Israel. We are satisfied that Hab. 2:6-8 is parallel with
Isa. 14:9-12. Isa. 14 gives us a glimpse of the Antichrist
being scoffed at in Hell, by the "chief ones of the earth"
because he, too, was unable to escape *their* awful fate. So
in Hab. 2, after stating that he "gathereth unto him all
nations" (v. 5) the prophet goes on to say "Shall not all
these take up a taunting proverb against him". The taunt
is, that though he had leagued himself with the mass of
Israel (*laden himself* "with thick clay"), yet it will be
"the remnant" of this *same people* that shall "spoil" him
(v. 8).

Another scripture which shows that in the End-time
apostate Israel will no longer be divided from and hated
by the Gentiles is found in Isa. 2, where we are told, "They
strike hands with the children *of strangers*" (v. 6 R.V.).
As the context here is of such deep interest, and as the
whole chapter supplies us with a most vivid picture of the
Jews in Palestine just before the Millennium, we shall stop
to give it a brief consideration. The first five verses present to us a millennial scene, and then, as is so frequently
the case in the prophecies of Isaiah, we are taken back to
be shown something of the conditions which shall precede
the establishing of the Lord's house in the top of the
mountains. This is clear from the twelfth verse, which
defines this period, preceding the Millennium, as "the
Day of the Lord". The section, then, which describes the
conditions which are to obtain in Palestine *immediately*

before the Day of the Lord dawns, begins with v. 6. We therefore quote from v. 5 to the end of v. 10:

"For thou hast forsaken thy people the house of Jacob, because they be filled with customs from the east, and are soothsayers like the Philistines, and they strike hands with the children of strangers. Their land also is full of silver and gold, neither is there any end of their treasures; their land also is full of horses, neither is there any end of their chariots. Their land also is full of idols; they worship the work of their own hands, that which their own fingers have made. And the mean man is bowed down, and the great man is brought low: therefore forgive them not. Enter into the rock, and hide thee in the dust, from before the terror of the Lord, and from the glory of His majesty". This most interesting passage shows us that apostate Israel will be on terms of intimacy with the Gentiles; that she will be the mistress of vast wealth; that she will be given up to idolatry. Their moral condition is described in vv. 11 to 17—note the repeated references to "lofty looks", "haughtiness of men", "high and lifted up", etc.

If Zech. 5 be read right after Isa. 2:6-9 we have the connecting link between it and Rev. 17. Isa. 2 shows us the Jews as the owners of fabulous wealth, as being in guilty fellowship with "strangers", and as universally given to idolatry. Zech. 5 reveals the emigration of apostate Israel (the "woman" in the midst of the Ephah) and the transference of her wealth to the land of Shinar. Rev. 17 and 18 give the ultimate outcome of this. Here we see apostate Israel in all her corrupt glory. She is pictured, first, as sitting upon many waters (v. 1), which signifies "peoples, and multitudes, and nations and tongues" (v. 15). These will support her by contributing to her revenues. The huge bond issues made by the nations to obtain loans, are rapidly finding their way into Jewish hands; and doubtless, it is the steadily accumulating interest from these which will soon make them the wealthiest nation of the world. That which has half bankrupted Europe will soon be used to array the Woman in purple and scarlet color and gold and precious stones and pearls (v. 4).

Second, the Woman is seen sitting upon the Beast (v. 3), which means that the Antichrist will use his great governmental power to insure her protection. How this harmonizes with Dan. 9:27, where we read of him making a seven-year *Covenant* with them, needs not to be pointed out. Then will poor blinded Israel believe that the Millennium has come. No longer the people of the weary foot and homeless stranger, but mistress of the greatest city in the world. No longer poor and needy, but possessor of the wealth of the earth. No longer the "tail" of the nations, but reigning over them as their financial Creditor and Dictator. No longer despised by the great and mighty, but sought after by the kings of the earth. Nothing withheld that the flesh can desire. The false Prince of Peace their benefactor. Yes, blinded Israel will verily conclude that at long last the millennial era has arrived, and such will be the Devil's imitation of that blessed time which shall be ushered in by the return of God's Son to this earth.

But not for long shall this satanic spell be enjoyed. Rudely shall it be broken. For, third, Rev. 17 shows us the ten horns and the Beast turning against the Whore, stripping her of her wealth, and despoiling her of her glory (v. 16). This, too, corresponds with Old Testament prophecy, for there we read of the Antichrist *breaking* his Covenant with Israel! As we are told in Psa. 55:20, "He hath put forth his hands *against* such as be at peace with him: he has broken his covenant", cf Isa. 33:8. And this very breaking of the Covenant is but the fulfillment of the Divine counsels. Thousands of years ago, Jehovah addressed Himself through Isaiah to apostate Israel, saying, "And your Covenant with Death shall be disannulled, and your agreement with Hell shall not stand; when the overflowing scourge shall pass through, then *ye shall be trodden down by it*".

Concerning Antichrist's relations with the godly Jewish Remnant, *that* has already been discussed in previous chapters, as also his final attack upon Jerusalem and his defeat and overthrow in the Valley of Armageddon. Apostate Israel, the Beast, and all his Gentile followers shall be destroyed. The faithful remnant of Israel, and those Gentiles who befriend them in the hour of their need, shall have their part in the millennial kingdom of David's Son and Lord (Matt. 25). Thus has God been pleased to unveil the future and make known to us the things which "must shortly come to pass". May it be ours to reverently search the more sure Word of Prophecy with increasing interest, and may an ever-deepening gratitude fill our hearts and be expressed by our lips, because all who are now saved by grace through faith shall be with our blessed Lord in the Father's House, when the Great Tribulation with all its attendant horrors shall come upon the world.

CONCLUSION

In bringing to a close this book on the Antichrist, we are conscious that "there remaineth yet very much land to be possessed" (John. 13:1). We have sought to present as comprehensive an outline of the subject as our present light and somewhat limited space would permit. But little more than an outline has been given. Abundant scope is still left for the interested reader and student to work out and fill in the details for himself. This, we trust, is what many will do. The subject, though solemn, is one full of interest.

No doubt the subject is new, and hence, mysterious, to some of our readers. These we would ask to turn back to the first chapter, and re-read the whole book. That God will yet permit the Devil to bring forth his satanic Masterpiece, who shall defy God and persecute His people, should scarcely be surprising. In each succeeding age there has been a Cain for every Abel; a Jannes and Jambres for every Moses and Aaron; a Babylon for every Jerusalem; an Herod for every John the Baptist. It has been so during this dispensation: the sowing of the Wheat, was followed by the sowing of the Tares. It will be so in the Tribulation period: not only will there be a faithful remnant of Israel, but there shall be an unfaithful company of that people, too. And just before the Christ of God returns to this earth to set up His kingdom, God will suffer His arch-enemy to bring forth the false christ, who will establish his kingdom.

And God's hour for this is not far distant. It was when "the iniquity of the Amorites" was come to the "full"

(Gen. 15:16) that God gave orders for their extermination (Deut. 7:1, 2). And Israel's transgressions (Dan. 8: 23) and the transgressions of Christendom (2 Thess. 2:11, 12), will only have come to "the full" when those who rejected the Christ of God, shall have received the christ of Satan. Then, shall God say to His avenging angel, "Thrust in thy sickle, and reap: for the time has come for thee to reap; for *the harvest of the earth is ripe*" (Rev. 14: 15). It is this which makes the subject so solemn.

What God has been pleased to make known concerning the Antichrist is not revealed in order to gratify carnal curiosity, but is of great moment for our daily lives. In the first place, a proper apprehension of these things should cause us to seriously search our hearts, and to examine carefully the foundation upon which our hopes are built, to discover whether or not they rest on the solid Rock Christ Jesus, or whether they stand upon nothing more stable than the shifting sands of human feelings, human resolutions, human efforts after self-improvement. Incalculably serious is the issue at stake, and we cannot afford to be uncertain about it. A mere "*hope* I am saved" is not sufficient. Nothing short of the full assurance of faith ought to suffice.

Unspeakably solemn is what we read of in 2 Thess. 2: 8-12: "And then shall that Wicked be revealed, whom the Lord shall consume with the spirit of His mouth, and shall destroy with the brightness of His coming: Even him, whose coming is after the working of Satan, with all power and signs and lying wonders, and with all deceivableness of unrighteousness in them that perish; because they *received not the love of the truth,* that they might be saved. And for this cause God shall send them strong delusion, that they should believe the Lie: That they all might be damned who *believed not the truth,* but had *pleasure in unrighteousness"*.

There are three points in the above verses by which the writer and the reader may *test* himself. First, have I *"believed* the Truth"? *"Thy Word* is Truth". Have I set to my seal that God is true? Have I applied the Word of God *to myself,* and taken it to *my own* heart? Have I *personally* received the Saviour that it reveals?

Second, do I have *"pleasure* in *un*righteousness"? There is a vast difference between *doing* an act of unrighteousness, and having "pleasure" therein. Scripture speaks of Moses "choosing rather to suffer affliction with the people of God, than to enjoy *the pleasures of sin* for a season" (Heb. 11:25). And again, it speaks of some who "knowing the judgment of God that they who commit such things are worthy of death, not only *do* the same, but *have pleasure* in them that do them" (Rom. 1:32). So it is here in the passage before us. They who "believe not the Truth", have *"pleasure* in unrighteousness". And here is one of the vital differences between an unbeliever and a genuine believer. The latter may be overtaken by a fault, his communion with Christ may be broken, he may sin grievously, but if he does, *he* will have no "pleasure" therein! Instead, he will *hate* the very unrighteousness into which he has fallen, and mourn bitterly for having done that which was so dishonoring to his Saviour.

Third, have I "received *the love* of the Truth"? Do I read God's Word daily, not simply as a duty, but as a delight; not merely to satisfy conscience, but because it rejoices my heart; not simply to gratify an idle curiosity, that I may acquire some knowledge of its contents, but because I desire above everything else to become better acquainted with its Author. Can I say with the Psalmist, "I

will *delight myself* in Thy statutes . . . . Thy commandments are *my delights*" (Psa. 119:16, 143). The wicked
love the "darkness"; but God's people *love* "the light"!

Here, then, are three tests by which we earnestly entreat
every reader to honestly examine himself, and see whether
he be in the faith. Awful beyond words is the only alternative, for Scripture declares of those who have "believed
not the Truth", who have "pleasure in unrighteousness",
and who have "received not the love of the Truth", that
"for this cause God shall send them strong delusion, that
they should believe the Lie: *that they all might be
damned*".

Again; if we diligently search the Scriptures to discover
what they teach concerning the Antichrist—his personality, his career, his ways, etc.—the more we are informed
about him the better shall we be prepared to detect the
many antichrists who are in the world today, now preparing the way for the appearing and career of the Man of
Sin. There is no reason why we should be *ignorant* of Satan's "devices". There is no valid excuse if we are deceived by his "false apostles", who transform themselves
into the apostles of Christ (2 Cor. 11:13). Christians
ought not to be misled by the many false prophets who are
gone out into the world (1 John 4:1). Nor will they be,
if they study diligently those things which God has recorded for our enlightenment and to safeguard us against
the subtle deceptions of the great Enemy.

Again; as we give diligent heed to the prophetic Word,
as we take its solemn warnings *to heart,* the effect must be
that we shall *separate ourselves* from everything which is
anti-Christian. "Be not unequally yoked together with
unbelievers: for what fellowship hath righteousness with
unrighteousness? and what communion hath light with

darkness? And what concord hath Christ with Belial? or what part hath he that believeth with an infidel? And what agreement hath the temple of God with idols? for ye are the temple of the living God; as God hath said, I will dwell in them, and walk in them; and I will be their God, and they shall be My people. Wherefore come out from among them, and be ye separate, saith the Lord, and touch not the unclean thing; and I will receive you" (2 Cor. 6: 14-17).

This Call is not directed toward Christians separating themselves from their fellow-Christians. How could it be? Scripture does not contradict itself. God's Word explicitly says, "Not forsaking the assembling *of ourselves together,* as the manner of some is; but exhorting one another: and so much the more, as ye see the day approaching" (Heb. 10:25). But the same Word which tells us not to forsake the assembling of ourselves together, commands us to have *"no fellowship* with the unfruitful works of darkness" (Eph. 5:11). God forbid that His people should be found helping forward the plans of the Prince of Darkness.

Finally; as we read prayerfully the teaching of Scripture concerning this Coming One, who shall embark upon the most awful course that has ever been run on their earth; as we learn of how he will ascend the Throne of the World, and be the director and dictator of human affairs; as we discover how he will employ the mighty power, with which Satan invests him, to openly defy God and everything which bears His name; and, as we are made aware of the unspeakably dreadful judgments which God will pour upon the world at that time, and the fearful doom which shall overtake the Antichrist and all his followers; our heart will be stirred within us, and we shall not hesitate to lift up our voices in warning. The world is in complete ignorance of what awaits it. The nations know not what is in store for them. Even Israel discern not the dark night which lies before them. But as God instructs us concerning what He is about to do, it is positively criminal to remain silent. The voices of all whom God has been pleased to enlighten ought to be raised in solemn and united testimony to the things which God has declared "*must* shortly come to pass".

THE COMING PRINCE   Sir Robert Anderson

This is the classic work on the marvelous prophecy of Daniel about the Antichrist and the seventy weeks. A classic interpretation of one of the key predictions of prophetic truth and long considered the standard work on the subject. Deals fully with the details of the chronology and the perplexing questions of the last of the seventy sevens. Valuable appendices cover matters of historical and chronological background.

"Christians everywhere should not only invest in this indispensible volume, but thoroughly digest it for a divine understanding of our times, and of those to follow."

—Herbert Lockyer

ISBN 0-8254-2115-2   384 pp.   paperback

CHRISTIANITY AND ANTI-CHRISTIANITY IN THEIR FINAL CONFLICT   Samuel J. Andrews

This "profound study of Antichrist and the apostasy of the last days is the finest that ever came from the pen of an American biblical scholar. . . ."   —Wilbur M. Smith

"After the Bible . . . I would recommend this book as indispensable for the library of the pastor, missionary or Christian worker of today."   —James M. Gray

ISBN 0-8254-5010-1   398 pp.   deluxe hardback

ISRAEL IN THE PLAN OF GOD   David Baron

Four major passages of Scripture, Deuteronomy 32, Psalm 105, 106, and Isaiah 51, which deal exclusively with Israel's history, are examined with biblical insight and spiritual application. Baron is meticulous in his study of Scripture with an emphasis on historical facts which bear on the passages involved. Throughout this volume, the author emphasises God's self-manifestation to the nation of Israel and His glorious and eternal promises to them.

ISBN 0-8254-2241-8   320 pp.   hardback

JESUS IS COMING — William E. Blackstone

A brief compendium on the subject of the Lord's Second Coming which provides a handy theasaurus for those looking into this important topic. Extensive Scripture references makes this volume a helpful resource for the study of eschatology.

ISBN 0-8254-2275-2   256 pp.   paperback

COMMENTARY ON DANIEL — Harry Bultema

A great contribution to studies in Daniel, written from a premillennial, dispensational perspective. Scholarship is combined with a spiritual emphasis to bring to bear God's great plan of the ages on the lives of believer's today. A unique chapter-by-chapter commentary, full of insights for pastors, teachers, and Bible students.

ISBN 0-8254-2262-0   368 pp.   paperback

MARANATHA! — Harry Bultema

In a careful and systematic manner, the author presents this classic premillennial study on the return of Christ. Having thoroughly researched the subject, Bultema supplies valuable biblical and historical material to enable the reader to understand fulfilled prophecies and those yet to be completed. The historical material alone provides a unique overview of premillennialism. This work is clear and interesting, reflecting no wild speculation, but the strong conviction of a warm heart that yearns for God's people to know His truth and to rejoice in the blessed hope of Christ's return.

Bultema's profound faith in the infallible Word of God, as seen in the 1700 Scriptural references contained in *Maranatha!*, helped him to rediscover the neglected truths keynoting the Lord's return. And *Maranatha!* can do the same for you!

ISBN 0-8254-2263-9   364 pp.   paperback

DANIEL — Arno C. Gaebelein

A chapter-by-chapter commentary by a well-known biblical expositor. Gaebelein offers a fine starting point for those beginning a study of this important prophetic book.

ISBN 0-8254-2701-0   212 pp.   paperback

THE COMING OF CHRIST: Both
Premillennial and Imminent   I. M. Haldeman

A classic, conservative study of God's plan for the ages. Surveys the connection of the church, the world, the kingdom, the witnesses, and prophecy with eschatology.

ISBN 0-8254-2844-0   326 pp.   hardback

CHRISTOLOGY OF THE
OLD TESTAMENT   E. W. Hengstenberg

This volume is one of the greatest works ever written on the messianic prophecies of the Old Testament. Full of profound scholarship, it confirms students in the deep truths of their faith. An indispensable reference work both for scholarship and Bible students, this study is a masterful example of scholarly research based on the integrity and authenticity of the Holy Scriptures. Christ is presented as the center of Old Testament revelation, both in type and in prophecy.

ISBN 0-8254-2835-1   715 pp.   paperback

CHRISTIAN EVIDENCES:
Fulfilled Bible Prophecy   Alexander Keith

This widely read author devoted much of his life to the study of fulfilled Bible prophecy. The results of his extensive research are here—available for the benefit of Bible students today. *The* standard work on Christian evidences.

ISBN 0-8254-5135-3   546 pp.   deluxe hardback

DAY X   Kurt E. Koch

The present world situation reviewed in the light of the nearness of the Lord's second coming.

ISBN 0-8254-3005-4   128 pp.   paperback

THE THEOCRATIC
KINGDOM   George N. H. Peters

This is one of the most exhaustive premillennial works ever

written on the kingdom of God. Manifesting profound scholarship and extensive reading in literature, history, science, theology, and prophecy, Peters quotes from over 4,000 different authorities, from the early church fathers to the end of the nineteenth century.

Out of a life-long study of biblical prophecy and pastoral ministry, Peters unfolds the entire scope of prophetic truth related to the kingdom. A series of 206 propositions, established from Scripture, forms the framework for an exegetical investigation of these great eschatological themes. These three volumes constitute a classic of monumental proportion.

"The greatest work on prophetic interpretation ever written."
—Lewis Sperry Chafer

"The most important single work on biblical predictive prophecy to appear."
—Wilbur M. Smith

". . . the most exhaustive, scholarly, reverent treatment of the questions of the kingdom of our Lord available today."
—Dwight D. Pentecost

ISBN 0-8254-3540-4 704/780/696 pp. (3 vol. set)   hardback

WHAT IN THE WORLD
WILL HAPPEN NEXT?   Ivor Powell

What lies ahead on God's timetable for the Christian? . . . for the unsaved? In his clear and concise way, Ivor Powell gives a panoramic view of future earth scenes. He covers many matters such as the Antichrist, the tribulation, Daniel's seventy weeks, and other themes. Powell also answers such intriguing questions as: Will the Mount of Olives be split in two? Will life expectancy be increased? What about Satan's final rebellion? Will there be a change in the earth's climate? What has God promised for His children?

ISBN 0-8254-3524-2   176 pp.   paperback

Available from your local Christian bookstore, or

kregel
PUBLICATIONS

P.O. Box 2607, Grand Rapids, MI 49501